THE INTERNET STRATEGY HANDBOOK

THE INTERNET STRATEGY HANDBOOK

Lessons from
the New Frontier of Business

EDITED BY MARY J. CRONIN

Harvard Business School Press
Boston, Massachusetts

Library of Congress Cataloging-in-Publication Data

```
The Internet strategy handbook : lessons from the new
frontier of business / edited by Mary J. Cronin.
   p. cm.
 Includes index.
 ISBN 0-87584-631-9(hc)
 ISBN 0-87584-720-X(pb)
 1. Business enterprises--Computer network.
2. Business--Computer network resources. 3. Business
information services. 4. Internet (Computer network)
I. Cronin, Mary J.
HD30.335.I57 1995
025.06'658--dc20                              95-19698
                                                 CIP
```

CONTENTS

v

INTRODUCTION

Suddenly it seems that the Internet is everywhere. After two decades of relative obscurity as a government and research network, the Internet burst upon the 1990s to penetrate the public consciousness, capturing headlines and attracting millions of users around the world. Analysts estimate that a new computer connects to the Internet about once every 30 minutes, propelling a rate of network expansion that tops 10 percent each month. Every indication points to even faster growth in the future. Hundreds of start-up businesses are designing software, offering connectivity, or giving advice about the Internet. The world's largest corporations are announcing Internet-related products. Companies of all sizes are registering their Internet addresses at a record pace, making commercial Internet domains the largest component of the global network.

As more businesses connect to the Internet, the potential for innovative commercial applications has expanded dramatically. The emergence of the World Wide Web (WWW, or the Web), with its intuitive interfaces and its system for organizing and locating resources through hypertext connections, has changed the look and feel of the Internet forever. By establishing Web sites and designing unique Web "home pages," businesses can present high-quality graphics, integrate multimedia components, and offer detailed product information via the Internet. Customers can browse catalogs, ask questions, see demonstrations, and make purchases using security-enhanced Web software.

The options available for Internet connectivity and establishing a presence on the Web are almost as diverse as the global network itself. Large corporations are most likely to invest in dedicated, high-speed Internet links that will support connections to multiple local area networks and thousands of simultaneous users and to set up secure gateways that include their own Web servers. Smaller companies and even individuals can obtain many of the same benefits with a lower-cost connection from an Internet service provider. Internet storefronts and entrepreneurs will also put company and catalog information onto the Web for businesses that lack the expertise to do it themselves. This range of services puts the Internet and the Web within easy reach of every type of company.

Making the leap from connectivity to competitive advantage on the Internet, however, takes more than a Web site. Where do managers turn for advice on making the best use of the global network? The Internet has spawned thousands of pundits, but its real experts are most readily found within leading companies that have a track record of innovative network applications. The Internet programs implemented at such companies provides a crucible in which ideas are tested, problems are solved, and value is created. Business practitioners with direct Internet experience, therefore, are the primary authors of *The Internet Strategy Handbook: Lessons from the New Frontier of Business.*

The lessons from outstanding corporate applications described in each chapter provide a framework that allows the reader to benefit from expert experience with critical issues of Internet planning, product development, cost-benefit analysis, implementation of core applications, staff training, and security. The strategies that have successfully provided competitive advantage from the Internet are described in the context of dealing with constant network evolution, adapting to unfamiliar tools and capabilities, and moving forward in the face of internal constraints—the real-world environment that every manager faces when introducing a new technology.

This book details the corporate planning and decision making that are required to develop and test programs that truly do harness the power of the global network. It is not, however, a collection of instant success stories. Each author offers insights derived from grappling with the complex issues involved in Internet applications. Each reflects on the false starts and the problems, the development of strategies, and the deployment of solutions associated with breaking new ground and acknowledges the challenges still ahead. Such candor makes *The Internet Strategy Handbook* a valuable resource for all types of businesses.

The first step in moving from Internet connectivity to competitive advantage is developing a strategic model for integrating network capabilities with key business objectives. Chapter 1, "The Internet as a Competitive Business Resource," provides an analytical framework for strategic positioning of Internet applications within different industries and discusses a model for placing interactive customer communications at the center of Internet implementation planning.

Successful Internet applications often translate into significant entrepreneurial business opportunities. Chapter 2, "Digital Equipment Corporation: Creating New Businesses," tracks the experience of Digital Equipment Corporation in transforming itself from Internet user to leading developer of Internet products and services, outlining the decision factors and milestones in DEC's establishment of an Internet-based business division.

The Internet presents new opportunities for every industry, but perhaps the most profound impact of ubiquitous connectivity to the global network will be on publishers and information providers. Chapter 3, "Dow Jones: Business Information Services on the Internet," outlines the issues facing all publishers in rethinking the content, the packaging, and the delivery mechanisms of information products in an online environment. Dow Jones's strategy of developing a news service product especially for the Internet and the issues involved in marketing and pricing such a product have implications for the future of business information services and networked publishing.

Research played a major part in the original development the Internet, and today's high-technology, research-intensive companies are more dependent than ever on the global network for access to essential resources. The strategies described in chapter 4, "Genentech, Inc.: Adding Value to Research and Development," apply to every company that competes on the basis of keeping up with leading-edge information and maintaining a rapid pace of development.

Despite its millions of resources, the Internet has no comprehensive index, which makes the Internet's information value one of its most important, yet most elusive, strategic benefits. Chapter 5, "Lockheed Martin: Integrating Information Resources," details the development of a project to enhance corporate information management using Internet standards and software tools and illustrates the importance of integrating new Internet capabilities into the corporate planning process.

Expanding market share and competing in the global economy are essential for corporate survival. Chapter 6, "Millipore: Marketing Products to the Global Desktop," describes how a manufacturing company responded to its customers' requests for expanded on-line product information, analyzed the opportunities, and discovered unexpected payoffs in establishing a multifaceted international presence on the Web.

The Internet's contribution to internal corporate communications and information management is discussed in chapter 7, "Schlumberger: The Internet Advantage across the Corporation." The network applications developed at Schlumberger—which include a dynamically updated staff resource directory, technology watch and "information harvesting," and recruitment of technical staff on the Web—demonstrate how bringing the capabilities of the global network directly to employees' desktops adds value to the whole organization.

Once network applications are up and running, companies need to know their impact on the bottom line. Determining the value of specific Internet applications, however, is a challenge for many organizations. Chapter 8, "Measuring the Value of the Internet for Business," presents a tested model for Internet cost-benefit analysis and describes of how it has worked in practice for different types of companies.

Does the Internet really enhance staff productivity? Only in those companies with a well-planned approach to training, according to chapter 9, "Productivity, Policy, and Internet Training Issues." With the use of the Internet becoming as widespread as the telephone and the personal computer in business, organizations need to develop policies to ensure that Internet use on the job effectively matches business priorities. The chapter discusses several approaches to integrating the Internet into work flow to improve productivity and presents a model training program to ensure that staff are well versed in using the Internet.

The growth of electronic commerce requires an infrastructure to support financial interchange and secure business-to-business transactions over the Internet. If the promise of the global network for transforming both corporate and consumer behavior is to be fulfilled, improved privacy and security are essential. Chapter 10, "Emerging Platforms for Commerce over the Internet," describes the challenges facing Internet commerce and discusses the latest offerings of electronic commerce, their vendors, and the evolution of the Internet marketplace.

Separately, each of these chapters represents the viewpoint of an individual Internet practitioner who is exploring and successfully adapting the core capabilities of the global network to meet particular business goals. Each author provides examples of how leading companies gain value, enhance performance, and improve interaction with customers through their Internet connections. Taken as a whole, *The Internet Strategy Handbook* offers a model for all companies interested in moving from basic Internet applications to gaining on-line competitive advantage. From the evaluation of strategic business opportunities to the discussions of network applications for different corporate environments, from the measurment of costs and benefits of Internet implementation to the necessity of staff training for increased productivity, this volume provides in-depth coverage of the key factors that make the Internet such a powerful business resource.

THE INTERNET STRATEGY HANDBOOK

The Internet as a Competitive Business Resource

1

Mary J. Cronin

Professor of Management, Boston College

FOR MANY BUSINESSES, the Internet is still a technology in search of strategy. Technology, as every successful manager knows, does not necessarily create change. People do. The most advanced technical infrastructure does not by itself generate revenues. Customers do. Nevertheless, the Internet makes headlines for the rapidity of its technical advances, the proliferation of its interconnected networks, and the multimedia capabilities of the World Wide Web far more frequently than for its strategic role within the corporation. Despite all the publicity, there are remarkably few models for integrating the global network into core business functions in ways that make a measurable difference. Yet this integration is the major challenge of any effective Internet business implementation.

Companies need a strategic framework that can bridge the gap between simply connecting to the Internet and harnessing its power for competitive advantage. The most valuable Internet applications allow companies to transcend communication barriers and establish connections that will enhance productivity, stimulate innovative development, and improve customer relations. Implementing such applications requires more than technical expertise. Managers must understand the competitive forces influencing electronic commerce today, evaluate the strengths and weaknesses of the

1

commercial Internet, and analyze the internal factors that will generate momentum and support for network programs.

This chapter provides an overview of the critical issues surrounding business on the Internet and offers a strategic framework for obtaining maximum value from the global network in a variety of corporate settings.

THE SEARCH FOR STRATEGY

Cyberspace is already crowded with start-up ventures, technical gurus, entrepreneurs, and established corporations staking their claims along the Information Highway. Thousands of new companies, eager to profit from the network's seemingly inexorable expansion, establish Internet connections each month. Businesses that made an early appearance on the Internet, especially those not involved with computer technology, were frequently highlighted by the media as pioneers in uncharted territory. But now commercial users are the largest group on the Net and Internet shopping malls number in the hundreds, leaving little gold to be mined from simply setting up shop on the World Wide Web. Companies should not assume that adopting the latest Web technology will guarantee profits on the global network. Internet applications need a distinctive strategy to stand out from the crowd. In the following subsections, we'll consider the contrasting experience of two businesses in moving to an on-line environment during the past year.

The Case of "Women's Gear"

"Women's Gear," a women's clothing retailer, embarks on an ambitious project to create an electronic storefront on the World Wide Web. Concerned about a two-year decline in revenues from traditional stores and looking for a way to establish a new customer base, Women's Gear executives analyze the prospects for setting up a mail-order catalog business but decide against it. Competitive data demonstrate that the women's mail-order field is already too crowded, profit margins are falling, and the prospects for significant growth are slim. Further analysis convinces them that on-line shopping will overtake and eventually supplant the mail-order business and that the Internet will be central to future expansion of this home shopping market.

After seeing a demonstration of electronic shopping on the Web, the executives direct Women's Gear's head of information technology to explore the capabilities, costs, and implementation requirements for creating a Web-based catalog of selected merchandise. Although the company has had little prior experience with the Internet, the steps to establish a Web home page linked to an extensive, fully illustrated catalog are quite straightforward. The major issue seems to be whether to expand the in-house Internet connection to accommodate the traffic and security requirements of an active Web site. Recognizing the lack of in-house Internet expertise and the complexities of security for taking orders and handling credit card transactions on-line, the head of IT recommends that the company contract an outside firm to design and maintain the publicly accessible Women's Gear Web catalog at a remote site, with a private network link to Women's Gear to transmit orders and track inventory information through the local area network.

Discussions among various departments at Women's Gear and the contractor about the catalog design and contents, and some debate about how frequently it will be updated, take several months. Finally, at the beginning of 1995, the Women's Gear home page is ready. It is quite attractive—with high-quality, fashion-conscious illustrations—and it features a short video modeling some of the merchandise. To facilitate on-line purchases, security and protection for credit card transactions, using state-of-the-art Web technology, are available for customers. Women's Gear advertises its new Web site through its traditional marketing channels and awaits the arrival of customers. The results, however, are disappointing. While thousands of browsers log on to the home page and look over the catalog in the first several weeks, there are few return visits. After the first month, new browser traffic slows to a trickle. Even those who do visit don't decide to buy. Very few orders come through the Internet; after six months on-line and an investment of several hundred thousand dollars, the Web site has generated only a fraction of the projected sales volume.

What went wrong? Among other things, the executives at Women's Gear focused too much on the technical capabilities of the World Wide Web and not enough on the match between the Internet community, their product, and their potential customer base. In the planning and implementation process, they misjudged three fundamental features of an Internet strategy: the demographics of connectivity, culture, and customer motivation.

The first issue is the number of Internet users who can readily access the Women's Gear Web site. While estimates of worldwide Internet connectivity range around 50 million users, this number includes everyone with electronic mail (e-mail), text-only access to the global network. A much smaller number, estimated at around 20 million, have the high-speed connection and the browser software to connect to the Web. A large percentage of all regular Web users are connected to the network through work or school rather than at home. The number of Web access points is increasing rapidly, but connectivity to the Internet in 1995 is still predominantly text oriented, limiting the potential customer base for the Women's Gear on-line catalog.

Even more problematic for the Women's Gear project is the demographic profile of those users who do have Web connectivity. While most mail-order and home shopping is done by women, Internet user surveys indicate that close to 70 percent of regular network users are men. Most report accessing the Web for work-related purposes; other frequently cited applications are to locate information or for entertainment. Only 9 percent of Web users at the beginning of 1995 reported any experience with shopping on-line.

Finally, Women's Gear Web did not make any special efforts to motivate customers to make the move to an on-line environment. Without a plan to capitalize on the capabilities of the Internet and the interests of its users, the Women's Gear home page was lost in a crowd of competitors and never connected with the electronic marketplace.

Given the demographic limitations of network connectivity and Web access encountered by Women's Gear, it might seem that the Internet is simply not ready for any applications that involve financial transactions with individual users regardless of the strategy involved. However, the success of other, more strategic approaches at reaching customers on the Internet demonstrates that this conclusion would be unduly pessimistic.

The Case of "Tech Books"

The Internet has delivered steady sales increases and an international group of customers to "Tech Books," a bookstore that specializes in computer and technical titles. The owner of Tech Books, himself a regular network user, first sets up an Internet e-mail connection for the store in 1992 to answer questions from customers at universities and computer firms in the Boston area. Several store employees share responsibility for managing the connection and responding to queries about titles and other customer requests. Tech Books begins advertising its e-mail address more broadly and offering an on-line order service in 1993; customers are encouraged to register their credit card numbers with the store via telephone or fax; in turn, they receive a personal identification number and password to confirm on-line book orders. Tech Books sends brief announcements about the availability of this service to a number of computer-related Internet discussion groups, and Internet queries from outside the local area increase significantly. By the end of the year, the store is handling several hundred title queries over the Internet each week. Many customers, especially those in other countries, make regular purchases over the Internet.

In 1993, store managers also set up an Internet planning group to evaluate the long-term potential for sales and marketing on the global network. The group determines that the priority should be providing more information and services on-line, with an expanded effort to reach national and international customers while improving service to existing patrons. The planning group designs additional services for Internet users, including a new-title notification service based on profiles of customer interests, on-line reviews of selected titles, and a complete on-line catalog of the Tech Books inventory.

Tech Books' interface for this information is a simple, text-only Gopher server maintained by existing staff. The staff publicize the new services by sending e-mail notices to customers who have already made Internet queries or registered for on-line purchases, and send postings to selected Internet discussion groups. The Tech Books server is included on numerous lists of Gopher servers at other Internet sites. Tech Books also highlights its Gopher and e-mail addresses on print and other marketing materials. The title catalog is a popular innovation; dozens of universities add it to their internal Gopher menus, and the number of on-line visitors increases by more than 50 percent within a month of its introduction. An unexpected benefit is that many customers begin to do their own title searches, freeing the bookstore staff to update information, post new reviews, and maintain the new-title notification program. An all-time Tech Books sales record for 1993 is attributed to a 35 percent increase in Internet-generated sales.

In 1994, Tech Books' Internet planning group begins to explore the advantages of a World Wide Web home page. Group members generate ideas about new content and features for a Tech Books home page from three sources: surfing the Web to find out what looks good and works well at other sites, brainstorming with Internet users on the staff, and surveying customers who have already used the e-mail and Gopher server. Based on these ideas, the group designs a home page that incorporates the title catalog and new-title announcements, expands the book reviews with links to reviews at other Web locations and customer-contributed reviews, and adds several features—"author forums" providing on-line commentary by best-selling authors, topical discussion groups for customer comments, and links to more extensive library collections in popular subject areas. Recognizing that many customers, especially those outside the United States, do not have access to the Web, the planning group decides to retain the Tech Books Gopher interface as well.

The Tech Books home page comes on-line at the end of 1994 with announcements to a number of public lists and notification to customers. The planning group makes a special effort to encourage links to Tech Books from other home pages, especially at universities and organizations interested in computer and technical materials. Home page "hits" at Tech Books start slowly but accelerate after the first month, to between 200 and 500 visits each day. Many of these visitors become new customers for Tech Books; for the first time, the percentage of books sold through the Internet overtakes the sales volume at the store. Tech Books is headed for another record year.

The contrast between the experiences of Women's Gear and Tech Books has much more to do with strategic positioning than with the intrinsic technical capabilities of the Internet. Tech Books started the pursuit of electronic commerce on the Internet with several advantages. Top management was already familiar with the global network and motivated to use the Internet to interact with customers even before the tools for on-line transactions were available. Because of its specialization in computer and technical books, the bookstore's customer base closely matches the demographics of the Internet. This early advantage was not enough to account for the success of Tech Books' home page, however. On the way to the World Wide Web, management made several strategic decisions that built on these early advantages to maximize the impact of the company's Internet presence.

One of the first was setting up an Internet planning group to map out a long-term plan for Internet commerce and to oversee its implementation. Tech Books' staff took the time to become familiar with the Internet, learning to use the available on-line channels appropriately to announce new services and to attract users. They also realized the importance of providing useful information for the Internet community in the form of the title catalog; this database gave customers an incentive to revisit the home page and motivated other Web sites to establish direct links to Tech Books for the convenience of their users. A particularly important aspect of Tech Books' strategy was the continued involvement of customers in developing the Web site, planning for enhancements, and interacting through discussion groups.

Real-World Strategies

Not every company can map out such a simple and readily implemented Internet strategy. Most business situations, as the authors of this collection will demonstrate, are far more complex. Nevertheless, the contrast between Women's Gear and Tech Books illustrates some basic lessons of Internet commerce. Companies doing business in a networked environment cannot rely on the strategies developed for traditional marketing, sales, and customer support activities. Effective Internet applications are grounded in an understanding of network limitations, demographics, and culture, as well as an analysis of internal and external opportunities. They are targeted to specific on-line customer groups and are dynamic enough to keep pace with developments in technology and the changing interests of customers. Small companies that are responsive, agile, and innovative, and large companies that manage to retain these characteristics, have a definite advantage in adapting to the demands of Internet commerce.

There is no single, foolproof strategy for gaining competitive advantage on the Internet. Every company needs to work through a process of assessing its particular environment, identifying opportunities, overcoming barriers to electronic commerce, and designing and implementing on-line programs that will add value to both the organization and the customer. Establishing this strategy-building process, and fine-tuning it frequently, is essential for continued success. Even the most carefully designed strategy will need regular course adjustments as the climate and the competition on the commercial Internet change from month to month. The components of a strategy-building process are described in more detail in the following sections.

The first step is a realistic assessment of the current barriers to commerce on the Internet, together with an overview of emerging solutions. The second step is an evaluation of the Internet's core capabilities, examining how companies are using the features of the global network in different corporate settings. This grounding in network obstacles and capabilities sets the stage for analyzing how the Internet can enhance internal information management, communications, and system performance. A strategic positioning matrix anchors potential Internet applications in a context of internal corporate needs and the external drivers of customer connectivity, competitive forces, and technical developments. Finally, a model for integrating Internet applications, which places interactions with the customer at the center of a networked information management system, provides a framework for redesigning traditional business functions for maximum advantage.

CHALLENGES OF INTERNET COMMERCE

In evaluating the value of the Internet for a particular business venture, it is salutary to start by scrutinizing the problems and challenges. Even for an Internet enthusiast, these are not hard to find. In fact, through the eyes of a skeptic—especially one seeking an ideal, business-friendly, and secure environment for global commerce—the Internet merits decidedly mixed reviews. Designed to facilitate research and government programs, the Internet has evolved into an extraordinarily decentralized, diverse, complex, and fundamentally ungovernable matrix of more than 60,000 separate networks. It works because all participants abide by the same fundamental Internet standards. However, the network configurations and protocols originally designed to maximize accessibility across multiple hardware platforms are difficult to retrofit into the secure gateways required for commercial traffic.

Since there are minimal restrictions on who participates and who publishes on the Internet, content considered objectionable, offensive, or even illegal can proliferate as rapidly as stock market reports and marketing data. To some Internet users, commercial applications still are unwelcome intrusions. Business ventures may attract negative attention ranging from a barrage of duplicate e-mail messages to attempts to break into confidential corporate data. On the other hand, products and services marketed inappropriately or tailored for customers not well represented on the global network may attract no attention at all.

How can business on the Internet be flourishing in the midst of such problems? One reason is that the networked environment stimulates innovations and encourages rapid adoption of new technology. For every barrier to electronic commerce on the global network, there are multiple, if sometimes competing, solutions. An even more compelling factor is a dawning recognition among business leaders that electronic commerce will dominate the future. The explosive growth of the Internet is not the only harbinger of a transition to networked enterprise; computer networks and connectivity have emerged as the crucial business tools of the decade. Companies that learn to cope with network vicissitudes and develop an interactive, on-line channel for working with customers, business partners, investors, and everyone else in cyberspace will have a definite edge in the next century. In the short term, however, they must also deal with the issues of Internet access limitations, cultural biases, and security problems.

Limits to Internet Access

Connectivity is the cornerstone of the new electronic commerce; the more companies and consumers are linked up to computer networks, the more business will be transacted on-line. If growth trends on the Internet and other on-line services continue at their current pace, network connections will be as ubiquitous as telephone lines within the decade and computer interfaces will be the conduit of choice for the majority of commercial transactions. But that is years in the future. Today there is no simple, linear process for reaching a critical mass of networked buyers and sellers in either the business-to-business or the consumer marketplace. Connectivity is coming at different rates to different industries and consumer groups. It is possible, however, to map out highly connected sectors, to pinpoint areas of rapid growth, and to identify persistent connectivity gaps whose correction may require new infrastructure breakthroughs.

Spurred by U.S. government subsidies for network connections and the needs of faculty researchers, colleges and universities have been heavy Internet users for the past decade. Many institutions of higher education now provide Internet access to all students and faculty through a campus network, allowing unlimited network use with no individual fees. An Internet access map would highlight college communities as sites of the greatest concentration of regular network users. Businesses interested in campus customers, therefore, will find them already well connected.

Beyond a few obvious early adopters such as computer and high-tech firms, it is more difficult in the corporate world to track network access. Internet domain registrations do reveal the major trends. The majority of *Fortune* 500 companies now have an Internet connection, as do research-intensive companies of all sizes. Among the industries experiencing the most rapid growth in connectivity are publishing, entertainment, health care, mail order, and financial services. The business connectivity map is the most volatile, since commercial domains have become the fastest-growing segment of the Internet. Each month, several thousand companies in the United States register an Internet domain for the first time, and business-related sites now dominate the traffic on the Web.

With press coverage of corporate Internet activities proliferating almost as quickly as network connections, it would be easy to assume that everyone has plans to link up to the global network in the near future. There are, however, still notable gaps in Internet access, some of which will probably persist into the next century. Only a small fraction of the hundreds of thousands of small and medium-sized U.S. manufacturing companies are current Internet users, and many such companies remain unconvinced that the Internet offers enough benefits to justify the cost of a corporate connection.

Another major connectivity gap is in Internet access to the home. The majority of home-based businesses do not have Internet access. Even those that do are more likely to be connected through a gateway from CompuServe, America Online, or another commercial network. Home-based consumers are the least likely of all to have an Internet connection. Statistics indicate that at the beginning of 1995, only 33 percent of households in the United States had home computers, and less than half of those computers had the software and hardware needed to connect to an outside network. Even the most optimistic projections don't envision the majority of American households' being connected to the Internet within the next five years.

Finally, there is a global gap, because Internet connections around the world tend to be more expensive and less accessible. In fact, the limitations of Internet access in the United States pale in comparison to the barriers to connectivity in many other countries. While Internet connections are growing at a faster rate in other countries, they are starting from a significantly lower base. Of the 4.8 million Internet host computers registered in all countries at the beginning of 1995, more than 60 percent were in the United States.

The popularity of the Web and the interest in accessing Web-based resources are spearheading a new rush to connect to the Internet. The graphical interface and multimedia that make the Web so attractive, however, also require higher-speed connections and more sophisticated hardware for effective access. In the short term, the requirements for Web access raise the threshold for full Internet participation above the level of many current users who rely on dial-in connections via low-speed modems. This divide between Web-accessible connections and text-only connections is part of a larger connectivity spectrum that ranges from direct, dedicated links to the Internet at universities and large corporations, to lower-speed direct connections for smaller organizations, to individuals dialing into a local Internet company using 2,400-baud modems. As the first step in building a strategy, companies need to establish where on this spectrum of Internet connectivity most of their customers will be found.

Recognizing, and planning within, today's connectivity limitations does not preclude an optimistic estimate of future Internet expansion. The key factors in developing a critical mass of users include availability of lower-cost, higher-speed options for global network access in the small office and the home, widespread deployment of solutions to ensure the security and privacy of network traffic, more intuitive interfaces between the end user and the network, and the continued expansion of content and services with high perceived value.

Analysis of Internet developments during 1994 and 1995 reveals significant progress on most of these fronts. Commercial hardware, software, and telecommunications providers are building Internet access capability and standard Internet protocols into new products. Announcements of Internet-compatible products and network access services from companies like IBM, Microsoft, Digital, Novell, AT&T, and MCI, together with hundreds of start-up companies established primarily to serve the Internet marketplace, have made it easier and cheaper than ever to establish network connectivity. With the competition for Internet access customers intensifying, it seems likely that connectivity products and performance will continue to improve. There has already been a marked increase in Internet connectivity options for businesses with internal corporate networks, including products to facilitate linking entire enterprise networks to the Internet, allowing easier integration of internal and external communication. Enhancing corporate Internet access has become a competitive selling point for hardware and software platforms.

The breakthrough in connectivity for smaller companies and home Internet users will depend on the current deregulation of telecommunications clearing the way for telephone, utility, and cable providers to create higher-speed options at even lower costs.

Commercial Culture Shock

Connectivity to the Internet is only one of the requirements for electronic commerce to flourish. Internet users must also be motivated to become customers, to change their patterns of buying, and to regard the on-line marketplace as an attractive shopping location. In many ways, the practices and culture that have heretofore contributed to the Internet's growth and success are at odds with such a transition.

For its first two decades, the hallmark of the Internet was open information access and free sharing of resources. Internet users typically had some definite purpose for participating in the global network, such as accessing research data stored in remote computers. Once connected, they identified with the overall good of the network infrastructure and were often directly involved in designing and improving it. Within this community, developing and sharing software that facilitated use of the network was a highly valued, and typically noncommercial, activity. Many of the most useful and popular Internet resources were distributed freely over the network; frequently, multiple enhancements and new versions were developed, announced, and circulated to hundreds of thousands of users. Among the positive results of this tradition are the extremely rapid dissemination and establishment of de facto standards for popular network resources that then become the basis for further development and applications in a number of different settings.

Parallel to the shared development of network software and standards is the tradition of free access to information resources. When university users and researchers made up the majority of the Internet community, this access was a fundamental feature of the global network. The growth of Web capabilities has made millions of other Internet users potential "publishers" and has created unprecedented numbers of electronic documents on all topics, most of them still available at no cost. With so many free Internet-based resources from which to choose, users are not flocking to the relatively few sites where payment is expected. As Greg Gerdy points out in his chapter on business information services on the Internet, corporate publishers are rapidly developing their own fee-based services for the Internet and are concerned that the surge in free networked information challenges the foundation of their whole industry.

As more fee-based and commercial offerings appear on the Internet, some network users express a different concern. The influx of business and individual Internet users who are primarily "takers" rather than "builders" of network resources is a departure from the tradition that created today's Internet. Companies attuned to this concern and familiar with the Internet's interactive culture make every effort to balance commercial activity with resources or information that adds value to the Internet as a whole. A value-added Web site is not simply a token of good network citizenship; it is also the best strategy for attracting on-line visitors and cultivating customer loyalty. The networked environment discourages the one-to-many broadcast approach to advertising and marketing. Unsolicited, mass e-mail and blatant promotions are likely to encounter resistance and negative responses. A successful Web site motivates customers to visit and do business because it offers something of value that they won't find anywhere else.

Combining information integration with active marketing on the Web is especially important for business-to-business commerce. Millipore Corporation, for example, attracts customers and potential buyers to its Web site by offering a well-designed, comprehensive front end for Internet-based resources of value to the pharmaceutical and microelectronics industries. This service attracts the attention of customers and researchers who will also utilize Millipore's on-line product catalogs and ordering forms. Millipore's interactive marketing strategy, described by Tom Anderson in chapter 6, is to create enough information value through the corporate Web server to merit a permanent spot on the customers' desktop.

Before inviting the world to visit via the Web, however, it is essential to address the issue of security on the global network.

Security

Some of the most intractable barriers to electronic commerce stem from security problems on a global network not originally designed to support transmission of confidential corporate and financial data. While the open structure and unhampered access to the Internet are strengths in promoting rapid, collective development of software tools and network capabilities, they become a weakness in the quest for security.

Actually, there are multiple security challenges on the Internet. The first is to establish secure corporate Internet gateways that can resist the random or malicious crackers who might try to use the global network as an entry point to break into company computers and steal or alter vital business data. When Internet use involved mainly research and information exchange, building a "fire wall," or barrier to outside intruders, at the point of Internet connectivity was the principal security issue preoccupying network managers and information technology directors. While a secure gateway is still the number one corporate priority, the growth of financial transactions and other confidential traffic on the Internet has made protection of information in transit a major security concern. Data encryption has emerged as the preferred method for protecting traffic moving across the public network from electronic eavesdropping. Despite some software advances that make encryption easier to implement, only a small percentage of the messages on the Internet are encrypted today.

One company's problem is another's business opportunity. Options for securing Internet connections against outside intruders are available from a number of vendors, as Joel Maloff discusses in his chapter on measuring the value of the Internet for business. The decision regarding how much to invest in network security varies from company to company, but some protection against outside intruders is mandatory. Corporations may opt for a customized, in-house Internet fire wall designed and installed by network staff, or they may purchase a secure gateway, complete with regular software upgrades. Either way, the issue of Internet security will not disappear. Corporate Internet gateways are regular targets for break-in attempts by crackers who have a knack for discovering unanticipated vulnerabilities. Outsiders are not the only threat. A large number of security breaches are due to poor password control and other internal network weaknesses. Managers need to develop policies to ensure that staff keep passwords confidential by following recommended security procedures.

Messages and information traveling across the network may be of little interest to anyone but the sender and recipient. However, passwords used to log in from remote locations are valuable tools in the hands of a cracker and should never be sent without precautions. Credit card and other financial information are obvious targets for network theft. Regular use of encryption offers the best protection from prying eyes. Standards for privacy-enhanced electronic mail and encryption of data between sender and recipient have been incorporated into a number of software products. Third-party Internet "storefronts," collections of product catalogs on the Web, frequently offer encryption to protect purchase transactions or require customers to register credit card information via phone or mail and issue authorization codes for on-line purchases. Posting product and sales information on a third-party server relieves companies of some of the administrative problems of electronic commerce.

With security solutions available at the gateway, at the workstation, and at the software level, a company must consider its security needs in relation to Internet applications. Will the company be expanding its use of the network to include applications requiring support for financial transactions or confidential exchanges? Are the company's customers ready to make purchases directly on the Internet, or are on-line sales several years in the future? Strategic decisions about security, like other aspects of Internet strategy development, will take into account the level of customer connectivity and other information about the competitive environment in a particular industry.

STRATEGIC POSITIONING ON THE INTERNET

Commercial applications do face significant challenges on the Internet, but for every barrier to commerce, there are multiple incentives for businesses to join the global network. If the current rate of network expansion continues, more than 200,000 U.S. companies will maintain Web servers by the year 2000. Many of them will be plugged in to the latest developments in connectivity and network security and ready to make the most of network capabilities. What network application will be most likely to give them competitive advantage?

As the chapters in this book illustrate, the Internet is as versatile as the companies that use it. Managers who look to the Internet for cost-effective ways to expand connectivity and communications or who seek to develop a new marketing channel may be interested in electronic publishing via the Web, in facilitating research and collaboration, or in offering global customer support services. The Internet can support all of these functions; its capabilities include communications, information management, connectivity for collaboration, product development, and interactive marketing. No matter what size or type of company connects to the global network, there is an Internet application to match its immediate needs. Separately, each of these applications will make an incremental contribution to organizational productivity and corporate competitiveness. The potential of the Internet to provide significant competitive advantage over the long term, however, can only be realized through a more strategic approach.

Establishing an Internet connection and planning the initial network applications is not sufficient for this rapidly evolving environment. Companies need to gear up to design, launch, and evaluate Internet-based programs on an ever-more-frequent cycle as more core business functions shift to cyberspace. Determining the priorities for implementation among dozens of potential network applications is frequently a daunting challenge. As the experience of Women's Gear indicates, the wrong decision may result in wasted dollars and lost momentum. Faced with uncertain outcomes, some companies opt for a conservative, wait-and-see approach, while others experiment with new network projects on a trial-and-error basis.

A better solution is to apply a consistent methodology to measure progress and to facilitate integration of expanded Internet capabilities into programs that will position a company to enhance its internal effectiveness and external market position. The process of developing, evaluating, and updating such a methodology can be described as an Internet strategy audit. Carrying out a strategy audit allows companies to analyze the strengths and weaknesses of their current Internet applications, to assess the competitive environment, and to determine the priorities for new network initiatives. It provides an end-to-end review of existing Internet utilization.

The starting point for an Internet strategy audit is a thorough analysis of the existing Internet connection. Typical questions that need to be answered in Phase 1 of the audit concern the type and speed of network connectivity, the percentage of employees who can access the Internet at their desktops, the amount of time and the budget devoted to all Internet activities, and the volume of internal and external use. This phase of the audit establishes a benchmark for future cost-benefit analysis and evaluation of network initiatives and also provides a capsule characterization of the existing level of Internet-based activity.

Phase 2 evaluates the company's internal Internet applications and develops models for substituting networked communications for more expensive alternatives. It provides an assessment of how effectively Internet-based resources can be accessed by various departments. This phase also includes an analysis of corporate communications strategies and proposes methods for integrating the Web into the company's overall publishing program. Finally, it looks at human resources issues: what skill sets will be most critical for planned applications, and in general, how do staff need to be trained to perform productively and interact effectively with the Internet?

The World Wide Web offers a new paradigm for organizing, retrieving, and publishing information in an on-line environment. Much of the attention focused on the Web highlights the rapid growth of public Web servers for marketing, sales, and product information. Less publicized, but of equal significance for many companies, are the uses of Web technology for managing and integrating a variety of information resources. With the Web, companies can streamline access to internal information residing on different computer platforms and create an efficient, customized front end for employees to move seamlessly between local and global data.

Web software simplifies the daunting challenges of resource discovery and information management, distribution, and updating by combining centralized control with decentralized access and interaction. As Scott Guthery describes in chapter 7, this capability allows Schlumberger to deliver information directly to staff desktops, saving time and central computing resources. Since the Web interface can easily be customized to provide different users with the most efficient pathway to frequently used resources, it is a useful tool for staff in every department.

Phase 3 of the strategy audit begins with a scan of the external environment. Questions addressed in this phase concern the level and results of Internet activity by competitors, the percentage of existing customers using the Internet, and the type of services or products most appealing to them. By the time they complete this phase, companies should know how the Internet is being used by competitors, how extensively the network has permeated its industry, and who are the leaders in deploying Internet technology. This phase also examines the technical developments that are most likely to have a significant impact on all companies doing business in the industry. What are the state-of-the-art programs, and how have they been implemented? How widespread is adoption of recent Internet developments?

Because network technology and Internet capabilities are evolving so quickly, companies that have been connected to the Internet for years may find that recent network applications provide solutions to long-standing problems. This is the case at Lockheed Martin Corporation, where an experimental program for networked information access has integrated Web browser and server software to enhance its latest release of information management tools. The Internet can also provide breakthroughs in marketing and sales strategy. Digital Equipment Corporation has made the Internet a key component of its interactions with customers. In his chapter, Russ Jones discusses how applications like on-line access to the company's Alpha computer platform take advantage of the remote access power of the network to "demonstrate" the system and software performance of Digital products for a user who is logging in over the Internet. Based on the success of its Internet marketing program, Digital has formed a new Internet Business Group dedicated to expanding opportunities and developing products to support Internet commerce.

The information derived from the Internet strategy audit allows companies to assess the internal and external conditions that will affect the impact of various network applica-

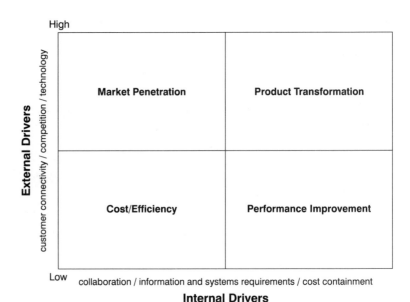

High

External Drivers
customer connectivity / competition / technology

| Market Penetration | Product Transformation |
| Cost/Efficiency | Performance Improvement |

Low

collaboration / information and systems requirements / cost containment

Internal Drivers

Figure 1-1 Strategic Positioning for Internet Applications

tions. Transferring the audit data to a strategic positioning matrix creates a graphic representation of the overall organizational use of the Internet compared to network applications of customers and competitors. As shown in Figure 1-1, this matrix provides a framework for identifying the forces that influence and shape the type of Internet applications most likely to add value and lead to competitive advantage at a particular stage of development. In combination with the Internet strategy audit, it offers a model for integrating the interactive communications and information management capabilities of the Internet into all core business functions to transform products and relationships.

While companies will typically have a number of network applications in each quadrant, the Internet's competitive value for a particular organization will reflect the interaction of customer connectivity and external competitive forces with internal network access and core applications. Competitive strategies cluster around the following approaches:

▶ *Cost/efficiency.* Low customer connectivity and little competitive activity combined with limited internal network access indicate the need for a strategy focusing on improving efficiency and lowering costs by substituting the Internet for other communications channels with vendors, information providers, and business partners. Extensive substitution will result in significant cost savings, but this strategy is likely to be superseded by shifting external conditions.

▶ *Performance improvement.* Low external connectivity combined with widespread internal access and pressures to redesign core functions indicate a performance-based Internet strategy. Adoption of Web tools to integrate information resources, support virtual teams, and facilitate distributed decision making, will enhance organizational flexibility and shorten the cycle from development to distribution.

▶ *Market penetration.* High external connectivity calls for applications that highlight customer interaction and build market share. Public Web sites, value-added information services, and on-line customer support provide a competitive presence in the global marketplace.

▶ *Product transformation.* To retain advantage when both customers and competitors are extensively networked calls for development of Internet-based services and products that redefine the company's strategic position.

The strategy audit also evaluates the company's customer relationships to determine the best use of Internet channels and interactive opportunities. Focusing on the customer viewpoint, it documents how networked customers are using the Internet in their own businesses and explores the potential for expanded applications. Using this information, companies can collaborate with their customers to think in more innovative terms about defining products and marketing. Once on-line partnerships are established, opportunities for network-based services and products can be identified and tested through the Internet with minimal risk. It may be profitable to provide specialized services and goods as long as there is a guaranteed market for them among the customer network.

Constant interaction with the customer base, feedback about every phase of product development, and the ability of multiple departments to serve as "customer support" and feedback teams all mean that the customer emerges as a central component of Internet-based applications. Strengthening the customer relationship, in turn, accelerates the integration of Internet capabilities into other areas of the organization. This integration prepares companies to recognize and capitalize on emerging network technologies that keep them ahead of the competition by creating even more advanced cycles of innovation and strategy development. One of the most profound, and least recognized, capabilities of the Internet is the channel it provides for interactive communication within the organization, with customers, and with the external world. Since customers ultimately determine revenues, any channel that improves communication, encourages customer feedback, and facilitates support services is a powerful competitive resource.

Integrating the capabilities of the network into every core business function requires a vision of how network capabilities can transform the flow of information and relationships throughout the organization. As Figure 1-2 illustrates, in a networked environment where the Internet is integrated into the work flow of core business functions, the customer naturally becomes the focal point for communications. When businesses link to their customers through the Internet, employees with network connections have a direct line to customer feedback. The customer contributes to an

Figure 1-2 Centering Customer Communications

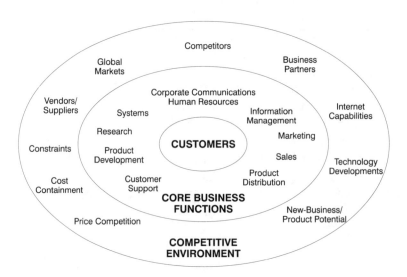

ongoing dialogue about products, support, information needs, and future development opportunities. Customer queries, complaints, product evaluations, purchasing decisions, and requests for support are not likely to be overlooked when they are visible on every workstation connected to the Web. Instead, they become the focus for interdepartmental discussion and problem-solving groups. Even departments such as systems and information management that do not traditionally communicate directly with customers are drawn into these discussions in a fully networked organization.

An orientation toward the customer also provides a context for companies to evaluate the competitive forces and opportunities at work in the external environment. A direct Internet link to a major supplier can, for example, ensure timely delivery of components for a product that the Internet-connected sales force knows is suddenly in demand. Customer comments on an Internet discussion group can alert development groups to situations requiring an immediate response. Centering Internet applications around the customer increases the value of each application and makes the most effective use of the investment in network connectivity. It is a strategic direction that sets the stage for value.

The Internet will not stand still while companies discuss the optimal approach to electronic commerce or debate which applications belong on the global network. As a new wave of network users ready themselves for serious business, the competition is intensifying and the stakes are getting higher. The winners will have a strategy that sets the standards for the marketplace of the future, a strategy that will continue to evolve with the next phase of Internet commerce.

DIGITAL EQUIPMENT CORPORATION

Creating New Businesses

RUSS JONES

Director, Program Office, Internet Business Group

DIGITAL EQUIPMENT CORPORATION, based in Maynard, Massachusetts, is a leading worldwide supplier of networked computer systems, software, and services. With 61,700 employees, its annual revenues in fiscal year 1995 were $13.81 billion. An international company, Digital does more than half its business outside the United States, developing and manufacturing products and providing customer services in the Americas, Europe, Asia, and the Pacific Rim.

This chapter tells how Digital has retooled its marketing organization to lead the industry in aggressive use of the Internet. It describes how the company assessed on-line alternatives, chose the Internet, and implemented it as well as how Digital continues to use the Internet to reach its partners and customers and even to create new marketing vehicles.

WHY ON-LINE INTERACTIVE MARKETING?

In 1992, Digital began exploring alternative ways to reach the marketplace and provide customers, prospects, and business partners with information about its products and services. Digital wanted to use an on-line, electronic medium that would allow it to (1) take advantage of the tremendous ad-

25

vances in computer and telecommunications technology; (2) build a foundation in anticipation of the coming convergence of the computer, telecommunications, and consumer electronics industries; (3) offer customers next-generation interaction; and (4) perform many of the traditional marketing tasks quicker, cheaper, and better.

Traditionally, the term *on-line* information referred to information that was available on spinning magnetic disk, as opposed to off-line information on magnetic tape. In the spring of 1992, the combination of falling disk prices and the emergence of the CD-ROM was changing the definition of on-line information to mean information interactively available on demand from the system's local disk.

Digital had previously experimented with on-line distribution of product information, demonstration software, and third-party application sampler packs, and it was already shipping its entire product documentation set on CD-ROM. The technology was well understood and extensively used. In fact, Digital was making money helping other software vendors package and distribute their software on CD-ROM.

Nevertheless, while most viewed the CD-ROM as the emerging "alternative" distribution channel, there was a strong feeling at Digital that "on-line" was going to take on new meaning, one that would tie into electronic distribution of, and access to, information—independent of source and location. Digital felt that any emphasis on CD-ROM-based marketing, although perhaps tactically significant, would miss the opportunity over the long haul.

Evaluating the On-Line Alternatives

The emergence of the on-line industry was just starting to offer the sort of capabilities Digital was looking for, the most important of which would be the ability to move beyond a simple information publishing and distribution model to a more interactive environment. This new interactive environment would allow Digital to develop new forms of marketing that break down the traditional "stovepipes" between marketing, sales, and advertising. By providing the means for direct electronic distribution to and interaction with potential customers, for example, these new forms of marketing would allow Digital to sidestep the industry pundits, the press, and other traditional information channels and establish a direct dialogue with the marketplace. Digital saw this as a significant opportunity that would shorten sales cycles not only for itself but for its distributors and application partners as well.

In the early 1990s, most viewed the on-line industry as consisting of on-line service providers—such as CompuServe, Prodigy, America Online (AOL), GEnie, and BIX—and bulletin board systems (BBS). However, based on experience in its research labs, Digital knew of a third option—the Internet. To determine which on-line option was most appropriate to its needs, Digital evaluated the on-line service providers, BBS, and the Internet against the following requirements:

▸ *Customer demographics:* Digital wanted to reach a wide cross section of the information technology marketplace to interact with customers buying personal computers, workstations, file servers, printers, networking products, computer servers, and layered products and services.

▸ *Reach:* Digital was selling and servicing a broad range of products that were increasingly geared toward a multivendor, multiplatform client-server environment, and it did not want to place any artificial restrictions on customers in their selection of platforms, operating systems, or graphical user interfaces.

▸ *Global presence:* This was an important consideration to Digital, given its strong global customer base, over 50 percent of which is located outside the United States.

▸ *Time to market:* Digital did not want to go through protracted legal negotiations about what it could or could not do with any particular service.

▸ *Cost:* As this was a new marketing approach, Digital did not want to incur unreasonable costs for itself or its users and potential customers (i.e., it did not want to bet the farm on any one on-line access provider since it was too early in the on-line information age to pick horses and crown winners).

After an extensive evaluation, the Internet emerged as Digital's on-line environment of choice.

The Internet Rationale

Demographically, the Internet made the most sense because Digital's customers were for the most part already on the Internet. The market research firm Dataquest Inc. estimated that 35 to 45 percent of *Fortune* 500 companies had access to the Internet. As Digital was primarily a supplier to businesses, it tended to be more oriented toward organizational access than an on-line service provider, which tended to be more oriented toward individual access. A vendor selling primarily to the consumer or home market would have reached the opposite conclusion for the same reasons.

In terms of reach, the Internet's multivendor, multiplatform environment was clearly superior. The Internet supports every information access tool on everything from Microsoft Windows to the Macintosh, to the X Window System, to character-cell terminals. By choosing the Internet option, Digital would not have to worry about the Macintosh port on a client access tool being 12 months behind the Windows port, nor would it have to worry about reaching the user base for Videotext terminals. The Internet was also a compelling choice in terms of available software tools. Instead of spending money and human resources on developing one-of-a-kind information-accessing tools, Digital would be able to concentrate on developing content, message, and customer support while leveraging the dozens of existing tools that were freely available on the Internet.

The Internet was the only option that offered Digital access to the global marketplace. Neither the on-line service providers nor the BBS could meet this key requirement.

Time to market also favored the Internet option. The Internet's decentralized nature meant that Digital was constrained only by how fast it could make things happen. Whereas on-line service providers required that Digital submit a detailed marketing plan describing what it intended to do, how it proposed to draw an audience to their services, and how it would market its subarea on their service, the Internet had no central organization to approve or require a review of marketing plans. In a world increasingly driven by competitive advantage, Digital made the decision not to spend six months waiting for its lawyers to negotiate with the lawyers for an on-line service provider.

Cost was the one area in which the Internet was not viewed as superior to the other on-line options. The Internet option would clearly cost Digital money, whereas an on-line service provider would pay a content provider to create an audience for its service. In other words, if Digital were to choose CompuServe as its primary on-line channel into the marketplace, it would be paid by CompuServe for bringing an audience to the service. Cost, however, can be a misleading indicator. In a pure marketing sense, the issue was not what it would cost Digital to do interactive on-line marketing but rather what it would cost customers, prospects, and partners to participate. This is where the strength of the Internet really became apparent.

Although the Internet is not free, its cost structure in the United States is based on a flat-rate model for connectivity. Companies connecting the Internet pay a flat rate for a set amount of bandwidth. Whether that bandwidth is used to 5 percent capacity or 95 percent capacity, the cost is the same. Therefore, whether the anticipated demand for a catalog is doubled or halved, the cost is the same. There is much more forgiveness built into the equation. This cost structure was particularly appealing to Digital because the company was already well connected to the Internet with multiple gateways, high-bandwidth connections, and redundant connectivity for high on-line availability. This meant that the uses of the Internet for marketing purposes could be incrementally built on top of the infrastructure already in place, and any additional marketing use would not add to the company's bandwidth cost, equipment cost, or annual fees. The initial cost was just the cost of human resources to start using the Internet proactively.

The Internet also promised to be particularly attractive for the distribution of product information and traditional marketing collateral. Product catalogs on the Internet can be kept up to date on a weekly or daily basis without regard for the quarterly or semiannual hard-copy production cycle. The latest information about a product can be accessed the second the product is ready for rollout. There are no production delays, and generally, the production process is not gated by capacity. In other words, the time to market is shorter and the revenue stream starts sooner.

Digital's evaluation of on-line options also indicated that

the trend was toward the Internet and not toward on-line service providers. Digital took a gamble that the on-line service providers would shift to embrace the Internet and eventually reposition themselves as personal Internet access providers. It hoped that by using the Internet as a marketing tool, it would be able to reach customers and prospects already directly connected to the Internet and that, over time, it would also be able to reach them indirectly via CompuServe, AOL, Prodigy, and other service providers.

Although it was not apparent at the time, the trend toward increased use of the Internet by the business community parallels other trends in the computer industry. The downsizing of computers (i.e., shifting from mainframes to desktops) over the last five years can be thought of as the dropping of the first shoe. The shift from private networks and private bandwidth to the Internet is the dropping of the second shoe. Among the business justifications for computer downsizing is the replacement of expensive computing power with inexpensive computing power. Among the justifications for implementing the Internet is the replacement of expensive private bandwidth, infrastructure, and connectivity with low-cost, public bandwidth, infrastructure, and connectivity. The business community is only now starting to appreciate the implications of this shift.

IMPLEMENTATION ISSUES

Once the Internet was selected, Digital quickly studied its landscape and terrain. This effort turned out to be critical because the Internet, like a foreign country, has its own culture and etiquette. Doing business on the Internet is much like doing business in any foreign country: the key to success is understanding, appreciating, and honoring the country's culture and etiquette.

Internet culture is characterized by cooperation and give-and-take between individuals who reach out to others with common interests and experiences. With access to the resources on the Internet comes the responsibility to give something back to the Internet community, to participate where you have expertise and to provide a service where you have the ability and the interest. This cultural rule applies as much to a business on the Internet as it does to an individual.

From a marketing point of view, the Internet is a *pull* as opposed to a *push* environment. The customer is always in the driver's seat. A marketer cannot push unwanted information on unsuspecting customers; rather, when customers request information or advice, the marketer supplies it. The response must be not only timely and accurate but also compatible with the access tool the customer happens to be using. For example, if the customer only has low-bandwidth access to e-mail on the Internet, he or she will not appreciate receiving technical specifications as a PostScript document on a file server.

Another sensitive area for the marketer to appreciate is proper use and reuse of e-mail distribution lists. When customers sign up for a newsletter or a mailing list devoted to a specific topic or purpose, it is counter to Internet culture to use that e-mail distribution list for other purposes. This has nothing to do with "advertising" on the Internet or misusing the Internet for business purposes. It is simply wrong to use a distribution list to disseminate so-called off-topic content. The corollary is that it is also culturally wrong to give, share, or worse still, sell a distribution list to other organizations.

Let's look at an example. Assume that a marketer establishes an e-mail distribution list to provide customers with usage tips and news about a given software product or product set. It is certainly in line with the intent of the distribution list to provide updates or new releases of the software, to advise customers of special promotions of complementary add-on products, to announce field-test software, or to solicit feedback on new features. However, it would be culturally off base to distribute other, unrelated information to customers on the list, even if such information comes from the same company. It would also be wrong (and probably unwise) to give or sell the list to another organization. A marketer must never lose the customer's trust, and nothing will do it quicker than to compromise his or her integrity in this fashion.

To help Digital's marketing community understand and correctly use the Internet, Digital established an Internet Program Office in the Marketing Communications organization in 1993. The Internet Program Office encourages creative use of the Internet across all marketing functions while coordinating consistent usage that reinforces Digital's overall brand identity and marketing goals. To this end, the Internet Program Office has developed an extensive guide that addresses proper usage of the Internet as a marketing tool. The guide describes the Internet access tools, relates each tool to its actual marketing use, and suggests opportunities that can be leveraged. In addition, the Internet Program Office has developed an internal newsletter to advise the marketing community of current marketing issues and opportunities as they relate to the Internet. The Internet Program Office has also developed companywide Internet-awareness campaigns that offer education on Internet culture and etiquette as well as cost-effective network usage tips.

With the increase in awareness of and interest in the Internet, particularly with regard to using the World Wide Web to reach the customer, the Internet Program Office has developed guidelines and assembled tool sets for hypertext authoring. Since Digital has an authoring community in the thousands, every conceivable approach to Web hypertext development, filtering, and conversion was being used, and the potential for inconsistent look, feel, navigation, and tone was very high. To continually reinforce Digital's brand identity, the hypertext style guidelines mandated logo usage that was consistent with guidelines for other communications vehicles such as glossy publications, advertising, and signage. However, the guidelines permitted layouts to vary according to function. The style of a detailed product technical overview is more functionally oriented, in keeping with its purpose, than the style used for press releases.

The coordination aspect of the Internet Program Office's role is particularly important because Digital provides Internet access to all its employees. Specifically, Digital has configured its security fire wall so that all employees have unrestricted send and receive e-mail support, as well as unrestricted post and read access to all newsgroups. Additionally, any employee with access to one of the 91,000 TCP/IP hosts in the company can use a WWW relay or an FTP relay to pull content from anywhere on the Internet to the desktop display. This capability is particularly attractive to the company's marketing and sales communities, which can now directly access information from the source. Both WWW and FTP relays can be used to:

- Ascertain availability of a product from an application partner
- Obtain product specifications from a competitor
- Obtain the office location and telephone number of a distributor
- Better understand customer requirements
- Check on government regulations that may affect customers
- Check the membership of a trade association
- Obtain conference registration information

Initially, access to this type of information was viewed as a way of increasing employee productivity. By mid-1995, all laptop computers distributed to Digital's sales force came with Netscape Navigator preinstalled with easy, simple Internet dial-up support to the local office.

Treating the Internet as a business tool, just like the telephone or fax machine, is an enlightened business practice. Most professionals expect to have access to telephones and fax machines in their work environment. But what about misuse? Significantly, Digital decided not to spell out a company-specific acceptable use policy (AUP) for the Internet. The creation of an Internet AUP would have made sense if Digital also had AUPs for the telephone and the fax machine. Instead, Digital chose to focus on behavior rather than mechanism. The company has produced a "Code of Ethics" for employees that clarifies how customers, partners, and competitors should be treated and how company assets should be used. The "Code of Ethics" spells out for employees the correct way to communicate, whether the instrument is a handwritten note, a letter printed on Digital stationery, a telephone call, a fax transmission, or an Internet e-mail message.

USING THE INTERNET TO REACH THE MARKETPLACE

The Internet, which is traditionally defined as the network of networks, is clearly not just a connectivity alternative to modems. Rather, it is a collection of applications or information services, with each service playing a different role, using different software, and reaching a different audience.

From a marketing perspective, the different Internet information services may be compared to different advertising media—newspapers, magazines, radio, and television. Although the marketer generally tries to deliver the same message regardless of the medium, each medium requires its own approach, with differences in ad sizes and layouts in newspapers, color usage schemes in magazines, audio and music in radio, and a balance of audio and visual media in television. To marketers, the principal difference between these advertising media is that, in the physical world, each medium is controlled by a different organization and has different associated costs. The Internet's flat-rate cost structure means that each incremental information service used simply reaches a wider audience.

A MARKETING STRATEGY DRIVEN BY INTERNET ACCESS DEMOGRAPHICS

Astute marketers understand the differences between the various Internet information services and the strengths of each service and use all the services to maximize their reach into the on-line marketplace. Because security and access policies differ by company and Internet service provider, information services do not have the same reach. For example, a purchasing agent in one company might have access to the Internet via a Web browser, whereas a purchasing agent in another company might only have e-mail access. At yet another company, some departments may have Internet access but the purchasing department that the marketer wants to reach does not. Because of these variances, the strategy for marketing on the Internet involves using all the Internet services in conjunction to reach the widest possible audience. Digital's strategy for marketing on the Internet is driven by just these differences in Internet access demographics. The following subsections describe the elements of the strategy on a service-by-service basis.

Electronic Mail

E-mail is the most ubiquitous of all Internet information services. Not only does it have the widest reach within a company, it can also reach far beyond the Internet. E-mail can be routed through the Internet's extensive e-mail gateways into MCImail, ATTmail, CompuServe, AOL, Prodigy, and other on-line e-mail systems. In other words, use of Internet e-mail gives the broadest reach into the on-line marketplace. From the start of 1993 to mid-1994, traffic through Digital's e-mail gateway increased threefold to 2 million messages a month.

There are many ways to use e-mail proactively. Digital's marketing organizations use Internet e-mail for:

> *Personal correspondence:* Digital's marketing personnel use e-mail to correspond with individual customers on product requirements, to deliver Post-Script files for conversion to 35-millimeter slides, to interact with contractors, to collaborate with partners on joint projects, or to obtain and respond to requests for proposals.

> *Corporate e-mail:* Digital maintains a general-information e-mail address, *info@digital.com,* for customer inquiries. Customers who send e-mail to this address automatically receive a response that describes all the different ways to reach Digital and gives detailed instructions on how to reach the company's various on-line Internet services, assorted fax-on-demand telephone numbers, and the telephone numbers of the major customer service functions. In early 1995, customers were sending approximately 500 messages per month to this address. An easily remembered, frequently referenced "info" e-mail address is the Internet equivalent of a toll-free 800 number.

> *Functional e-mail:* Digital's functional e-mail addresses enable customers and prospects to reach a department or function where they don't know (and don't really care) who receives the message, as long as someone responds with the requested

information. Examples include customers wanting to ask a technical question before placing an order or resolve an issue involving a distributor or register for a seminar. Customers can request Digital's extensive set of functional e-mail addresses by sending e-mail to: *help@digital.com.*

▸ *Electronic newsletters:* Many of Digital's marketing groups publish electronic newsletters that condense information about broad corporate programs and products to make it more relevant for their target markets and customers. For example, Digital's Education Marketing Group distributes a monthly newsletter summarizing activities at Digital and in the world of educational computing to any customer on request. Readership of the newsletter is distributed across the United States (60 percent), Europe (30 percent), and all other parts of the world (10 percent). An e-mail distribution list represents the most focused group of potential customers possible.

Digital also maintains a distribution list containing the e-mail addresses of members of the press and system analysts who have requested that press releases be sent to them over the Internet. The current distribution list contains the addresses of thousands of contacts, all of whom were added over a four-year period. Press releases sent via e-mail are delivered directly to the recipient's electronic in-box, and each recipient uses his or her software of choice to sort, route, or delete the press releases by subject. More important, information delivered electronically can be easily cut and pasted into news stories. Sending press releases via e-mail is the on-line equivalent of submitting film footage to the local television station. Marketing information stands a better chance of being picked up and carried if the reporter is able to integrate quotes, facts, and product specifications into news articles immediately.

From Digital's vantage point, news releases distributed via Internet e-mail are not under the copyright of the distribution channel and may be forwarded and propagated to others. End-user organizations often register an internal e-mail "exploder" on the distribution list. When the press release hits the e-mail exploder, it is propagated to dozens of people in that organization.

Digital regularly includes its functional e-mail addresses and its corporate e-mail address in direct-marketing material, advertisements, and product information. These corporate-level e-mail addresses are maintained by Digital's Marketing Communications function.

Newsgroups

Newsgroups support informal customer interaction and discussion. Access demographics are much looser with newsgroups. The marketer may know how many people are estimated to read postings to a particular newsgroup on a regular basis but not know who the individuals are. Nor is there a guarantee that any of the estimated readers will actually read any specific article posted.

Vendors find newsgroups useful as support vehicles and presales support tools. They may also find it useful to maintain and manage a Frequently Asked Questions (FAQ) document. Companies that ignore their own customer discussion forums do so at their own risk. Digital's customers have formed a number of newsgroups on the Internet to discuss the company and its products. The readership of the main Digital newsgroup, *comp.sys.dec,* is estimated at over 100,000. Although the newsgroup is not a corporate function, about 50 individuals in diverse functions across the corporation regularly read and respond to newsgroup postings and participate in newsgroups on behalf of Digital.

Digital has also created a series of newsgroups for the dissemination of information. For example, at the same time a press release is distributed to the e-mail distribution list, it is also posted to the newsgroup *biz.digital.announce,* which carries news releases and announcements from Digital. This newsgroup is clearly identified as business related. This is common Internet etiquette, and other organizations on the Internet, knowing that the newsgroup's contents are business related, can choose whether or not to carry it. The readership of biz.digital.announce is significantly higher than that of a direct e-mail distribution list, but Digital has no guarantee that a customer will catch every announcement, nor can it be sure that any given customer actually got the announcement from this newsgroup.

Digital moderates the newsgroup biz.digital.announce because it is a well-defined broadcast newsgroup that is not intended to support discussions. Discussions are redirected to the main Digital newsgroup, which is used as a customer-oriented discussion forum. Also, the moderation filter allows Digital to keep inappropriate, off-topic postings out of the newsgroup. Moderation can be used to block the so-called junk advertising of the Internet.

File Transfer Protocol Archives

File transfer protocol (FTP) archives facilitate the on-line distribution of product collateral, documentation, software, technical specifications, and the latest product information that does not make it into hard-copy material. FTP archives are also used to make available to customers information that is updated on a weekly or daily basis and cannot be cost-effectively delivered using traditional means of communication.

Digital's marketing organization uses the FTP archive, *ftp.digital.com,* to distribute product specifications, service descriptions, buyers' guides, demonstration disks, technical summaries, and performance information. Since each press release, in addition to being posted to the e-mail distribution list and newsgroup, is also placed in an FTP archive and indexed as part of that archive, customers who prefer not to receive every announcement have the option of accessing the archive to search for a specific announcement. Customers retrieve about 250,000 documents per year from the FTP archive at a considerable savings to the company. By continually adding to the FTP archive, Digital is also creating an important store of company information dating back to the early 1990s.

Wide Area Information Servers

Wide area information servers (WAIS) is a protocol that presents on-line information as a distributed collection of searchable databases. Digital makes extensive use of WAIS.

Everything in the FTP archive is indexed overnight and placed in a WAIS database, partly as a service to the WAIS user community and partly to place Digital's news releases and product information into the world of global searching. For example, an individual who subscribes to America Online can use WAIS to seek information about laser printers. From the WAIS directory of directories, the individual learns that Digital has a WAIS database with information about laser printers. When the individual inquires against Digital's WAIS database, *wais.digital.com,* he or she can quickly locate the latest information about Digital's laser printer products.

World Wide Web

The Web is the Cadillac of Internet information services. It allows the marketer to add visual and multimedia components and hyperlink product-related materials to a company's on-line information. In October 1993, Digital became the first *Fortune* 500 company to launch a WWW server. The Web gives Digital's customers and prospects the ability to point-and-click their way smoothly from one document to another, following the thread of interest from product to product and service to service. Figure 2-1 shows Digital's interactive catalog on the World Wide Web.

Digital's Web server unifies many of the Internet access services described in this chapter:

> ► Customers can browse through Digital's latest product announcements, search an archive of historical announcement material, or subscribe directly to e-mail distribution lists. Product announcement material is hyperlinked to other related materials or to the Web servers of other companies that are described in the product announcements.

> ► Customers can learn about the experiences of other users of Digital's products, learn about various newsgroups and customer-supported mailing lists, or search through an archive of technical problems and solutions reported by other customers. If interested, customers can join mailing lists directly from the Web server.

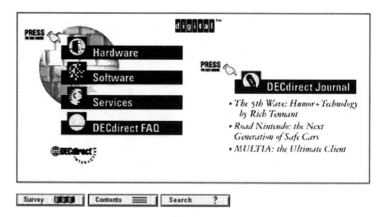

Welcome to *DECdirect Interactive*, Digital Equipment Corporation's World Wide Web catalog of Hardware, Software, and Services.

You will find Digital's latest products with up–to–date prices here along with the DI Journal and other useful information. You may browse through the various product headings to find the products that meet your needs. Or if you already know what you want you can use the Search engine to directly lookup a specific product or a group of related products.

The DECdirect catalog is also available in other media. Use the Catalog Request Form to obtain a printed version. You may also obtain a free one year subscription to the DECdirect Interactive CD–ROM for Microsoft Windows(TM) by filling out our reader survey or by calling 1–800–DIGITAL.

Figure 2-1 Digital's Inter-active Product Catalog

This is the U.S. edition of DECdirect. Pricing and ordering information applies only to U.S. customers.

> ► First-time users of Digital's Alpha system can learn about the Internet Alpha "Test Drive" Program, establish an account, and log on to the test-drive systems.

> ► Customers can use Digital's Document Search Engine (WAIS) to locate information about Digital's products and services quickly and with varying degrees of granularity. For example, a customer searching for information about Digital's TeamLinks product is given a list of TeamLinks documents with information describing publication date, document length, and document category. This list spans all document categories and provides information ranging from product specifications to technical specifications, technical white papers, related articles from the *Digital Technical Journal,* and in some cases, the actual product documentation.

- Customers can look through Digital's interactive catalogs, which contain detailed ordering information and information about application partners. Subdocument searching capabilities within the interactive catalogs go beyond the serverwide Document Search Engine. (Figure 2-1 shows Digital's interactive product catalog.)

- Customers can view demonstrations of personal computer software and presentations that can be downloaded and employed for user group meetings.

- Customers can use feedback mechanisms to enter their comments, suggestions, and questions about products. The use of feedback mechanisms brings Digital closer to the customer and begins to approach the type of next-generation, on-line marketing marketing environment that Digital wants to use increasingly.

In addition to allowing the integration of multiple information services into a unified customer-oriented environment, the Web server enables Digital's marketers to move beyond a simple publishing model in the following ways:

- By enriching on-line product information with hyperlinks to related information and color photographs and illustrations that clarify concepts that are difficult to articulate using text only. Figure 2-2 shows a typical product information sheet from Digital's WWW server.

- By adding audio and video multimedia components to enhance content with material that illustrates particular product features or examples of usage. For example, Digital put its television advertising campaign on the Web server to add sizzle and tie the company's Internet presence more closely to the brand identity established through nationwide television advertising.

- By introducing interactive tools that engage the customer in a dialogue with the vendor about product requirements or usage ideas. For example, Digital used the Web server to demonstrate a prototype

digital

Alpha AXP Systems Summary

A Complete Family of Open Systems

Figure 2-2 Typical Product Information Sheet from Digital's World Wide Web Server

Alpha AXP is Digital's commitment to open computing leadership through the nineties and beyond. It was inspired by today's need for low-cost computing with tremendous power. Tomorrow's need to capitalize on more advanced information technology. And the long-term need to sustain a competitive advantage into the 21st century.

and conduct a customer survey about next-generation PC requirements; Digital's Personal Computer Business Unit compressed six weeks' worth of focus group feedback into three days on the Internet with much broader worldwide customer coverage.

In the first two years of deployment, Digital's WWW server was accessed 43,000,000 times by over 100,000 customers.

With 200,000 Web servers in the world and 10 million on-line documents, how do customers locate a specific company on the Internet? Just as in the physical world, advertising becomes key. The advertising models on the Web are built around listing services and sponsorships.

There are two kinds of listing services—active and passive. Active listing services, or indexing services, seek out company Web servers to add to their lists. Passive listing services leave it to the company to register its Web server. The different passive listing services can be thought of as competing yellow pages. The marketer's objective is simply to be listed with as many of these services as possible.

Most listing services are free. These are sometimes called "metaindexes" or "metalibraries." The for-fee listing services should be evaluated individually. As a general policy, Digital registers with as many free listing services as possible and will register with a for-fee listing service after evaluation and only if the payback is obvious.

Sponsorship provides a company with the opportunity to associate its Web server with another Web server that in its own right draws a certain audience. In some cases, sponsorship simply buys name association with a particularly popular service; in other cases it buys on-line icons that can be hyperlinked to a Web-based advertisement that is further hyperlinked to richer promotional material, special offers, and other product information. For example, when Digital advertised in the innovative electronic magazine *Global Network Navigator,* Digital's Marketing Communications function was able to sprinkle electronic ads across the magazine by using an icon at the bottom of featured articles. By clicking on the icon (in this case, the Digital logo), an on-line magazine reader would go directly to an on-line Digital advertisement. The unique aspect of this electronic advertising was the advertisement's call to action. Instead of referring the customer to an 800 telephone number, as in traditional magazine advertising, the electronic advertisement invited the customer to jump from the page of the electronic magazine onto Digital's Web server for on-line product and service information. Thus, after reading about Digital's latest Alpha server, a reader could click and log on to public-access Alpha systems over the Internet. If satisfied with the on-line trial, the reader could click and jump to Digital's Internet Electronic Connection for on-line configuration and ordering support. Sponsorship fits in with the norms of the Internet (i.e., it is nonintrusive but available to those who want it). It can be thought of as "advertising on demand."

Many books oriented toward the Internet user discuss

techniques for resource discovery. Resource discovery is a useful technique when the user knows what to look for but not where to find it. The challenge to the Internet marketer is not resource discovery but being discovered. To facilitate discovery, Digital cross-references all its Internet information services to one another, so that when a customer receives a news release via e-mail, he or she knows where to go to find related information, back issues of customer magazines, and other on-line resources that could be of value.

Marketing on the Internet does not eliminate the traditional expenses and overhead of marketing; rather, it allows the marketer to reach the marketplace quicker and in a way that offers many different types of interactive capabilities.

A company's coordinated Internet information services establish its Internet "presence," which is critical to building the foundation that a business needs in order to use the Internet effectively for marketing.

INTERNET ALPHA "TEST DRIVE" PROGRAM

The interactive nature of the Internet presents many opportunities to create completely new marketing vehicles. A good example of such a vehicle is Digital's Internet Alpha "Test Drive" Program. In late 1992, Digital launched Alpha, a completely new 64-bit computer architecture, and the initial server and workstation product lines based on the Alpha architecture. To get the product into customers' hands, the company developed the Internet Alpha "Test Drive" Program in early 1993 and formally launched it in May of that year. The strategy was to place multiple Alpha systems on the Internet, provide unrestricted public access, and let potential customers "test-drive" the systems over the Internet from their offices or homes. First, each potential customer was asked to use Telnet to remotely log on to one of the systems and complete a simple questionnaire. Then the test-drive system would establish a private account and allocate disk space for the test drive. Test drivers were allowed unrestricted access to the system and could use all the local utilities, layered products, compilers, and software development tools. They could also use FTP to pull over their own software and tools from their own systems and log on and off as many times as they liked. There were no restrictions on what they could or could not do or on how long they could keep their private account.

Two equivalent Alpha systems were placed on-line for public access by two different types of customers—the UNIX customer and the OpenVMS customer. Digital wanted both UNIX and OpenVMS customers to evaluate the responsiveness and overall performance of the Alpha systems. Both systems were configured as general-purpose time-sharing systems. In other words, when a customer is accessing a test-drive system, he or she would be sharing the resources of the system with other test drivers. Although not ideal for true benchmarking, the configuration proved very effective nonetheless.

Once the Alpha "Test Drive" systems were available on the Internet, Digital started marketing them aggressively and integrating the marketing program into the company's other marketing programs. Initially, the program was announced to Digital-related newsgroups and profiled in all of Digital's Internet-related newsletters. Using the Internet to market the program directly to Digital's customers was cost-free, and it created an initial surge of test drivers who helped to shake down the account registration process and systems support. Next, Digital reached beyond its existing customers by issuing a press release that described the Internet Alpha "Test Drive" Program and explained how anyone could get unrestricted access to free, near-supercomputer computing cycles over the Internet. Needless to say, the response went through the roof.

The program was also announced to Digital's sales force and positioned as a way to (1) sustain customer interest in the new Alpha systems by providing immediate access over the Internet and (2) shorten the sales cycle by eliminating the delay associated with deploying a loaner system for on-site test-drive purposes. In addition, Digital started including access instructions in materials handed out at trade shows and, eventually, incorporated access instructions into magazine advertising aimed at Internet-savvy vertical markets (i.e., users in education and government).

The response to the Internet Alpha "Test Drive" Program from customers and prospects was immediate and extremely positive. After the first six months, demand on the systems was so high that two additional test-drive systems were implemented (at customer sites rather than Digital's gateway). After a year, 7,500 customers from around the world had established personal accounts on just one of the systems, the Digital UNIX Alpha system. Another 100 individuals open new accounts every week. The number of log-ins a day is 1,400, which is roughly one log-in per minute.

To track strategic usage of the on-line Alpha systems, Digital has sent surveys to the top 50 users once a month asking how they are using the systems, how the test drive has progressed, and whether they plan to purchase the systems. From this small sampling, Digital has been able to identify $15 million of incremental revenue.

The target customer for the program was the end-user purchaser of Alpha workstations and servers. To Digital's surprise, the application development community has latched onto the program. Once the developers realized how to access the systems, many of them preferred using the on-line Alpha systems to port their applications from another vendor's UNIX platform to the Digital UNIX environment. Application developers could have a port underway and completed over the Internet within days—before their own loaner systems (shipped almost immediately from Digital's factory) could even arrive.

Once the Internet Alpha "Test Drive" systems were formally integrated into Digital's support program for developers, the benefits were immediate. Application developers could start porting sooner and be done sooner than had traditionally been the case. Significantly, Digital was able to redirect dozens of systems to paying customers instead of nonpaying application developers. Not only did this have a positive effect on revenue, but it also minimized the cost of carrying the loaner systems in inventory. Furthermore, Digital's sales organization did not have to spend hours setting up loans and coordinating test drives. Instead, the sales staff is spending the time pursuing additional business opportunities.

After three years, Digital's Internet Alpha "Test Drive" Program is still unique in the computer industry. Digital believes the success of this program is directly tied to how well it mapped against the culture of the Internet. The Alpha systems were open for unrestricted access and in many ways positioned as a *service* that Digital provided for the Internet user. Digital did not place any unnecessary restrictions on the systems; it simply encouraged others to practice Internet etiquette, as Digital tries to do.

Ultimately, for many customers, what mattered most was not what they were actually able to accomplish with these on-line systems. Rather, it was the very fact that Digital had made them available for unrestricted, public access. In a subtle way, exposing the first-generation Alpha systems to the rough-and-tumble world of the Internet showed more about our confidence in the systems—their actual performance, software robustness, and overall reliability—than any amount of advertising or personal handshakes could ever convey.

INTERACTIVE ORDERING

In late 1993, as Digital started to embrace the Internet further for marketing, the company began to explore ways of leveraging its interactive ordering facility, the Electronic Connection, with the Internet. The Electronic Connection had been developed in the mid-1980s around a terminal-oriented, time-sharing model with remote access over dial-up modem and Tymnet. The system was heavily used by non-Internet customers in the United States to obtain pricing, generate quotes, place orders, and track order status against Digital's full product catalog. Although the initial development and deployment of the Electronic Connection predated Digital's use of the Internet as a business tool, Digital believed that a simple phased approach could be used to connect customers on the Internet with the existing Electronic Connection.

It was determined that the quickest way to leverage the Electronic Connection over the Internet was to add Internet connectivity to the on-line store and let customers Telnet to the system as an alternative to using a dial-up modem. As the first step in a phased approach, this had several benefits. First, it would be relatively straightforward to accomplish and would not break the existing on-line buying model used by the Electronic Connection. Second, it would let Digital test the acceptance of interactive ordering on the Internet, which, in 1993, was still being viewed as counter to the Internet's academic and research orientation.

The system went on-line in January 1994 in a limited

trial with just customers in the domestic education market-place. The education market was selected because most customers in that market were already connected to the Internet, and typically, all who were connected had access to Telnet. The initial trial was successful, with an immediate increase in orders estimated at $1 million per month. After the initial shakedown (and the upgrade of Electronic Connection systems in anticipation of an increase in demand), the Internet Electronic Connection was launched to the national market-place in June 1994.

At the launch, access to the Electronic Connection was added to the home page of Digital's Web server. Although the ordering facility was not yet based on Web technology, this underscored how the Web can be used to unify Internet information services and how marketers can create a larger Internet presence for a corporation by stressing a comprehensive approach to the Internet market.

The second phase of implementing the Internet Electronic Connection was to complement the Telnet access with direct Web access. In this phase, an alternative point-and-click interface was developed that allowed customers to order products directly from their Web browser. This Web interface enabled Digital to reach its "Click Here to Order" vision for its full 20,000-item product catalog. Digital generated $150 million in revenue over the Internet in fiscal year 1995.

FUTURE DIRECTIONS

Some view the Internet as the prototype of the so-called Information Superhighway, which will someday provide a wide range of benefits. But aggressive organizations are using the Internet to provide those same benefits today. Digital's future direction is twofold: to lead in (1) using the Internet as a business tool and (2) helping customers use the Internet to achieve business results.

To Lead in Using the Internet

Digital's goal is to be one of the first companies to totally leverage the Internet throughout all phases of the product life cycle. Beyond what Digital has already accomplished, the challenge is to assure that the Internet is being used consistently in a coordinated and integrated fashion to determine market requirements, provide individualized presales support, deliver the actual software products, and generate after-market follow-on sales and upgrades. Once this electronic business state is achieved, the global nature of the Internet assures worldwide leverage.

The heart of Digital's direction is a global electronic channel based on World Wide Web technology. Such a channel will allow Digital to take orders and deliver software products electronically over the Internet from anywhere in the world.

The Internet obviously supplies the infrastructure to reach a global marketplace. The key to leveraging this infrastructure is the global product set. To the extent that a vendor has a global product set with consistent worldwide business practices, it will be just that much easier (and quicker) to reach the desired end state. Digital has been moving over the last three years to behave much more like a global corporation than a multinational corporation. Companies that are not prepared for a truly global marketplace will have a much more difficult time adapting to the business environment found in the emerging, electronic global village.

A global electronic channel will generate revenue by reaching broadly into a marketplace that isn't always reachable by other traditional channels. Is there incremental revenue in the extra 16 hours of the day when the local distribution channel is asleep or not working? Of course there is. A customer might need a feature that is in the latest shipping version of a layered product. But the customer can't wait to buy the upgrade: it's 8:00 P.M. and the new feature is needed now to complete the project by tomorrow morning. This is analogous to a photocopy shop or grocery store's staying open 24 hours a day. In large metropolitan areas, more stores stay open all night because there is a critical mass of customers up all night. In the global electronic marketplace, there is a critical mass 24 hours a day.

There are many ways to think of the cost reductions associated with a global electronic channel—savings from not pressing CD-ROMs, not printing documentation, not shipping products to distributors. Some of these savings are the traditional hard and measurable costs of doing business. Others are more intangible because they reduce the total cycle time for the business transaction. The window between winning the order and delivering the product is the same window your competitor has to unhook the order.

The Internet Business Group

In August 1994, Digital formed the Internet Business Group. Its charter is to help customers achieve business results from the use of the Internet, much as Digital has achieved in its use of the Internet. Through this initial thrust into the emerging Internet market, Digital is helping customers:

- ► Create new business structures on the Internet
- ► Enhance business and market development programs via the Internet
- ► Improve employee productivity by using the Internet
- ► Reduce their overall cost of doing business by leveraging the Internet
- ► Improve the quality of business decisions and results through access to information over the Internet

Digital and its partners are delivering these results to customers today, primarily through distribution channels, with a comprehensive Internet product and service portfolio. With security as its foundation, this portfolio helps customers safely access the Internet and use the Internet to collaborate with partners, distribute information to prospects, and perform secure electronic commerce with customers and suppliers.

Digital believes that the Internet is revolutionizing mainstream business practices to the same extent that open systems revolutionized the computer industry. Digital's goal is not only to be the lead company within the computer industry driving the Internet business opportunity but also to be at the forefront of how to use distributed, networked computing for a distinct competitive business advantage. Helping our customers benefit from the Internet opportunity is now the top priority of Digital's Internet Business Group.

DOW JONES

Business Information Services on the Internet

GREGORY P. GERDY

Director of Enterprise Products

THE COMMERCIALIZATION OF the Internet promises to be an exciting time for entrepreneurs and corporate giants alike. New industries will spring up and old industries will be challenged as never before. One such mainstay, the publishing industry, faces challenges and opportunities unlike any since the dawn of television.

Dow Jones, like other publishers, has paid close attention to the arrival of the Internet. One of Dow Jones's responses to the challenges and opportunities in this new era is Ask Dow Jones (AJD) on the Web, a business information library that combines proprietary Dow Jones content with selected data from third-party sources to provide timely, tactical news and broad coverage of the important business news on any given day.

ADJ is built around the technology of the World Wide Web (WWW) and wide area information servers (WAIS). WAIS Inc. built ADJ under contract with Dow Jones and also contracted to provide operations services in the initial period. This chapter provides a brief background on Dow Jones and the electronic publishing projects leading to ADJ, discusses the major issues addressed during the development of the service, and examines some larger issues facing the publishing industry in the era of the Internet.

DOW JONES AND ELECTRONIC PUBLISHING

Dow Jones has been a publisher of business and financial information for more than 100 years. This brief background on Dow Jones and electronic publishing is necessary to place into context the enormous changes that are occurring on the Internet. It shows how the company has adapted well through the years to become an electronic publisher while retaining the recognition and success of its print publishing business.

Dow Jones News/Retrieval

The world of Wall Street has its own rhythms, demands, and idiosyncrasies. In 1977, Dow Jones moved its electronic-publishing efforts off "the Street" to Main Street with a new venture called Dow Jones News/Retrieval. The service, aimed at the emerging market for businesspeople who used modems to connect to remote databases, was part of the Information Services Group.

News/Retrieval drew on Dow Jones News, the newswire of record in the securities industry, for its content. Stories from Dow Jones News were put into a database for access by individuals using dedicated terminals, small teleprinter devices, and other systems just starting to emerge in forward-thinking companies. Corporate libraries and some individuals were the early subscribers. Shortly after News/Retrieval was launched, an important addition was made to the service: stock quotes.

This undertaking received a boost when the first personal computers appeared on the market. Initially, news and stock quotes from News/Retrieval appeared on Apple Computer's Apple II machines, marking a significant move into the electronic age for the company. The arrival of the IBM Personal Computer a few years later expanded market opportunities for the service among companies and personal investors tracking their portfolios.

As News/Retrieval added new databases and gained new customers, the Information Services Group was developing a full-text database that was to include the full text of *The Wall Street Journal*. Although there was much discussion about cannibalization of the print business, the company made the transition smoothly, and in 1984, the database was unveiled. Users were primarily corporate librarians, who had the budgets to pay for the expensive services and the knowledge of the complex search protocols that were then state of the art.

Through the 1980s, News/Retrieval increasingly focused on the business market, adding many databases to serve business users trying to gain an edge, track competitors, and make sound investment decisions. Toward the end of the decade, there were two developments that are part of the story leading up to ADJ: (1) the development of DowQuest, a natural-language retrieval system, and (2) the formation of a business plan for a service called DowVision.

DowQuest

In 1987, Dow Jones and The Thinking Machines, a small firm located in Cambridge, Massachusetts, started collaboration on a service using the Connection Machine, a massively parallel processing supercomputer. Most of the Connection Machines in use were in government and defense applications. For The Thinking Machines, a project in the commercial market with Dow Jones was viewed as an attractive first step toward diversifying its client base and moving the company forward. For Dow Jones, the possibility of finding a text engine that would bring text retrieval out of the corporate libraries and onto desktops to be used by "mere mortals" had tremendous appeal.

The algorithms used in DowQuest were based on work done by Brewster Kahle and others at The Thinking Machines. They implemented relevance feedback, which used natural-language query to build an index that allowed for rapid "feedback" to find stories that meet "fuzzy" search criteria. The feedback loop involves multiple queries of the database in which the user asks to see more stories like the ones that best meet the original criteria. It is an iterative process that requires no understanding of Boolean search strategy and complicated print and display commands.

Work on DowQuest was ultimately to dovetail with a major new initiative from Dow Jones called DowVision.

DowVision

DowVision is a news delivery system aimed at the corporate market. It offers broadcast delivery of real-time news and information from Dow Jones and other third-party sources. The news is sent over a proprietary, high-speed X.25 network directly into customer computing systems. The DowVision operation is similar to that of other financial industry vendors like Automated Data Processing and Track Data. These vendors take news from Dow Jones and other third parties in real time and display it to brokers and analysts in the securities industry.

The WAIS Project

As an offshoot of DowQuest and DowVision, the WAIS project was started in 1989 to try to break new ground in the field of widespread search and retrieval for "mere mortals." The concept of wide area information servers was driven by Kahle as a result of his work on DowQuest. The project was formed as a way of determining how to allow users to reach multiple databases anywhere in the world with one search and one search protocol. Dow Jones and The Thinking Machines approached two forward-thinking firms to round out the project: Apple Computer was brought in as a client software developer, and the accounting giant KPMG Peat Marwick, known for actively testing new technologies, was enlisted as a test customer.

The architecture for most of the project life included access to internal KPMG files and to the DowQuest server, which by then contained one year of the contents of over 500 business publications. Apple provided enhanced client software, which was built on the WAIS protocol and code-named Rosebud, to allow for tighter integration into the Macintosh operating environment. Interestingly enough, and more apparent in hindsight, the architecture anticipated the Internet services appearing today. In the diagrams prepared by the WAIS project team, boxes and lines connected servers all over the world containing multiple types of files, such as text, numbers, graphics, audio, and video. These diagrams could be dropped into today's Internet presentations, particularly World Wide Web presentations, and hold up quite well.

By the end of 1990, the project group had developed an effective prototype that was used at KPMG. The most immediate commercial success story involved the integration of internal information with news from Dow Jones to shorten a proposal cycle from three days to one day. This success story begged the question, "What next?"

By early 1991, the four participants had gone their separate ways. However, the project's reputation continued to have "legs" in the information retrieval and Internet communities. The WAIS project was viewed as an attempt to take a technology leap.

ASK DOW JONES ON THE WEB

After a lapse of about a year—during which Brewster Kahle founded WAIS Inc. in Menlo Park, California, and Dow Jones consolidated all electronic-publishing efforts aimed at the corporate market in a group called Business Information Services (BIS) in Princeton, New Jersey—Dow Jones and WAIS Inc. officials renewed their ties and began to discuss potential projects. The result of those discussions was a formal proposal to put Dow Jones content on a WAIS server on the Internet, creating a retrieval service.

Although Dow Jones News/Retrieval already contained everything contemplated for the Internet service, the idea was appealing for a number of reasons. First, it was a way for the company to experiment on the Internet without competing with its existing businesses. BIS was ready to take a gamble on what was viewed even as late as 1993 as the province of hackers and "university types." Second, WAIS Inc. had a strong presence on the Internet and a proven technology. It was believed that by working with WAIS, Dow Jones could learn about publishing on the Internet without having to build up a staff and start a new internal project on top of an already full plate. Finally, history played a bit of a role since both parties already knew each other.

From Conception to Announcement

The ADJ service was to operate in the manner shown in Figure 3-1. A file server at WAIS Inc. would be set up to

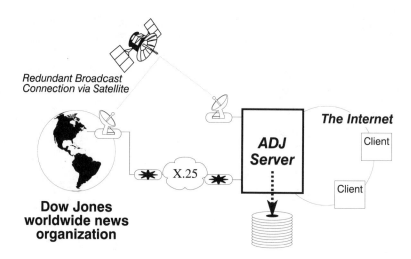

Figure 3-1   Ask Dow Jones on the Web

process the feed, index it, and put it in a WAIS database for retrieval over the Internet. The contents would be searched by using free-text terms and relevance feedback or by using the metadata (company codes, industry codes, and so forth) as applied by the Dow Jones editors. For client software, ADJ was to take advantage of free clients in widespread use on the Internet: Gopher, WAIS, and a new entrant, Mosaic.

Gopher was designed at the University of Minnesota for searching structured databases, which are best accessed through folders describing the contents within. The WAIS client software, as noted above, is an extension of the WAIS protocol to allow searching across all WAIS servers on the Internet. Mosaic, developed at the University of Illinois' National Center for Supercomputing Applications, takes advantage of WWW, the new Internet protocol, which allows for hyperlinking of information within and across Web servers anywhere on the Internet. Web servers are inexpensive to develop for content sets that are small and uniform. ADJ would be Web-compliant, but the WAIS engine would still be required as the server-based retrieval software for the service.

ADJ was to be a flat-fee monthly service. Initial thinking was that the fee would be in the $50-per-month-per-user range. Since the Internet was still not well known, difficult to reach, and subject to wide ranges of communications charges, there was not much concern about the impact of a product with this price/value equation on Dow Jones's existing businesses, although some News/Retrieval accounts and a few small DowVision accounts were deemed vulnerable. Therefore there was not initially a lot of analysis of possible impact. Instead, gut feelings were relied on to conclude that the service would reach people not necessarily using Dow Jones BIS products. The ideal target was envisioned as a consultant, a professional in a small private practice, or the president of a small business who had never used an information service but needed high-quality information.

Due to other internal demands at both organizations, a contract was not signed until January 1994. Minutes later, a prototype of ADJ was demonstrated at Demo '94 in Indian Wells, California. Demo brings together new products in the computer, software, and information industries.

The service was well received, though certainly not the hit of the show. However, the show did confirm the potential of reaching consultants and other small practitioners because many of the attendees were people operating in small firms or on their own. With the contract completed, it was time to build the product.

Major Issues

As the project moved through 1994, a number of issues emerged. Addressing the issues in any new venture can be the most challenging, frustrating, and exhilarating experience in business. This project was no exception.

Software clients. It became evident by the end of the first quarter of 1994 that Mosaic, the most prominent Web browser, was becoming the clear winner in the battle for client access. Less visible early in the year, but more important, WWW servers were appearing at the rate of 5 or 10 new ones each week, a figure dramatically eclipsed in early 1995 by a factor of at least 20. Although the Gopher client was never formally eliminated, the rise of Mosaic permanently pushed it to a back burner. Even the WAIS client technology was relegated to the background as Mosaic and the Web started to take off.

Target markets. Technology often drives a market, though not always successfully. The ADJ project was certainly driven by technology, but it was also a case of a perceived audience's driving a product. Internet technology had been evolving over the years, with certain protocols and conventions well established. The Internet, however, was not a market for business news and information. As word started to filter through the Internet community that commercialization was acceptable, it was the promise of the potential market that spurred the early initiatives.

In early 1993, published reports were identifying millions of users on the Internet. Deeper analysis, however, showed that most of these users were exchanging electronic mail (e-mail) messages only and not roaming around the many Internet databases. In guessing who would be the likely target markets, Dow Jones conducted informal surveys of its existing customers, which indicated that the number of end users moving to the Internet was very small. Informal assessments by the WAIS community—which included developers and others who talked to people who accessed the Internet or who monitored download logs from these databases—also indicated that business end users were not moving to the Interent in large numbers. In fact, if formal studies had been done in late 1992 and early 1993, the results might have led Dow Jones to the conclusion, "Don't bother." Nevertheless, a modest forecast was developed identifying business end users, small practitioners, and consultants as good candidates for an Internet-based service. These users were deemed likely never to have used Dow Jones News/Retrieval.

By early 1994, little had changed with respect to the proposed target market. There were no meaningful surveys. All download statistics were suspect because no one was charging. And finally, the growing hype about the Internet was just adding to the confusion. Later in the year, there were stronger indications that the Internet market really existed and that perhaps several million users had full access. Characterizing those users was still difficult, and few surveys offered the kind of insight that would help businesses understand the true potential of the market. When all was said and done, it was an exercise in flying blind.

Publishing ventures involving large and small companies.
In general, the dynamics of large and small companies are different. Large companies are formal, structured, and slow

to move. Small companies are informal, generally less structured, and usually quick to respond. But it would be wrong to read too much into the big company/small company characterization. Groups at Dow Jones have demonstrated the ability to move quickly like start-ups. BIS has had to move quickly through the years in the face of stiff competition. Other groups, such as The Wall Street Journal Classroom Edition, came to market entirely as entrepreneurial operations.

The ADJ venture is a match of two very different companies with complementary contributions to make. Dow Jones has high-value content, vast experience in traditional print and electronic publishing, and considerable brand identity with the business populace. WAIS Inc. brings Internet expertise, extensive contacts in the Internet community, and a retrieval technology that is pioneering the difficult path of text retrieval for mere mortals. The pairing of large and small is best done as a match of complementary skills required to reach a goal.

Meeting dates. As the project entered its second phase in the summer of 1994, it was clear that the original target date of Fall 1994 would not be met. There were more unknowns than first anticipated, and the members of the project team continued to juggle other responsibilities, consistent with the original decision to develop a low-key, modest service. In addition, developing the search engine and marrying it to a Web server was not something done overnight. It was known from traditional, LAN-based DowVision business that it often takes twice as long as anticipated to achieve stability in a product that is doing real-time or near real-time indexing and updating than in a static database in which the updates might be batched or might contain few records. ADJ was to handle dozens of news stories every minute during business hours.

As the summer wore on, the hype about the Internet and the Information Superhighway reached new levels, which was good news and bad news. The good news was that customers were signing on, drawn by the promise of exciting technologies, products, and services to come. Dow Jones customers were finally starting to ask questions about Internet access. The Internet was becoming very real as a commercial opportunity. The bad news, of course, was that the competition was out in force. Some announcements were substantive; others, a placeholder for things to come. The terrain had shifted significantly.

Security.   The ADJ project was undertaken on a leap of faith that the security issues on the Internet would be solved or that security would be deemed no more risky than in any other medium in which Dow Jones operates. At numerous points along the way, senior management at Dow Jones peppered the BIS group with questions about Internet security. Although these questions were answered responsibly and in detail each time, it seemed that, every month or so, a story about a new violation of copyright law, a break-in at a database, or some similar event would make headlines.

Fortunately, progress has been made in the area of security on the Internet. In fact, it is being driven as much as anything by the promise of electronic commerce. Companies like RSA Data Security and Terisa Systems have developed software that will allow for secure transactions. These developments will benefit all Internet service providers looking for the best possible security measures at parity with those available in closed systems.

Intellectual property rights.   The question of intellectual property rights is a major issue for publishers on the Internet. This is not a new issue in electronic publishing. On-line services have faced it for years, and the problem has been exacerbated by the proliferation of local area networks (LANs) and e-mail in corporate environments. It takes no stretch of the imagination to understand how users may attempt to forward articles, a form of electronic copying and distribution questionable under current copyright law.

The experience of ADJ to date has brought a few surprises. There have been two incidents in which possible intellectual property and contract right violations were caught and corrected. In the first instance, a user posted an article from *The Wall Street Journal* in a newsgroup. The group self-policed the matter at once and sent Dow Jones a finished "report" within hours of the incident. In the other instance, a branch of a multisite institution posted several *Journal* articles on its server under the mistaken impression that the server was local only and that this use of the content was within the scope of its agreement with Dow Jones. When it came to Dow Jones's attention that the material was generally accessible throughout the Internet, a "cease and desist" notice was sent to the organization and the matter was dealt with promptly to Dow Jones's satisfaction.

There is no question that the burgeoning Internet community must be made aware of the law. Publishers and Internet leaders must continue to press hard for public education and for legal reforms that address the ways that electronic publishing differs from traditional print publishing.

Pricing. The general premise for most of 1994 had been that the price of the service should be $49.95 per month for access to the full service with no time restrictions. In late 1994 and early 1995, external and internal factors came into play. Externally, several new electronic services that were oriented toward current awareness were announced. For example, the *San Jose Mercury News* unveiled a broadcast clipping service for which it charged $9.95 per month. In addition, a price battle among the commercial Internet service providers—America Online, CompuServe, and Prodigy—was establishing pricing expectations that had ramifications beyond the consumer market. These developments led to thoughts of either lowering the price to $29.95 to get widespread distribution or perhaps even creating a lower-tier service that did not include the *Journal.*

Internally, the positioning of ADJ was eyed much more critically. One view was that the $49.95 price was potentially low enough to draw some business from News/Retrieval yet not low enough to meet the new expectations in the marketplace. On the other hand, there was a view that it was easier to roll out ADJ at $49.95 and lower the price later if necessary. As is so often the case, pricing was to be one of the final decisions prior to launch.

The Internet Opportunity

As ADJ moved toward a mid-year 1995 launch, final issues of pricing, packaging, and rollout were being addressed. In addition, other initiatives related to the Internet were under development. Consistent with the company's mission to provide global business information in whatever form, wherever and whenever the user needs it, new products for several markets were set for unveiling.

OBSERVATIONS ON PUBLISHING ON THE INTERNET

Although the print world is not going to disappear, the impending changes in electronic publishing will result in new media that will change the fundamental definition of publishing. The Internet is leading the charge as publishers of all types race to put up servers. The following observations on publishing on the Internet are the preliminary conclusions derived from Dow Jones's experience in developing ADJ over the last year.

The Value of Information in the Information Age

Through early 1994, most people's perception of the Internet was of a democratic domain that had its own culture. By the end of the year, that perception was lost in the heightened awareness of the Internet and other media collectively known as the "Information Superhighway." The rush to commercialization was overshadowing many of the early cultural elements of the Internet.

One of those early elements was the view that information on the Internet should be free. Indeed, few Internet services were charging for information in the early 1990s. Even then, the price per company or per user was equivalent to the price of a magazine subscription. One pioneer, Brad Templeton, offered his Clarinet news service at a very low cost. But "low-cost" and "free" were viewed as practically synonymous in many Internet circles.

Users gained value either by culling information from the Internet or by using the Internet as a transport medium. However, it is one thing to draw from a university archive, where the presence of the content on the Internet was almost an afterthought, consistent with the free flow of information in academia, and another thing to transfer the publishing industry and the demands of running a business to this environment.

Lost in the hype is the fact that branding is going to be critical for publishers getting onto the Internet. In fact, when numerous publishers announced the availability of their print publications on Web servers on the Internet in the fourth quarter of 1994, the more ambitious ventures took elements of their existing print publications and combined them with flavors of interactivity (e.g., inviting customers to send e-mail to editors) or new types of content written specifically for the Internet service.

The promise of these new efforts is that branding will remain secure and that new value can be created. One immediate benefit of Internet publishing for newspapers is that it will be easier to reach constituencies outside the range of the print product. For example, people with an interest in Los Angeles because of travel, birthplace roots, or other factors would likely subscribe to an electronic version of *The Los Angeles Times* if it were available, appealing, and appropriately priced. In this way, newspaper publishers will be challenged to create new value for far-flung constituencies.

A second element of early Internet culture that is overshadowed by the rush to commercialization is the arrival of innovative information tools and utilities. New software routines and new filtering and agent software will bring only the most relevant information to the user. The combination of features and appropriate content is a high-value proposition.

Finally, the highest-value information will remain highest-value. Although it is going to be relatively easy for anyone to start a publishing business on the Internet, it still comes down to reporting and editing clout. Obviously, large publishers like Dow Jones have a tremendous advantage over small publishers or start-ups. That said, however, users who gather what information they need with filtering and agent software can assemble powerful packages derived from a wide range of sources, some free and some fee-based. The challenge for publishers is to stay competitive with their competitors *and* with the personalized newspapers that people will assemble because the technology is now available.

The electronic information revolution is currently in a phase in which the value equation for information appears to be up for grabs. After all, the old line goes, "bits are bits."

In a primarily text-based domain, it is harder and harder to make sense of where the value lies. Is it in the software? Is it with the publisher? Is it with the reporter? Or is it in the local area network? As all of these elements merge and bring significant value to consumers and business people, it is actually the publishing industry that may be facing change.

The Changing Nature of Publishing

Publishing is currently entering one of the most dynamic periods in the history of the industry. Arguably, the assault on the print medium from all media types is as dramatic as the change brought about by the introduction of television. Compounding the "bits are bits" dilemma is the rapidly changing terrain of the Internet. At least three factors—the World Wide Web, changing economics, and information overload—are acting in confluence to bring about a change in the publishing industry.

The World Wide Web.   The Web is the first mass-creation, mass-distribution, mass-consumption medium in which the user can participate in all phases of the process. The creation, production, distribution, and consumption of information are literally within the same operating environment. The intellectual connection is made within the same electronic universe. In the traditional print model, there are clearly some distinctions and distance between publisher and distribution channels and readers. Although they are within one "system," there are distinct physical steps in the form of printers, mail houses, and all the other steps in the process. In some electronic systems, creation, production, and distribution are

Figure 3-2 Evolution of Publishing

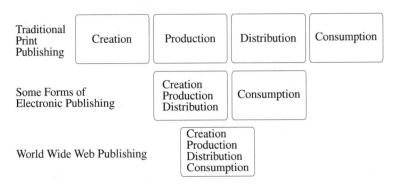

within the same system, whereas the user is generally still a user and outside the publishing system. As shown in Figure 3-2, with publishing on the Web, creation, production, distribution, and consumption are all in the same system.

Changing economics.   The Web is changing the economics of electronic publishing. The cost of entry has been reduced dramatically. Anyone can now "publish" on the Internet with an investment of several thousand to several hundred thousand dollars. This contrasts with the significant start-up costs for many types of hard-copy publications. (Newsletters, of course, can be an exception in some cases.) On the other hand, the large publishers will continue to have an advantage through their reporting and editing organizations and strong brand name carried forward from print.

Over the last 20 years, all publishers have been watching the on-line world in anticipation of developments that would turn promise *and* threat into an imperative. The year 1994 will be viewed as the point when that imperative took its first shape. The Internet, Mosaic, and the Web have been at the forefront of that change.

Context sensitivity will spur new types of electronic publications and new user experiences. Early activity on the Web is an indication of this change. For example, a user could be browsing a *Wall Street Journal* story on Coca-Cola in ADJ and go in several directions to dig for more information:

- Within the *Journal* for additional similar stories
- To a database on the Internet that has information on a new book about Coca-Cola
- To a newsgroup in China where there is a discussion about the impact of Western brands on local culture

These searches are not far-fetched; they are representative of the kinds of searches that are being done today. What remains to be seen is how the elements of the dynamic relationship of content to format (see Exhibit 3-1) will continue to evolve as new kinds of electronic publications emerge. It even begs the question as to whether the concept of a publication will be redefined in the new electronic world.

On the distribution front, electronic delivery of docu-

Type of content domain	Example
Internal to a publication	Article in *The Wall Street Journal*
External to the publication	Book review database
"Live" public debate	Newsgroup

Exhibit 3-1 Relationship between Content and Format

ments will change the established patterns of the print world. Electronic delivery can be nearly instantaneous, whereas print delivery takes days.

Information overload.   It took centuries for the publishing and information industries to become the giant entities they are today. Information overload in the electronic publishing industry is already matching the information overload from print, with e-mail the major force driving this development. Dozens and even hundreds of messages are moving to the user's desktop every day.

As the personal computer becomes the primary medium for exchange of nonverbal information in companies, and as electronic clipping services emerge to alleviate information overload by bringing tailored content directly to users, publishers face challenges in standing out from the electronic noise. The price for some publishers will be invisibility in the information ocean. The opportunity for others will be to build successful new business models.

Publishing Ventures Involving Large and Small Companies

Although all industries have their share of ventures involving large and small companies, the software industry has had some highly visible examples of such partnering. Even within that industry, there are only a few cases in which old-line companies successfully partnered with small software companies to gain entry into the software business. Most of today's software giants—Microsoft, Novell, and others—were founded in the early 1980s, started small, and grew to the highly respected companies that they now are.

An open question for the publishing industry at the start of this new electronic era is, What will be the model for getting off the ground? Dow Jones elected to work with WAIS Inc. to put a service out on the Internet after years of operating successful electronic publishing ventures of several types. Publishers like Encyclopaedia Britannica are also working with WAIS Inc. to produce electronic services. Other software companies are pitching themselves as enablers of electronic publishing. Not all of them are small. For example, Microsoft is entering the on-line world with a new service. One of the important ideas being put forward by these new entrants is that they can create content areas in which branding will be kept distinct for the publisher. Clearly, this is an appealing development for all publishers.

Dow Jones started investigating the Internet more deeply in 1993 as a reaction to a new business opportunity offering the possibility of a new market served by an emerging commercial technology, the Internet. At the time, it was not clear how quickly the mainstream business world would "get on the Net." But because the Internet was being commercialized through the door of the computer industry, it was apparent that the pace of change would be driven by the unleashing of the talent of the computer industry, where so many individuals and companies are looking for the next big hit. And it stood to reason that the evolution of the Internet would be governed by the ability of these talented people to create useful and meaningful services. In 1993, none of this was clear. But the Internet still looked like a small, safe bet.

In reviewing the developments of 1994 and early 1995, it is astonishing to see how compressed the time frame has been for anyone attempting to help publishers with their electronic efforts. The window for the small companies has been very short, yet it remains to be seen whether Microsoft and others can attract publishers, old and new.

When larger and small companies undertake partnerships in electronic publishing, they will face the challenge of remaining as nimble as possible and recognizing each partner's strengths and weaknesses in performing various tasks. Although, on the surface, it appears that smaller companies can move faster, many small publishing companies decidedly do not move quickly in the technology arena. Careful identification of the respective strengths and weaknesses of the organizations at the outset of the business relationship can pay off with faster marketplace response.

Agility in the New World of Business

The publishing industry must become nimble in the new world of business. Publishers will need to adopt attitudes and processes that will enable them to keep pace with the most agile companies in the world—the software companies. Small new entrants will be able to package content through licensing arrangements in such a way that they create ad hoc reporting organizations. Large new entrants with clout, such as Microsoft, can still move fast when required (though with increasing difficulty). For all entrants, a new level of agility is required as far as reacting to change. In fact, the sheer quantity of new entrants on the Internet scene could result in either a highly compressed rise to maturity for the Internet or just a lot of noise and a more moderate growth path.

ADJ AND THE FUTURE OF ELECTRONIC PUBLISHING

ADJ has been an experimental effort designed to enable Dow Jones to take advantage of and learn from the exploding Internet arena. Although many of the business issues are the same as in any other industry, there are factors that are unique to the publishing industry. It is probably a safe bet to say that the changes in the industry will be dramatic over the next 10 years. What remains unclear is what the publishing landscape will look like in 10 years. What companies will be the big electronic publishers? What new technologies will emerge as the creative talents of the information industry are unleashed on the publishing industry? What will the user experience be like? It promises to be a very exciting decade.

GENENTECH, INC.

Adding Value to Research and Development

JOHN "SCOOTER" MORRIS

Manager, Computing Technology Development

GENENTECH, INC., WAS founded in 1976 by Bob Swanson, a San Francisco entrepreneur, and Herb Boyer, a professor of biochemistry at the University of California, San Francisco (UCSF). The company's purpose was to apply recombinant DNA technology to the development of pharmaceuticals for the treatment of human disease. Today, Genentech has offices in the United States, Canada, Europe, and Japan and employs over 2,500 people, the majority of whom work at corporate headquarters in South San Francisco, California. The company's 1994 revenues were $795.4 million, with 40 percent dedicated to research and development.

Genentech scientists developed the first pharmaceutical based on recombinant DNA technology to be approved for human use, recombinant human insulin, which was licensed to Eli Lilly Company and sold under the brand name Humulin. In 1985, the Food and Drug Administration (FDA) approved the first product that Genentech itself was to market, a recombinant form of human growth hormone sold under the brand name Protropin. Since then, Genentech has received approval to market four additional products, all of which are human proteins that have been isolated and manufactured using recombinant DNA technology: Activase, for treating myocardial infarctions (heart attacks); Actimmune, for treating chronic granulatomous disease (a rare immune disorder); Nutropin, a human growth hormone for treating growth deficiency due to chronic renal insufficiency; and Pulmozyme, for treating symptoms resulting from cystic fibrosis.

By 1992, Genentech had published more than 2,100 papers and held more than 1,200 patents worldwide, with 1,100 additional patents pending. In that same year, a study by the Institute for Scientific Information cited Genentech's scientific achievements as having the leading impact on the biotechnology and pharmaceutical industries. In 1993, Science Watch reported that research papers on AIDS published by Genentech scientists had more impact than papers coming out of any other major AIDS research institute.

From a business standpoint, Genentech's success depends on the quick identification, development, testing, and marketing of new therapeutic agents. The more potential products the company can identify, and the sooner the products are prepared for testing and marketing, the better its business. Much of Genentech's success is due to its scientists, who contribute basic research to advance the state of knowledge in process sciences, biochemistry, molecular biology, protein chemistry, and a number of related areas. The company's founders recognized this and created an environment that attracts the top scientists in the relevant areas of basic research and supports those scientists with the tools and technologies to maximize their efforts.

The Internet, to which Genentech has been connected since 1990, is one of the tools that enhances Genentech's core business. For Genentech researchers and project scientists, it provides not only access to a wealth of information (e.g., biological databases, computing resources, scientific publications, conference registration information, and activities of various professional societies) but also a mechanism for exchanging information with collaborators. This chapter reviews Genentech's initial experience in using the Internet, describes examples of major current uses and potential new uses, and examines the impact of the Internet on the organization as well as concerns regarding Internet use.

USE OF COMPUTING TECHNOLOGY AT GENENTECH

Computing technology has always been an important component of Genentech's scientific environment. In the early 1980s, Genentech was connected to the outside world through a Unix-to-Unix Copy Program (UUCP) link to UCSF. This modem and phone link gave Genentech scientists and programmers the ability to communicate via electronic mail (e-mail) with collaborators and consultants at universities and at other sites connected to the Internet either directly or via UUCP links. To maintain security, Genentech computers initiated all calls to UCSF.

Genentech's use of UUCP for outside communications grew until it became economical to consider a direct connection. Uncomfortable with the possibility of UCSF students' having easy access to the company's computing environment, Genentech's computing staff modified some of the Berkeley Unix networking software to block access from outside the corporate network. This primitive "fire wall" provided enough security that it became reasonable to connect Genentech's science computer directly to the outside electronic world. In 1988, when Robert Morris's worm rampaged through many hosts on the Internet, the fire wall was severely tested but successfully thwarted a serious invasion of Genentech's computers. The connection was established by installing special serial interfaces in both the Genentech computer and the UCSF computer and a dedicated 56-kilobits-per-second (Kbps) line between the two institutions. The routes to Genentech's network were not advertised outside the UCSF machine, and Genentech's network was not accessible from the Internet at large.

In 1987, Genentech registered its Internet address and its Internet domain, *gene.com,* with the Network Information Center. The use of the Internet connection was initially restricted to e-mail, Usenet news, and Telnet (remote terminal access) and FTP (remote file transfer) services for those staff members who had accounts on the UCSF computer. During this period, various biotechnology databases and data sources increasingly became available on the Internet, and there was mounting pressure to allow additional users access to the Internet. When GENBANK, a key DNA sequence database on which Genentech scientists rely for information about potentially useful sequences, became available on the Internet—in a more frequently updated form than the quarterly updates on tape—additional users gained access to the Internet for regular downloading of the most recent versions of GENBANK to Genentech computers.

In 1990, Genentech became an affiliate member of the Bay Area Regional Research Network, or BARRNet, which began advertising a route to Genentech's network. The physical connection to the Internet continued to go through UCSF, but employees with demonstrated need could now directly access the Internet from Genentech computers. Because security continued to be a concern, the Genentech fire wall received ongoing enhancements. In addition to the fire wall software developed at Genentech, special software was implemented to allow users inside Genentech's network to employ the fire wall computer as a proxy for accessing host systems on the Internet, which enabled these internal systems to avoid exposure to access from systems on the Internet. Eventually, the connection to the Internet was moved off a production system onto a dedicated machine. In 1994, Genentech became a full member of BARRNet and connected directly to the BARRNet core with a T1 (1.5-megabits-per-second [Mbps]) dedicated link. By then, Genentech's business needs and the uses of the Internet for Genentech scientists and staff justified both the increased access and the increased bandwidth.

The period of growth in external access was accompanied by the growth of Genentech's internal computing resources. The adoption of Transmission Control Protocol/Internet Protocol (TCP/IP) as Genentech's major networking protocol enabled the company to link all the buildings at corporate headquarters in South San Francisco, the European office in Basel, Switzerland, and the Canadian office in Toronto. Within Genentech, interest in the Internet rose dramatically as a result of both heightened media attention and the rapid increase in valuable scientific resources available via the Net. The ease of Internet access provided by Mosaic, Netscape, and other World Wide Web (WWW) browsers also contributed significantly to the growing interest in the Internet among Genentech's researchers.

The growth of Genentech's use of the Internet has far exceeded the company's original expectations. The fact that this growth was achieved with limited resources is attributable to a combination of careful planning and lucky decisions at the outset. One of the lucky decisions made early on was the adoption of TCP/IP as the company's interoperability standard. This meant that most of the desktop devices and all the servers in Genentech's environment were capable of participating in an internetworked environment. The development of an e-mail system that could easily exchange messages with the Internet and the early attention paid to security were also fortuitous. A critical decision was the adoption of a phased approach to Internet implementation, as it allowed key members of Genentech's management to become comfortable with the technology as the corporation's use of it increased and ensured that the implications for corporate computing security at each step in the process were discussed and addressed.

Figure 4-1 shows Genentech's use of the Internet since the connection was first made in 1990. As the figure demonstrates, use was relatively low initially but increased steadily after 1992. In December 1994 alone, Genentech exchanged 2.3 gigabytes (GB) of data with sites on the Internet. Although

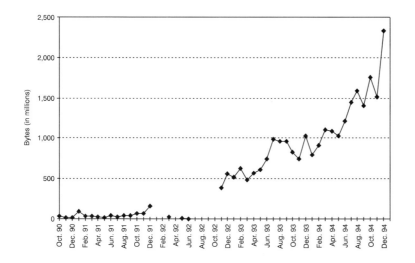

Figure 4-1 Genentech's Internet Usage (October 1990–December 1994)

much of this data exchange consisted of e-mail, the regular transfer of large data files, such as the GENBANK updates, represented a significant portion of the overall traffic. Currently, Genentech's gateway processes 14,000 mail messages a week to or from the Internet. With the increased use of the Web, the volume of traffic will inevitably grow. As Genentech's experience indicates, even if the initial level of Internet use is low, it can rise dramatically in a relatively short time. Therefore, one of the key criteria in choosing an Internet access provider should be the provider's level of connectivity to the backbone, which must be sufficient to support a potentially rapid increase in traffic load over time.

GENENTECH'S INTERNET ARCHITECTURE

Genentech's connection to the Internet is via BARRNet, which was the designated National Science Foundation (NSF) network in the San Francisco Bay Area. In one of its computer rooms, Genentech maintains a Cisco router connected to a dedicated T1 (1.5-Mbps) line. At the other end of the T1 circuit is a BARRNet core router. The BARRNet connects to an MCI T3 (45-Mbps) backbone network, which has replaced the old NSFNET backbone. The BARRNet also maintains a connection to the Commercial Internet Exchange (CIX).

The Genentech Internet router (Gtech-open-gw) is connected to an "open" network. Because it is assumed that all hosts connected to the open network are subject to attempts to gain unauthorized access, these hosts are very well protected against potential damage from such access. One very well protected host on that network is the fire wall computer. This machine runs the fire wall software, which includes modified versions of some system utilities; the most recent versions of the mail program, *sendmail;* the externally visible name server; and the low-level proxy program, *socks.*

Outside the fire wall is another network that utilizes private leased lines and frame-relay links to connect Genentech with selected business partners that require a more secure, direct connection to Genentech. This network (labeled "Limited Access Net" in Figure 4-2) was comparatively easy to add to the original network architecture because it is based

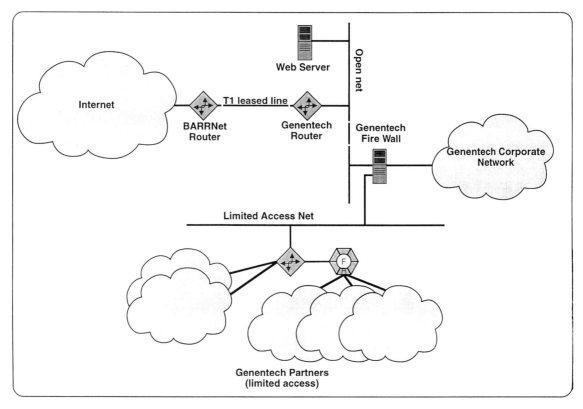

Figure 4-2 Genentech's External Network Architecture

on the same protocols and fire wall technology used between Genentech and the Internet.

The current network architecture depicted in Figure 4-2 should provide Genentech with a foundation for continued growth as the company's uses of the Internet continue to grow. Eventually, higher-bandwidth connections to the Internet and additional fire walls will be required to provide redundancy and higher throughput. The security of the existing arrangement has been evaluated through one formal audit and one informal external audit, and the auditors have concluded that the current architecture provides a reasonable balance between security and access.

MAJOR USES OF THE INTERNET AT GENENTECH

The four major uses of the Internet at Genentech are: (1) acquiring data or computer programs for use at Genentech; (2) collaborating with colleagues at other institutions; (3) participating in electronic forums; and (4) finding and using data, information, or computing resources available outside Genentech. Each of these uses has important business implications for Genentech.

Acquiring Data or Computer Programs for In-House Use

One of Genentech's principal uses of the Internet is accessing the most current versions of critical scientific databases and resources, such as the latest versions of the DNA sequence database GENBANK and the protein sequence database SWISSPROT, as well as the Brookhaven Protein DataBank, which is now available for electronic searching. Other public databases are becoming available as a result of the Human Genome Project. By comparing sequences in these databases with newly isolated DNA sequences, Genentech scientists can determine to which gene family a sequence might be similar and whether the protein coded for by the DNA has already been identified and researched. Access to this information can save a scientist potentially hundreds of hours devoted to further isolation and identification of a protein that is already known. With the rate of sequence identification increasing dramatically, access to the most current versions of protein and DNA sequence databases is critical and can produce cost savings in the millions of dollars.

The key DNA and protein databases were the original justification for Genentech's connection to the Internet. New databases that contain important data for Genentech research projects and that are expected to become available in the near future include cancer and neurobiology databases, on-line digital brain atlases, and other specialized data stores. If Genentech scientists obtain access to such data before competing scientists at other pharmaceutical companies can, they will have an edge in deriving any significant discoveries of commercial relevance.

Genentech scientists use the Internet to access another key resource: software. Some of the best software for analyzing DNA and protein sequences has been developed at academic institutions or federally sponsored laboratories, and much of this software is made available on the Internet. Enhancements to analysis software, which may be released far faster than commercial software enhancements, generally improve product performance. Occasionally, however, they modify the algorithms to improve sensitivity or to provide additional controls. These enhancements give Genentech scientists the best possible tools for analyzing DNA and protein sequences. Increasingly, software for molecular modeling and computational chemistry is also becoming available via the Internet.

Access to current databases and analysis software results in two major benefits for Genentech's business. First, there is the obvious benefit that data pulled from the Internet might provide a clue to a new therapeutic agent, thereby saving the effort that would otherwise have been spent on pursuing proteins whose functions are already known and shortening the time from discovery to marketing of a new therapeutic agent. The result can be significant cost savings or a significant new or more timely income stream. Second, the reputation of having the best databases and high-quality tools can help Genentech recruit the best scientists in order to hire or collaborate with them. It is currently the case that researchers in or from academia expect easy Internet access; it is quickly becoming the case that scientists working in commercial biotechnology expect easy Internet access as well.

Collaborating with Colleagues at Other Institutions

To avoid duplication of effort and to pool resources for various aspects of research and development, Genentech scientists use the Internet connection to exchange information in a timely and efficient manner with collaborators inside the company as well as with consultants and business partners at institutions throughout the world. Internally, this exchange relies heavily on Genentech's corporate e-mail system. When collaboration involves other institutions, the collaborators occasionally need access to Genentech's network in order to exchange e-mail and electronic documents. More often, however, electronic correspondence can be exchanged over the Internet, which is preferable in terms of both convenience and performance.

Collaboration is also supported by other forms of Internet access, such as Telnet or FTP, which are most often used to retrieve data files from shared instrumentation located at the collaborators' or contractors' facilities. Previously, all data files of this sort were stored on nine-track magnetic tape, which had to be hand-carried or delivered to the recipient.

Collaborations with colleagues at other institutions are not restricted to Genentech scientists. Staff members in information technology, medical affairs, and regulatory affairs also conduct ongoing collaborations or regular interactions that rely on the exchange of documents, data, or correspondence via the Internet. The Genentech library staff uses the Internet to search for literature and access various data sources made available by search bureaus. Recently, the library added a regular feature on electronic information resources to its monthly newsletter.

Participating in Electronic Forums

While most collaboration is carried on between individual scientists or between groups of scientists, collaboration on Internet tools and techniques occasionally takes place in forums that have wider audiences. Participating in electronic forums can help scientists to reduce the amount of effort they might otherwise expend in attempting to solve problems with a computer program or tool that others have already solved, with obvious advantages in terms of efficiency and cost savings.

Access to Usenet newsgroups was one of the original uses of Genentech's connection to the Internet. These newsgroups continue to proliferate, and the variety and amount of information available from these sources continue to increase. Of special interest to Genentech are two newsgroup hierarchies: the bionet.* newgroups and the comp.* newsgroups. The bionet.* newsgroup hierarchy provides a mechanism for the exchange of information among researchers in various disciplines related to biotechnology (molecular biology, plant biology, immunology, and so forth). It also provides a forum for the release of job announcements, tips on various related software packages, and announcements of general interest to the biology community. The comp.* newsgroup hierarchy is tracked closely by the computing professionals at Genentech. These newsgroups—which cover all the operating systems, hardware platforms, and software development environments at Genentech, as well as a variety of public-domain software systems—help keep the Genentech staff aware of developments in networking, client-server architectures, operating systems, user interfaces, databases, and other relevant areas such as the Internet and TCP/IP.

The mailing list, or distribution list, is another Internet mechanism that facilitates the exchange of information among those with shared interests. Genentech staff receive a variety of distribution lists, including those relevant to users of a common scientific software package and those relevant to specific advances in computing technology. Distribution lists are also used either formally or informally to support professional affiliations of Genentech staff and communications among colleagues with shared interests.

Finding and Using Outside Sources of Data, Information, and Computational Resources

The Web browser, which was developed to support the high-energy physics community at CERN, is easer to use than either FTP or Telnet and has been enthusiastically embraced by the biomedical community. At Genentech, scientists have begun demanding increasingly better access to the Web to locate information resources relevant to their research or development efforts, perform literature searches, or obtain computing services.

Of course, Genentech staff access the Web not only to search for scientific information relevant to their research but also to make travel arrangements to conferences, check on the weather or cultural activities in cities they will be visiting, or look up the latest stock prices for Genentech or other companies. The number and types of information sources available on the Web are growing at a phenomenal rate. Figure 4-3 shows some Web sites of particular interest to the Genentech community.

National Institutes of Health Molecular Modeling Home Page
 (*http://www.nih.gov/molecular_modeling/mmhome.html*)

World Wide Web Virtual Library: Biosciences
 (*http://golgi.harvard.edu/biopages.html*)

National Center for Biotechnology Information
 (*http://www.ncbi.nlm.nih.gov/*)

On-Line Mendelian Inheritance in Man
 (*http://gdbwww.gdb.org/omimdoc/omimtop.html*)

European Molecular Biology Laboratory (EMBL)
 (*http://www.embl-heidelberg.de/*)

Johns Hopkins University BioInformatics Web Server
 (*http://www.gdb.org/hopkins.html*)

Biotech Industry Organization Home Page
 (*http://www.bio.org/pub/home.html*)

Figure 4-3   World Wide Web Sites of Interest to Genentech

EXAMPLES OF THE INTERNET'S IMPACT ON GENENTECH'S BUSINESS

This section discusses two specific examples that illustrate the positive impact of the Internet on some aspect of Genentech's business plus a third example involving an application that may not be "ready for prime time." The first example shows how on-line databases accessed via the Internet, particularly the Web, provide support for important research projects; the second demonstrates the advantages of using the Internet to foster communication with a business partner in the product development process; the third concerns literature searches, an area in which use of the Net has not yet achieved significant success.

Providing Support for a Key Research Project

A Genentech scientist came across an issue of *Nucleic Acids Research,* a common reference for molecular biology, that contained a series of articles discussing on-line databases.

The scientist was interested in potential links between a surprising result obtained in one of his research projects and any similar condition that has been discovered in humans. If such a link were found, it might provide important clues to the behavior of the molecule in which the scientist was interested and might suggest possible commercial opportunities for development of the molecule or an antagonist to the molecule.

The scientist started his search by looking at the "On-Line Mendelian Inheritance in Man" database. Historically, the information in this database had been available only in book form, and the scientist had manually searched this literature for a possible link without success. When the scientist used a simple key word search in the on-line version of the database, however, he found a literature reference describing a human condition closely resembling the result obtained in his research. In the scientist's own words, "It would be difficult to underestimate the importance of rapid access to these databases." Although this unexpected link may never result in the development of a new product, the scientist's use of the Internet saved him a substantial amount of time that would otherwise have been needed to manually search through various literature references. Moreover, the ease of electronic access and searching kept the scientist from abandoning a potentially fruitful avenue of research.

Fostering Communication with a Business Partner during Product Development

The development of a potential therapeutic agent is a long and costly process. Near the end of this process, clinical trials are conducted in several phases to determine the appropriate dosage, efficacy, and safety of the new agent. Clinical trials are generally conducted by multiple physicians at multiple sites. Often, a pharmaceutical company will work with an outside group of specialists who will organize and manage the clinical trial, provide impartial oversight of the conduct of the trial, and analyze and interpret the data. When a pharmaceutical company works with a contract research organization, communication between that organization and the statisticians, clinicians, and computing professionals at the company is critical to ensure timely analysis of test data that the company hopes to include in a submission to the FDA. On one occasion, Genentech selected a university-based research organization on the East Coast to manage a clinical trial. Initially, dial-up accounts were created to enable the clinicians and statisticians at the university to access Genentech's computers in order to exchange electronic messages about patient enrollment and project status with the company's scientists. (Test data cannot be discussed except at certain points in the trial to ensure a "blind" study.) This mode of communication was deemed unsatisfactory because it did not integrate well with the work habits of the relevant individuals at the university. It was discovered, however, that all of these individuals could be accessed via Internet mail. This discovery led to the creation of mail "aliases" on Genentech's computers to facilitate naming conventions for Genentech users, and the project participants at each end used Internet mail for coordination and communication during the clinical trial.

The impact of using this "friendlier" technology is difficult to assess. However, considering that each day the approval of a potential therapeutic agent is delayed, the potential revenues lost can amount to hundreds of thousands of dollars, or even a million dollars, even small efficiencies can result in large payoffs. By providing convenient, reliable, easy-to-use tools, the Internet can contribute to those efficiencies.

Conducting Literature Searches

Because many (if not most) vendors of on-line literature databases can now be accessed via the Internet, interested parties can theoretically use the Net to perform literature searches. However, Genentech has encountered certain problems with performing such searches.

The first problem involves the issue of conducting searches in the most cost-effective manner. Literature searches have traditionally been performed by connecting a modem to a public data network that relies on X.25 to construct a circuit to the search vendors' computers. This access method uses serial communications for everything. In particular, a serial "break" is used to abort a query to download in progress. Because each download costs money—and incorrect or unnecessary downloads cost the same as downloads that provide the desired information—the serial bank feature is an important part of the search process. The Telnet protocol used by the Internet does define an out-of-band signal, referred to as a "TELNET BREAK." Unfortunately, not all on-line database vendors' implementations catch the signal and perform the expected action (i.e., abort the query or the download in progress), thereby unnecessarily raising the cost of Net searches.

Furthermore, the vendors' connectivity speeds and reliability are not up to the same levels as their X.25 access, perhaps because searches conducted via the Internet currently represent only a small portion of their business.

Despite these problems, it is still faster and less costly to conduct literature searches via the Internet than to conduct them manually. Hence, Genentech intends to continue using its Internet connection to perform these searches, in the hope that the database vendors will eventually improve their Internet connectivity and services.

POTENTIAL NEW USES FOR THE INTERNET AT GENENTECH

As discussed above, the wealth of information available through the Internet is extremely valuable to Genentech's ability to remain competitive. It is clear to Genentech's scientists and management that the Internet will play an increasingly vital role in the company's overall research and development effort, in part because of the phenomenal growth of the World Wide Web. More and more corporations and laboratories are using Web technology to "publish" various kinds of information. A number of genomic research efforts have already adopted Web technology and use the Web to make their results available to the larger community. Other providers of information relevant to Genentech researchers are rapidly following suit. In 1995, when Genentech's external Web server is up; Genentech will also become a publisher on the Net, providing information about the company, its products, its collaborative research efforts, and possibly, about its employees and employment opportunities.

New uses of the Internet are suggested constantly, both within Genentech and externally. One suggestion involves a Genentech-sponsored program for high school biology teachers called Access Excellence. The program would help participants develop teaching materials and exchange them with their colleagues. Providing the instructors with their own Web pages, where they could "publish" their projects, would enhance their experience as well as their opportunities for collaboration with other teachers. The Internet could also provide teachers participating in the Access Excellence program with the means to communicate with Genentech scientists participating in the program.

Another possible new use that has been suggested involves "virtual presentations"—i.e., using the Web to broadcast live audio and video events to any site. Virtual presentations could greatly promote collaboration while simultaneously reducing travel costs. Suggestions for commercial uses have also been made; for example, an application that would allow Genentech employees to look up information about an item in a catalog using a Web browser, order the desired item, and pay for it using a personal or corporate encryption key. The seller would use the key to authenticate the order and debit the appropriate account.

ORGANIZATIONAL IMPACT OF INTERNET USE AT GENENTECH

The advent and phenomenal growth of the Internet have not led to any appreciable organizational changes within Genentech as a whole or within the computing support groups. Most Genentech employees have readily absorbed Internet technologies into their daily work, and these technologies are becoming a key part of the company's computing infrastructure.

Within Genentech, several groups cooperate in the management, planning, and deployment of Internet technologies. Initially, the scientific computing group provided the primary impetus for the use of Internet technologies such as SMTP-based mail, Telnet, FTP, and X-Windows. As Internet technologies gained commercial exposure, other computing groups within the company expressed growing interest in these technologies. At present, virtually all the computing groups participate in some way in the development, evaluation, support, or deployment of Internet technologies. The scientists and others within the company who are potential users of the Internet or resources on the Internet also play a major role. Recently, the corporate communications department, which is responsible for Genentech's external communications, has started developing a Web server that will provide Internet users who are not employees of Genentech with access to the company's official press releases, announcements of research collaborations, job postings, and other company information.

Genentech is also using Web technology to implement an internal information service for its employees. This service, called *gWiz!,* is expected to provide information about Web sites of particular relevance to Genentech employees, companywide announcements, press releases, the company phone list, and news about company activities and interests.

GENENTECH'S CONTINUING CONCERNS ABOUT INTERNET USE

Security concerns remain the chief impediment to the increased use of the Internet. At Genentech, these concerns surface in a number of areas, which range from conducting transactions over the Internet to ensuring the privacy of e-mail messages. These concerns are exacerbated by "spoofing"—i.e., users pretending to be somebody else. A number of possible solutions to these problems have been suggested, such as privacy-enhanced mail (PEM), pretty good privacy (PGP), and the inclusion of public key encryption into Web servers and browsers. Continued expansion of the use of the Internet as a corporate resource depends on the establishment of security standards and their adoption by computer vendors and the Internet community within the United States and abroad.

Another impediment to the continued expansion of the

Internet is the architecture and technology of the Net itself. As new uses of the Internet such as those described above become more generally available, additional bandwidth will be required. The next-generation IP protocol, IPng, should constitute a solid foundation for growth. The yet to be determined National Information Infrastructure (NII) will serve as the political counterpart to the technical solutions offered by IPng. The NII will provide the hardware as well as the political, and possibly regulatory, infrastructure for the development of the next-generation Internet. As the dialogue surrounding the NII continues, one point that is very relevant to the future uses of the Internet should be considered—namely, that academia is an essential part of the Internet. Much of the key information of interest to Genentech scientists is "published" via the Internet by academic institutions, and many of Genentech's collaborators are academics or academic institutions. It is Genentech's hope that the next-generation Internet, as articulated by the various committees involved in the NII, will recognize the value provided by the exchange of information between industry and academia.

Finally, there are important concerns about what access to information on the Internet implies for copyright and intellectual property laws. Publishers are rapidly trying to come to terms with the copyright issues associated with electronic publishing, but little has been said about how the use of Internet-based resources affects intellectual property laws. At the heart of this concern are the differences between U.S. patent law and international patent law. Under international patent law, any public disclosure of information prior to patent filing invalidates the patent. The issue, relative to the Internet, is what constitutes "public disclosure." If information about a research effort is available somewhere on the Internet, and Genentech scientists independently arrive at the same result, how can the scientists prove that they had no access to the published information? What are the implications if they cannot? Answering these questions will require much more experience with Internet publishing and an understanding of what rights authors retain and what rights they implicitly relinquish. This is one of many legal issues relative to the Internet (but not particularly central to Genentech's usage) that will need to be resolved as the commercial uses of the Internet grow and mature.

Genentech's success depends on the success of its research and development efforts. The Internet is one of the resources that the company uses to support those efforts. Access to the Internet significantly enhances the process of scientific collaboration and discovery, as well as the company's ability to attract new scientists. In addition, the Internet and the opportunities for collaboration that its use provides are critical to the dynamic scientific culture that thrives at Genentech.

Although this chapter has focused on the benefits that accrue to Genentech from its use of the Internet, costs are also involved, including the costs of the network connection, the BARRNet membership, and the staff to maintain and support network connectivity, as well as the costs implicit in the security risks associated with the Net. At Genentech—thanks to careful planning, fortuitous decisions, and management support—these costs are clearly outweighed by the benefits of Internet use.

LOCKHEED MARTIN

Integrating Information Resources

STEVE L. SWENSON

Manager, R&DD Information Resources

FOR 40 YEARS AFTER the end of World War II, the U.S. government supported industrial research as being fundamentally good for the nation and for business. Over the last few years, this support and the accompanying funding have been sharply reduced as the Cold War ended and as U.S. industry lost its dominance in global business. Deeply affected by severe budget cuts, all aerospace companies have massively downsized. The irony is that these cuts have reduced research and development (R&D) spending just as the companies supplying the government are finding that they need to develop technology and products to move into new commercial markets.

Aerospace companies find that customers have changed from making a "lifetime of the program" commitment to making a commitment by phase, with follow-on work depending on the success of the preceding phase. Both new and

The author wishes to acknowledge the important contribution of Chris Rhode, who developed and integrated the software tools that enabled his vision to become a reality. Chris saw this development as a challenge—finding the best way to get this done while maintaining a sensitivity to overall integration, cost of maintenance, and ease of use. His expertise and willingness to risk and try new things has been invaluable in developing these systems. The author would like to thank the Lockheed Research and Development Division for giving him the challenge of supporting the dramatic changes under way at the laboratory, for its willingness to experiment, and for its support in shaping new ideas into useful tools for the laboratory.

traditional customers are demanding improved efficiency, better value, and reduced cycle times. These customer demands have forced the aerospace industry to adopt a different business model—one characterized by competition, increased attention to product quality and service, price sensitivity, and deemphasis of leading-edge technology.

This new business model runs on information—information about the customer, customer values, alternatives, competition, and cost. Current and accurate information—and timely action on that information—is critical to winning contracts in this new environment. Companies cannot afford long management chains, extended meetings, or waiting until everyone has time available on crowded calendars to make decisions. If you wait, others will meet the need. As a result of this new business model, many companies are struggling to change, whereas others are being acquired or closed.

The Research and Development Division (R&DD) of the Lockheed Missiles and Space Company (LMSC), which has been in business for 38 years, has undergone major change as a result of this new business model.* The traditional mission of the R&DD has been the development of technologies required by the LMSC. When the LMSC made the strategic decision in the late 1980s to diversify into commercial businesses in addition to maintaining a strong defense business, it triggered a series of changes in the R&DD to accommodate the complex of new businesses.

Over the past five years, the R&DD has fundamentally reengineered and optimized its business processes, removing any parts that do not add value in the new business climate—such as shortening the procurement process to 3.1 working days from a previous average of 15 working days. Emphasis has shifted from research by individual contributors to development of product-focused technology by cross-disciplinary teams that often partner with non-Lockheed companies to share technology development. As a result of the shift from competency in individual disciplines to the ability to syner-

---

*In early 1995, Lockheed Corporation and Martin Marietta Corporation merged to become the Lockheed Martin Corporation. The Information technology changes discussed in this chapter all occurred within the Lockheed Missiles and Space Company of the Lockheed Corporation, prior to the merger. The merger has increased the opportunities for wider use of these tools and information concepts.

gize and integrate several disciplines into cost-effective technology solutions to specific business problems, timely access to information about current research and potential applications has become increasingly important for effective collaboration between the R&DD and its potential customers and partners. Responsibility, decision making, and accountability have been pushed lower in the organization through the use of teams and collaboration, increasing the importance of timely communication of directions, goals, marketing intelligence, and information to all decision makers. In response to customer demand for improved visibility into the progress of their contracts and for a richer, more frequent, less formal interchange of information with the company, the LMSC now formulates plans for information exchange with companies with which it teams up to perform on contracts and presents the plans in LMSC proposals for contracts. Customers closely evaluate these plans, regarding them as a significant part of the company's projected capability to perform on the contracts.

All these changes underscore the critical importance of the R&DD's information flow and the need to improve that flow. Individuals working in teams or work groups need improved capabilities for communicating across time and distance. Managers want to lower their organizations' collaboration costs by replacing meetings and time- and labor-intensive processes, such as reproducing and routing documents and papers, with tools and systems that can accomplish those functions electronically.

This chapter looks at how the R&DD has improved its information flow to meet the challenges of the new business environment successfully and what lessons it has learned along the way.

A NEW MODEL FOR INFORMATION MANAGEMENT

A key activity in business process reengineering is to thoroughly understand the assumptions and business drivers behind the organization's existing systems and processes, identify current business drivers and needs, and rethink the systems, processes, and solutions in light of the current business drivers. Accordingly, the R&DD reexamined the fundamental assumptions of its business and reshaped those assumptions, where necessary, to ensure the lowest-cost, focused delivery of key information. Using current-day computing technology, the R&DD determined that labor was the key cost driver of the business, accounting for most of the cost of creating, obtaining, using, and storing information. Labor was driving the cost of information delivery in three areas: (1) accessing and using information; (2) creating the systems to acquire, store, and use information; and (3) enabling the "reuse" of information through the maintenance of a "corporate memory" of information already acquired. Moreover, trends—stable over the 15 preceding years—indicated that labor cost as a portion of the cost of information could be expected to increase, whereas all other information costs would decline rapidly.

The R&DD then looked at various commercially available software programs to determine the potential for reducing the labor content of its information systems. It found that commercially available information applications had several disadvantages, such as requiring users to maintain multiple directories (grouping information by topic) and "in-baskets" (computer locations where incoming information is placed) and offering different user interfaces, commands, and capabilities. It was also extremely difficult if not impossible to use these applications to integrate information such as technical drawings, three-dimensional models, and pictures from multiple sources. The net result was hodgepodge computing rather than a seamless information "system."

The R&DD decided that commercially available applications were not the fundamental reengineering for which it was looking and that the then-available versions incorporated design choices that limited the return on investment to a range far short of the R&DD's goals. Further, after assessing the impact of its own near-term vision of the coming technology, the R&DD felt that the life of commercially available systems was too short. What the R&DD required was a common information infrastructure—one that would provide a single computer location where all information and tools would be accessible to the user and easy to use.

The R&DD studied the successes and failures of previous

systems implementation efforts, both internal and external to Lockheed, most of which used some form of database technology to centralize information in a single location. Without exception, the implementations that the R&DD examined had ended up with performance, cost, licensing, deployment, or modification problems. The R&DD was determined to avoid, through appropriate design, as many problems as possible.

The Internet provided the R&DD with both a source of information and a model for the exchange of information among independent but cooperating organizations. Many of the tools and techniques used on the Internet were transformed into low-cost and highly reliable support tools for gathering, organizing, searching, distributing, and archiving information developed internally or obtained from external sources. A key strategy was the R&DD's use of the Internet technology known as the World Wide Web (or the Web) to define a standard user access.

The R&DD's new model for information management is based on Web technology, which enables a user to access, search, display, and transfer information from a server to the user's desktop. Specialized information or a specialized method of displaying information is programmed only on the server, leaving the user's desktop software unchanged to provide a "one size fits all" display, no matter what information or application system the user is accessing. This technology, which the R&DD refers to as a "common user interface," is defined by the Hyper/Text Markup Language (HTML) protocol embodied in Internet specifications and is implemented in Internet tools such as Mosaic and Netscape Navigator.

FUNDAMENTAL CONCEPTS OF THE R&DD'S INFORMATION MANAGEMENT

As the R&DD gained a better understanding of its information needs and business drivers, it developed a set of five fundamental concepts for managing information. These concepts have been found valuable as criteria against which to evaluate potential approaches and technologies.

1. *Deliver information in the user's paradigm.* The R&DD

mitigated the effect of the high cost of labor by forcing all information to be delivered via a single consistent interface and toolset that the user specifies and manages to suit his or her preference, giving the user a consistent view of all information. The R&DD chose a standard, simple, button-driven graphical interface that links data to other desktop toolset applications as well as to other information sources. This interface supports the lab's "standard platform set"—which includes Apple Macintosh, Windows, DOS, and UNIX platforms—and the lab's standard desktop toolset (i.e., word processors and spreadsheets). Use of the single interface has minimized both the number of systems deployed on each desktop and user training needs, thereby reducing the total cost of information delivery. It is far less costly to have a single complex information provider than to have many complex information users.

2. *Supplement existing systems.* Given the pace of business, now measured in days rather than years, it makes sense to supplement existing information systems rather than develop a new system for each new information need. Information systems must be able to anticipate a company's rapidly changing business. The ability to develop and modify information tools within several weeks is critical to the longevity and adaptability of the system.

The old model of software system development at the LMSC consisted of a series of steps performed as isolated, sequential tasks, with rigid control and verification at each step. Given the model and the potential delays due to work backlog, limited funding, coordination processes, and the developer's mind-set, the development of any information system tended to be a multiyear process. The original drivers for this development model included an expected system lifetime of 15 or more years, a perceived need for rigid control to ensure stability of the entire information system, and the high value of machine time compared to the labor involved in the development process. The LMSC ended up with many customized systems, each tailored to provide maximum performance and stability for its own specific purpose, with little interaction between the systems. Any interaction between systems was achieved through custom-tailored programs and maintained at a high labor cost.

These drivers are no longer valid in today's computing

environment, with its low-cost workstations, cheap disk storage, high percentage of read-only information, rapid changes in the business climate, expected system lifetime of three to four years, and high labor cost. The new business drivers mandate a rapid development system of a few weeks, which demands a standard information delivery system and the maximum use of commercial off-the-shelf products in the system. In a dramatic change from the previous one- to two-year development cycle for information systems, the R&DD has reduced systems modification times to between 2 and 4 *hours,* systems development times to between 30 and 40 hours, and system deployment times to 15 *minutes.*

3. *Reuse information from internal and external sources.* R&DD scientists are encouraged to draw on other information sources whenever they can, to avoid "reinventing the wheel." At each information need point, a scientist makes an informal trade-off among the available options for acquiring the needed information—developing the information from scratch, doing a literature search, asking someone else for the information, or using commercial information services. The decision is primarily influenced by (1) the scientist's *perception* of the degree of difficulty of exercising an available option, (2) the cost of each option, (3) the scientist's personal experience with such options, and (4) the extent to which the scientist is willing to interact with other individuals or groups.

In the past, R&DD scientists usually chose to rely on their own resources—either rediscovering the information for themselves or using their personal archive of stored journals, textbooks, research papers, and friends in industry. They were reluctant to ask in-house librarians and information researchers who had access to commercial information services to help identify journal articles through keyword searches. This resistance was due to the *perceived* discomfort of social contact, the lack of success, or the desire to "do it myself."

The R&DD has achieved significant savings in labor costs by implementing systems that enable its scientists to reuse information provided by others rather than having to re-create the information themselves or using the labor of laboratory personnel to find the information. It refers to this leveraging of existing information systems as "information reuse" internal and external to the LMSC. R&DD personnel generally do not re-create, rekey, or copy information; instead, they try to access the information in its original location. Exceptions to this approach are made for performance or other reasons.

4. *Use information experts.* An ocean of information is available. Seeking a specific item of information in this ocean is like being in a sailboat that is caught between high waves most of the time: you see only the wave behind the boat and the wave directly ahead, but you lose sight of where the boat is headed. The R&DD recognized this feeling of "being lost among the waves" as a problem and decided that the best approach to supporting information users would be to organize information into a hierarchy. In an information hierarchy, users are always in a context of more detailed information "within" a more general information structure and can move around that structure easily while retaining a sense of "where they are" in the information. Although this approach is frequently used in information delivery, the R&DD chose to emphasize the simplicity of navigation for the users and the ability of users to retrace their steps and regain their landmarks.

Interviews with R&DD personnel revealed that information users have different paradigms of the information catalog needed to access the *same* information. Although most of the R&DD's then-existing information systems were based on a specific catalog, one information catalog definitely did not fit all users. With this knowledge, the R&DD designed a toolset and an approach that can rapidly and inexpensively create many alternative information catalogs to match the paradigms of different user groups while employing the *same* information elements. This made it possible for the R&DD to use experts in library science to locate, organize, and index overall information and use individual paradigm experts to design each alternative information catalog. Thus, a cost manager designed the catalog for cost managers, a scientist/researcher designed the catalog for scientists, a marketing expert designed the catalog for users of marketing information, and so on, with each catalog employing a different sequence and a different search-refinement algorithm.

Program-specific and contract-specific information catalogs have been set up. Each catalog is in the language and the information search/access paradigm of the information user, but all catalogs access the *same* underlying information elements.

5. *Employ a pervasive common user interface.* The data repositories first developed at the LMSC consisted of various forms of fielded financial databases because they contained the information most desperately needed for day-to-day monitoring of the company's business activities. Each system was different in its operation and user interface. Information the systems delivered was late, triggering the development of small, informal data-capture and reporting systems, each with a different user interface. This environment of inconsistent interfaces caused many training and use problems. Support and maintenance labor costs skyrocketed.

The R&DD overcame these problems by delivering all information into a common user interface. To handle a broader range of information needs, it developed access to "helper applications," with all the helper applications controlled and managed by the common user interface. This change significantly reduced labor support costs and facilitated training. Users were very happy. Attention then shifted to the larger information exchange necessary for effective and efficient collaboration, which resulted in the broad and increasingly aggressive effort to improve information access, availability, and use over the 1992–1995 period.

EVOLUTION OF AN INTEGRATED INFORMATION MANAGEMENT STRATEGY

The first system the R&DD chose to develop was one that made available to other organizations within the LMSC all the technology developed at the R&DD. This was called the technology broker system in recognition of the R&DD's charter to transfer technology from the research laboratory into development processes and customer product. In the past five years, the R&DD has used a consensus-based continuous improvement (CI) process to develop other integrated information systems. Exhibit 5-1 summarizes key attributes of the phases in the evolution of the R&DD's information management strategy.

	1989	1992–1993	1994	1995
Type of information system	Technology broker system	NetNews and WAIS (wide area information servers)	Information architecture	Pervasive common user interface
Business driver	To improve business relationship between the lab and customers within LMSC	To use inexpensive, valuable information tools to save time, share information, and access outside discussions	To provide wider easy access to information	To achieve integration and radically lower cost of system development
Sponsor	CI team	R&DD CI team	R&DD CI team and R&DD computer services Demand and use by some programs/contracts	R&DD directors R&DD computer services
Architecture	Mainframe with dumb terminal interface	Client-server with graphical user interface, but only text is displayed Clients for Macintosh, PC, UNIX, VMS, and OV/VM WAIS has extensions for graphics	Client-server World Wide Web Clients for Macintosh, PC, and UNIX; limited clients for VM and VMS	Client-server World Wide Web Clients for Macintosh, PC, and UNIX
Features	Supported submission of customers' questions to the R&DD via e-mail Supported conferencing within the R&DD for discussion Supported a database (yellow pages) of internal R&D resources (people, labs, equipment) and R&DD literature	NetNews: provides electronic bulletin board system with topical hierarchy of current news and Q&A forum WAIS: provides search tool with full-text and Boolean search capability NetNews and WAIS can be used alternately; some information is exclusively in WAIS	Supports a single wraparound tool incorporating all previous tools (i.e., NetNews, WAIS, FTP [file transfer protocol], Telnet, Gopher, and Archie) Supports hyperlinks and bookmarks Supports multimedia (e.g., graphics, CADAM [computer-aided design and manufacturing], movies)	Formats information to user's specifications Delivers information in user's choice of desktop tools

	1989	1992–1993	1994	1995
Cost	$5,000	$20,000	$30,000	$30,000
Problems	Lack of updating support Security concerns Size of documents versus printer speed Printers not widely available Poor connectivity	Could not handle graphics or formatted documents Client not user-friendly; bugs in public-domain software Finding and updating information Creating custom filter scripts	Slow deployment Security concerns Gathering information from sources onto servers	Changing the R&DD's culture and paradigm Standardizing the systems Formatting information from sources onto servers

Exhibit 5-1   Evolution of the R&DD's Information Management Strategy

The Technology Broker System

The technology broker system was implemented in 1989 by a CI team with the charter to "improve the business relationship between the lab (the R&DD) and customers within Lockheed (the Corporation)." The system was to "broker" information between the originator (the R&DD) and the consumers (programs and customers within the LMSC) to facilitate the technology transfer process. The system supported (1) submission of customers' questions to the R&DD via electronic mail (e-mail) for review, discussion, and consensus response by R&DD personnel; (2) conferencing within the R&DD to arrive at the consensus response; and (3) a "yellow pages" database of internal R&DD information, resources (people, specialty areas, equipment), and R&DD literature.

The system was developed at a cost of $5,000, using the available tools on a VAX mainframe feeding dumb terminals on a user desktop. The system worked, but the information was not always updated in a timely fashion. In addition, senior management (mostly through paranoia, but driven by a security-conscious culture) had concerns about the protection of sensitive and/or proprietary information. Also, most printers did not do justice to the nice formatting of the documents supplied by the system. Finally, many of the customers targeted by the R&DD did not have access to the system because they lacked robust connectivity to the mainframe. All this bred discontent. However, the technology broker system was sufficient for R&DD management to see the potential and hungered for more.

NetNews and WAIS

In 1992, another CI team picked up the challenge. The 1992 team's charter was to "use cheap and good information tools to save time, share information, and access outside information discussions." About this time, Internet discussion groups had gained a wide enough audience and participation that they contained information that the R&DD found useful. The lab decided to use the Internet tool called NetNews to access the Usenet groups on the Internet as well as to store LMSC and R&DD information. NetNews had client-server architecture and a graphical user interface (as long as the desktop had graphics capability) and nicely supported much of the dialogue that R&DD personnel needed for collaboration. However, users found NetNews's topical information structure cumbersome at times. To remedy this, the R&DD added wide area information servers (WAIS) that offered full-text and Boolean search capability, and made the same information that was in NetNews available through WAIS. This system allowed users to alternate between keyword searches and topical searches as well as to follow the "thread" of a collaborative "conversation" from the asking of the question to the various replies and, through the consensus process, to the final "group answer."

Essentially, NetNews is like the daily edition of a newspaper that delivers a day's worth of current information, whereas WAIS is like an "index" to a year's worth of the newspaper and answers the question, "Where did I see that?" NetNews is an excellent support tool for work groups, especially when the members of the group are not physically in the same location. NetNews's "post when you can" feature eliminates problems of scheduling meetings across time zones. It automatically maintains an electronic history of comments and inputs, thereby reducing time lost waiting for mail to arrive. At the time the system was implemented, however, the Lockheed culture still favored face-to-face meetings and, to a lesser extent, video teleconferencing over electronic meetings.

The Internet may provide a great deal of very useful information with potential to help employees work better, but it is difficult to locate specific information sources on the Net. Usenet can have a low signal to noise ratio. Since LMSC management continues to be concerned about "junk" on the Internet and employees' wasting time reading "junk," the R&DD has explored the possibility of creating a team of employees to monitor the Usenet discussion groups and bring "the best of the best" to LMSC desktops. The company has so far chosen an ad hoc solution: certain topic areas are "managed" by volunteer content experts, whereas others are managed by staff librarians and users who have a business interest or an organizational charter to monitor a particular area of information. The information hierarchy provided by this informal team of interested, engaged people is better than one that a more bureaucratic, chartered service organization could provide, but the quality of the resulting information varies.

Deployment of NetNews and WAIS was slow, as the R&DD team took the "If you build it, they will come" approach. The system did not gracefully handle graphics or formatted documents, and there were bugs in the public-domain software tools. The WAIS interface, although new and clever, was not particularly user-friendly and left unresolved the problems of finding, loading, and updating information in the tools. The R&DD built custom filter scripts to convert the original form of the information into a form palatable to NetNews and WAIS. Examples of information available included the contents of *The Commerce Business Daily,* LMSC management policies and procedures, and activity reports. Putting this software in place and loading it with information cost $20,000. This system worked well through 1993, but the success bred "if only" wishes for more.

Information Architecture

By 1994, another CI team was in place with a charter to "provide wider easy access to information." The R&DD computer services support team was by this time tired of supporting this series of information systems in addition to a large group of specialized reporting systems and joined forces with the CI team. The teams settled on a single wraparound tool that eased user training requirements, allowed wider information access, and enabled single point-and-click access to the next level of information. This tool was the Web, which was embodied in the desktop software application called Mosaic and supported on PCs, Macintoshes, and UNIX platforms.

The Web includes previous Internet tools (NetNews, WAIS, file transfer protocol [FTP], and Telnet) and Internet services (such as Archie and Gopher), and it pleases all users by hiding most of the complexity of using these earlier tools and services. The Web handles multimedia, graphics, and computer-aided design and manufacturing (CADAM) transparently. It allows users to "jump" from one information resource to another, even to different servers, with a single click of a mouse or by typing in a single line specifying the next information resource.

This phase was called the "information architecture," emphasizing the shift from a tool-driven approach to an information-driven approach and minimizing tool complexity, tool operation, and tool learning. With the tool steps out of the way, the user perceives information in a structure that he or she can understand and that contains embedded "hot buttons" that respond to a single click of the mouse.

As developed at the R&DD, the Web has many capabilities that are not obvious from first use. The basic interface, Mosaic, provides one-click retrieval and display of documents containing text and graphics, with embedded "hot buttons" that act as pointers (called hypertext links) to related documents located somewhere on the internal network or on the Internet. Mosaic also incorporates "helper" applications that display documents in specialized spreadsheets, word-processing formats, pictures, movies, sounds, schedules, presentations, or three-dimensional models. To speed the process of adding information and rebuilding the information structure, the R&DD developed tools that automatically generate the linked document structure from an indented outline format. It extends the functionality of the system through the use of scripts that enable rapid searching of text for combinations of words or partial words, and a "sounds like" phonetic search. The R&DD intended to use Mosaic and the current information structure as a "front-end" menu to access all other R&DD information system tools and information. The system provided "forms capability," which allows information to be entered in a "fill in the boxes" model. The information can then be used to develop forms-based "databases" at low cost. Apple Macintosh, PC, and UNIX platforms that display full graphics natively are supported by Mosaic. A limited character-based interface without graphics is available for VAX and IBM mainframes and other character-limited machines. Access to NetNews and WAIS is available. Both server and client software allow for a "sensing" of the desktop tools available and delivery of the appropriate representation of information driven by the display toolset available on the individual client platform as well as by user preference. When information is to be shared with non-Lockheed customers or team members, the R&DD can replicate selected information from a master server to a slave server accessible to systems outside LMSC's security fire walls.

The Web was well received within the R&DD, but its deployment was slow, as the lab was still using the "If you build it, they will come" approach. Concerns about information labeling, data integrity, and security on the Web persisted, and there was still a cost to making new or additional information available through the system.

A Pervasive Common User Interface

During 1995, R&DD senior management sponsored an improved concept of the 1994 toolset as a way to "achieve integration and radically lower cost of information system development." This concept involved using the Web toolset as the infrastructure for delivering all the required R&DD information *into* the desktop tools, displaying that information (typically graphs and charts) in a meaningful way to the user, and allowing the user at that point to *manipulate* the information using the desktop tools. The information is formatted by the user to suit his or her needs and is delivered into the *user's* choice of desktop tools.

Previously, the R&DD had developed a specific report system for each specific information set, using labor-intensive software programming to customize the reports to the user's specification. Each new demand for information meant time spent developing the feed of information, the integration of that information with other information, and the presentation of that information to the user. The process of developing a new system by this method could take anywhere from three months to two years, depending on complexity.

The pervasive common user interface goes beyond the conceptualization of a rich information structure to focus on the entire information process—beyond obtaining the information to *using* the information. The R&DD looked at what users did, from start to finish: how they accessed information, the purposes for which they used the information, the locations to which they moved it, what information they merged, and how they changed the information to make the "product" they delivered to other users. It was discovered that information was not just read but was in fact "reused," changed in form, merged with other information, summarized or consolidated, reworded, shaped, and then delivered to others. The extraction of the information from Mosaic or other sources and the insertion of the information into desktop tools consumed a significant portion of the user's time and was responsible for a large part of the user's problems and frustrations and the customer's dissatisfaction. The R&DD decided to address this problem, starting with its conceptualization of what the "problem" really was and ending with a "near-seamless" integration of the information system with the desktop toolset, enabling the desktop customer to move smoothly from information gathering to information use to product delivery.

To achieve maximum stability and reuse of information in the new system, the R&DD chose to isolate the information from the tools used to access data. The tools contain no rules or hard coding that are data-related; the "data" comprise the information, links to other information, display information, and access information. As a result, a single system can be used to provide all information. To add information to the system, it is only necessary to add data. No programming changes are needed either on the server or on the clients. The information structure is stored centrally to allow "instant" updating and modification of information; only the initial-access pointer and a "hot list" of pointers to frequently accessed information are maintained individually by each user.

The "hot list" and initial-access pointer can be modified by each user with no need for system programming. In addition, the system has been made self-documenting through the use of hypertext.

As of mid-1995, the LMSC had a series of specialized information servers, each focused on the area of information content available on a particular server, with hypertext links in the hierarchy on the individual server to other servers. These specialized servers are distributed within the LMSC and provide links to information outside the company. The value of the information provided by these systems is clear, and business metrics show positive results where the "information architecture" concept is used. In addition, some Lockheed programs use the desktop toolset as a marketing feature and to distinguish the LMSC from its competitors. Customers are impressed with the toolset, which they see as adding value to contract performance. This success has gotten management's attention.

TYPES OF COMMUNICATION

To meet its business goals, the R&DD communicates electronically with other organizations within LMSC, with customers, and with non-Lockheed partners. The four types of communication involved are:

1. *Reference communication:* communication that supports read-only access to laboratory and nonlaboratory (internal and external) information from a server where the information has been stored by the information provider. LMSC uses Web technology, either public-domain or commercial, to support read-only access to reference information such as scope-of-work specifications, customer information, miscellaneous design reference material, and information about company policies, procedures, and operations. The public-domain software for this type of information access is "free."

2. *Collaborative communication:* communication that supports the initial design and modification of in-

formation such as engineering drawings, procedures, and plans. At LMSC, critical development processes (e.g., check-in/check-out of documents, revision control, and voting by product development teams [PDTs], concurrent engineering, and design for manufacture) require coordinated efforts and teamwork. Collaborative information is readable and modifiable, is controlled by a PDT or some other team, and typically is checked into a database server by the creator of the information for access by users. LMSC's "engineering design release waterfall" is a sequential review of a document by many individuals at different times and places. The company's "change control process" requires the negotiated concurrence of many people. Each member of a development work group may work separately on a component of a larger integrated product while maintaining integration, consistency, and overall product function. Members of a PDT must meet frequently and be able to coordinate work between meetings. To modify collaborative information, a team member "checks out" the information (locking it so no one else will make changes), makes the changes, checks the changed information back into the server, and obtains the concurrence of the team by having the members vote on the changes. The team leader then upgrades the attribute of the changed information to "current version." LMSC uses a commercial database software program to support access to collaborative information. The software costs roughly $1,000 per user desktop plus $50,000 for a 20-user concurrent server license.

3. *Notification communication:* timely communication to laboratory personnel of information that they need to know or in which they have an interest. Notification information is sent via e-mail to interested R&DD personnel (who only need to be linked to a standard information location to be assured of full notification of interest information). Notification information is read-only, is usually controlled by the information provider, and typically is routed from desktop to desktop by a mail server. LMSC uses a

commercial database software program to support access to notification information. The software costs roughly $50 per user desktop plus $500 for a 200-user server license.

4. *One-on-one communication:* communication that supports the exchange of information between the R&DD team and the customer. Communication with the customer is read-only, is usually controlled by the person at LMSC who is responsible for program/contract management, and typically is conducted person-to-person through a limited access server. When multiple companies team up on a project, one-on-one communication typically goes to all team members as well as to the customer, following the model for collaborative communication, but the communication cannot be modified. LMSC uses Web technology, either public-domain or commercial, to support this type of information access. The public-domain software is "free."

CURRENT TOOLS

It is critical to the R&DD's success that each employee desktop contain an appropriate set of tools for working with electronic information. At a minimum, the following tools must be available:

1. *Common laboratory tools:* These tools support creation and manipulation of information by laboratory personnel at their desktops. Since LMSC already had a site license for a comprehensive toolset, and these tools were "good enough" for 95 percent of the laboratory's uses, the R&DD used the existing word-processing, spreadsheet, presentation, e-mail, scheduling, and project-planning applications. Site license costs involve an initial fee plus a quarterly maintenance charge. These charges, however, are less costly than acquiring the unique applications preferred by each user, so standardization was forced as a cost saving to the company. Individual

acquisition of other additional tools is permitted, but deviation from the standard toolset is strongly discouraged.

2. *Interactive collaboration tools:* These tools support the real-time interaction of people using various communication techniques, including telephones, audio teleconferences, video teleconferences, and electronic whiteboarding over networks. Because interactive collaboration requires information delivery to desktops, electronic whiteboarding with an added voice telephone connection best meets that need. This communication capability, which requires low-cost and easy-to-use support tools, is expected to be made pervasive at the R&DD.

The features of various electronic information tools currently implemented at the R&DD are summarized in Exhibit 5-2.

ISSUES OF IMPLEMENTATION AND EVALUATION

In moving from a paper-based information system to a computerized information system, the R&DD has encountered all the problems inherent in reengineering: resistance to cultural change, need for user training, need for consensus building, and so forth. In addition, the move from a centralized, tightly controlled environment to a decentralized, looser, user-controlled environment has caused a significant amount of initial discomfort. However, no alternatives were suggested with better potential for payback, efficiencies, and return on investment.

The first step in implementation was to identify the kinds of information that users wanted every day (e.g., phone book/e-mail address directories, company news, and company "how-to" guides). Next, the R&DD team focused on providing added value to existing mechanisms, including faster access, special features (e.g., phonetic searches for last names and on-line searching), and fresher data. The team polled users to determine where they spend their time seeking and collating information and made efforts to automate or simplify their work. The team incrementally refined ideas

Tool Name	Features	Used in Current System?
Telnet	Dumb terminal emulation	Yes
WAIS	Information searching, full-context searching	Yes
NetNews	Topical bulletin board system	Yes
FTP	File transfer	Yes
Gopher	File retrieval	Add-on tool
Archie	Information cataloging	No
Mosaic	Hyper/Text Markup Language viewer	Yes
NetScape	Hyper/Text Markup Language viewer; alternative to Mosaic	Yes
Word processor	Edit/modify/view text documents	Add-on tool
Spreadsheet	Edit/modify/view spreadsheet documents	Add-on tool
Presentation	Edit/modify/view presentations	Add-on tool
Project management	Edit/modify/view project management schedules, tasks, and plans	Add-on tool
Phonetic search	Search text matching on "sounds like" match (e.g., "gud" matches "good")	Yes
Server replication	Replicate information, in a controlled way, to other servers when information is updated	Yes
GIF viewer	View Graphics Interchange Format (GIF)-encoded graphics files	Yes
Graphics viewer	View graphics and images	Add-on tool
HTML forms	Display forms and retrieve fields in viewer	Yes
Server Structured Query Language (SQL) connection	Gives the server SQL query access to SQL-compliant databases on other machines accessible through TCP/IP (Transmission Control Protocol/Internet Protocol)	Yes

Exhibit 5-2   Information Tools Currently Used at the R&DD

and tools with lots of feedback and suggestions, asking at each stage, "Can we do this better?" Development efforts focused on adding high-value, low-cost information sources to satisfy users. Users were kept informed through "what's new" bulletins about new information sources that were available on-line long enough that everybody eventually read them. In addition, the R&DD team designed and built in a "Click to submit comments and suggestions" on-line capability and positioned it visibly near the top of the main home page (see Appendix E).

One of the early implementation problems was obtaining permission to access information from the Web through the company's fire wall. The R&DD had a tremendous problem balancing the pull between computer security people who wanted to put locks on every information item in sight and users who wanted robust Internet access to everything in sight. The two sides eventually reached a reasonable middle ground, but the debate continues and emotions explode at the slightest spark.

Maintaining the privacy and proprietary ownership of company information is an ongoing valid concern in the world of electronic communications. The R&DD chose to make each information provider responsible for determining the sensitivity of the information provided and for marking and storing it appropriately. Because the impact of a security breach in the electronic world is far greater than that in the "paper world," the information provider must make an informed decision from a companywide perspective—not a parochial, limited, uninformed decision. The rule used at the R&DD is, "When in doubt, ask."

The R&DD is clearly experiencing a revolution in its information delivery system. Nevertheless, progress seems agonizingly slow. Although "early adopters" eagerly advocate and use the new systems, 60 percent of the potential users are leery of the new technology and are waiting until there is a compelling reason (such as a management directive) to move to adoption.

The response of the R&DD population to this latest technology upheaval is very similar to the response following the earlier shift from a "host with dumb terminal" environment to the PC and Apple Macintosh desktop environment. Attempts to force early adoption are rarely successful. For users to "buy in" to the technology, they must understand

and accept its benefits. At the R&DD, the surge in e-mail usage occurred about three years after the service was introduced. In the case of the Internet, the R&DD has had little success in shortening the lag in cultural change. User acceptance is directly proportional to need, perceived value, and ease of use.

The dramatic improvement in information flow has clearly had a positive impact, reducing business costs, improving capabilities, and enhancing business processes. To achieve a large benefit rapidly, management must direct and strongly support the early adoption and infusion of this kind of technology.

The R&DD has managed to keep costs low, build user trust, and increase the use of its information systems by automating information updates whenever possible and marking manual information updates on a calendar and sticking to them. It balances the cost of automation versus the frequency of updates; thus, if it takes 30 minutes a week to update the database manually, an investment of 10 hours in devising an automated solution pays for itself in less than five months.

To the extent possible, owners of data (rather than the computer systems personnel) are made responsible for providing updates. The data owners understand that this will be an ongoing commitment, but their pride in the information provided tends to commit them. When information becomes obsolete, it is ruthlessly identified and purged. The R&DD tries to give users the sense that the information server is always "well housekept."

The R&DD works to structure its information hierarchies cleanly, limiting the number of points of departure and providing each division of the company with a home page with pointers to all the other home pages. Since users will store paths and names of links in local bookmark lists, the R&DD avoids changing paths once they are established. It uses hyperlinks to store information only once and then reuses the information.

Given the distributed nature of the system and information servers, it is difficult to measure system use and growth accurately. The NetNews portion of the system logs over 25,000 accesses per day, not including accesses for copying of information to other servers. Within several months of start-up, users would fill the initial 56K baud Internet link to capacity during peak usage periods (midmorning and mid-afternoon). The R&DD has since upgraded to a 1.544M baud line. At present, peak usage runs at about 150 kilobits per second for minutes at a time for external access, with internal servers on individual Ethernet legs filling the Ethernet leg during peak usage. High-use servers have been moved to high-speed FDDI (optical fiber–based) lines. Although these are not precise measures, they give a sense of the usage of the information systems at the laboratory.

The business impact of the R&DD's information systems is difficult to measure, as the effects are both subtle and global. Also, other continuous improvement activities at the laboratory—including changes in process, focus, and customer awareness—have contributed to rather dramatic improvements in the laboratory's business measures. The information systems that support the laboratory have made strong contributions to the success; more important, they have enabled changes that would have been impossible otherwise.

Several business measures indicate an increase in the R&DD's business during a very tough time for defense contractors and a dramatic improvement in the capture of new business. In 1991, the laboratory won 37 percent of the jobs for which it submitted proposals. Following the change in process and the shift of emphasis to collaboration within the laboratory as well as between the laboratory and its customers, the value of jobs won increased to 52 percent of those bid in 1992, to 78 percent in 1993, and to 95 percent in 1994. With e-mail, word processing, and information exchange playing a strong supporting role, the R&DD has increased the value generated by each employee by 45 percent over the 1990 to 1994 period.

Another critical measure that may be used as a reliable indicator of the business impact of the R&DD's new information systems is the time from a system failure until the help desk phone rings, which is now seconds after a failure affects service.

OPPORTUNITIES FOR IMPROVEMENT

The R&DD's current communications model offers a number of opportunities for further refinement and improvement. First, there are software technology groups within the laboratory that have expertise in artificial intelligence, software tools, and other technologies, and their expertise could be useful in information access. The R&DD is currently not capturing any information about the results of information searches and accesses. If captured, that "knowledge" could be used to provide "smart" help to other searches based on captured previous experience. This is an aspect of capturing "corporate knowledge/technology" and reusing it—gaining through economy of scale and shared expertise. If the lab needs to perform many searches, it should be much better at later searches based on prior experience. At present, expertise is shared by word of mouth.

Second, information maintenance is a critical aspect of the information environment. Users expect the information to be current, well-organized, and always available. The R&DD needs to establish a clear infrastructure for maintenance and management of information servers, software, and information.

Third, the R&DD's information toolset can be most valuable as a pervasive information infrastructure for the Lockheed Martin Corporation. So far, most of the R&DD's "business" has come through word of mouth and referrals.

Fourth, there is a move toward charging for information services on the Internet. This move has the potential to dramatically change the R&DD's cost drivers and business assumptions and the implementation of the integrated information system as previously described. With the potential for payment, many additional information sources may become available on the Internet. This can only increase the usefulness of the system.

THE FUTURE OF INFORMATION MANAGEMENT AT LOCKHEED MARTIN

The Internet plays a critical role in the R&DD's information model, both as a source of information and collaboration and as a source of powerful tools built to support a distributed model of information deployment. The tools are quickly tested in a wide environment, and the rate of bugs fixed and improvements is higher than that for typical commercial software providers. Most Internet tools are built collaboratively, resulting in better and more comprehensive tools at an earlier stage of development.

Much of the information that the R&DD needs is in the public domain. Locating the information and obtaining delivery of it are the critical factors. The Internet offers near-instantaneous access and delivery to match a specific user need. This is a wonderful example of on-demand, just-in-time delivery.

The R&DD expects a wider implementation of the current toolset within the LMSC. Already, several Lockheed Martin programs have recognized the toolset's potential value and have decided to implement it. Other divisions of LMSC have seen demonstrations and are considering adopting this technology. The R&DD is in the process of building critical mass. It will probably take another year or so before information delivery using the Web server becomes an obvious choice and then another year or so before the rest of the corporation adopts the toolset. The LMSC currently has a significantly higher percentage of desktop computers than any other company within the Lockheed Martin Corporation. However, word of the strongly positive business outcomes achieved as a result of reengineering is spreading, and the laboratory is beginning a series of metrics and sharing of best practices that should drive the implementation across the corporation.

Competition in the defense industry is forcing this change. The LMSC has learned to embrace change and try to make it work to the company's advantage. However, change is a continuing process—not just a single step—and the R&DD is already asking itself, "What next?"

There is an old story about two hunters being chased by a bear. The first hunter gasps out his worry about not outrunning the bear. The second hunter replies that he is worried about not outrunning the first hunter. The R&DD does not have specific required targets for its information systems; it just needs to develop, use, and evolve the information systems faster, at lower cost, and with more benefits than can any of its competitors. The R&DD thinks it can do that.

6

MILLIPORE
Marketing Products to the Global Desktop

THOMAS ANDERSON

Director of Corporate Communications

MILLIPORE IS A 41-YEAR-OLD, $500-million high-technology company headquartered in Bedford, Massachusetts. The company focuses on applying purification technology to critical research and manufacturing problems, such as purifying the gases used to manufacture semiconductor chips, sterilizing biotechnology-derived drugs, monitoring bacteria levels in municipal water supplies, and testing for chemical and biological pollution in soil and air. Millipore offers several thousand products and accessories targeted at different industries and market niches and has a worldwide sales and marketing infrastructure. In each of the market niches that it serves, Millipore is either the number one or number two player. The company has an outstanding reputation among its customers, as measured by external and internal studies. Indeed, many of Millipore's employees are the company's former customers.

Millipore faces challenges, however: running a knowledge-based business is more costly and complex than running a widget-based business; a relentless focus on individual customers and their needs has resulted in a large number of innovative products and accessories that have created new markets but have also spawned imitators and knockoffs. Millipore has responded to these challenges by providing customers with "added value" in terms of documentation, applications assistance, and technical support and has used innovative marketing tools, such as satellite teleseminars and CD-ROMs, along with more traditional vehicles such as seminars, trade shows, and newsletters to get the message out. It has placed major emphasis on building relationships with multinational customers as well as with the regulatory agencies that set testing standards in various industries. The company has adopted an "infrastructure marketing" approach that makes the easy availability of technical information as important as—if not more important than—typical advertising or direct mail. The field sales force has been automated, and portable computers and modems accelerate information flow and customer support to the Millipore applications specialist sitting in front of the customer.

Millipore has had access to the Internet since 1987 in terms of electronic mail (e-mail) and various file transfer protocol and Telnet connections. True marketing on the Internet, however, was initiated in 1994, after the advent of the World Wide Web (WWW) and the creation of a robust and transferable relational database of Millipore products.

Millipore's customers and potential customers match the demographics of the Internet. A cross-match of Millipore's top customers and Internet "domains" in early 1994 indicated that about 40 percent of the company's top 500 customers were on the Internet in one form or another. Microelectronics companies were strongly represented. Pharmaceutical and biotechnology companies were on the Internet, although few had publicly accessible servers. All major universities were on the Internet, with fascinating and robust databases. Key regulatory agencies, such as the Food and Drug Administration (FDA) and the Environmental Protection Agency (EPA), were on the Internet. The EPA had a robust Mosaic-based server; the FDA had a popular Telnet- and Gopher-based server that the agency supplemented in early 1995 with a WWW server. It was not known exactly who at these companies was "wired"—the network managers or the librarians or the scientists and engineers who purchased Millipore products—but based on the university model, it seemed safe to assume that scientists and engineers at these organizations were, or soon would be, using this tool.

Increasingly, Millipore's own scientists were using the Internet for collaborative research. The Internet permitted faster and more efficient transmission of information than telephones, faxes, modems, or any other means. It simplified the collection of data and accelerated the exchange of creative ideas. In addition to speed, the Internet gave researchers a larger palette from which to work.

Given Millipore's knowledge-based business, focus on the individual customer, and marketing challenges, going "on-line" was predictable and inevitable. It did, however, take a customer to get Millipore started on the Web with its own server.

DOWN THE BIKE PATH

Johns Hopkins University operates a data-rich server for the bioscience research community—with protein databases, owl and mouse DNA sequence databases, and links to all the leading biodatabases around the world. Over 9,000 scientists a day surf the Hopkins server looking for information.

The webmaster at Johns Hopkins thought it might be useful and convenient for these scientists to have on-line access to product information as well as technical databases. In early 1994, he made a request of Millipore's technical service department: could he have Millipore's product catalog in an electronic format? The request went to a marketing support person at Millipore who had created a number of electronic programs based on various protocols and programs. The response was simple: provide an ASCII file that would be converted from the latest desktop published catalog. Work started on this ASCII conversion.

But during lunchtime one day, Millipore's expert took a ride down the bike path that runs behind Millipore from Bedford through Lexington to Cambridge, approximately the same route taken by the Redcoats and Minutemen a few hundred years before. He was going to see a friend, a rocket scientist at the Harvard Smithsonian Astrophysics laboratory, which was located in a converted Sears department store building in Porter Square. At the laboratory, the rocket scientist showed Millipore's in-house expert a new Internet application called Mosaic. It was a revelation. The expert realized that Millipore could offer the Johns Hopkins webmaster a *real* catalog with photos, charts, and diagrams as well as search capabilities and hyperlinks, a more attractive, functional, and complete solution than a simple ASCII flood of words.

Rocket scientists. Minutemen. Laboratories in converted department stores. A paradigm shift was underway. Responding to a customer, having catalog content, having the right people, being opportunistic—all of this put Millipore way ahead of its competition and right where many of its customers were heading.

When Millipore's laboratory product catalog went up on the Hopkins server in March 1994, it was as though a "fast filter" restaurant had opened on the information freeway. In the first 90 days, scientists accessing the Hopkins server pulled down 14,000 files from the Millipore catalog. And that was all "drive-by" traffic, with no promotion and no electronic alerts. Given this response, Millipore decided to develop its own server, make more information available, and embark on its own cyberquest. Traffic on the Hopkins server did not stop, however. In the next eight months, 44,000 additional catalog files were downloaded from the Hopkins server, with each access session pulling down an average of 7 files. Millipore was clearly in the right place: the Web was where leading-edge scientists were collecting the latest information.

THE PLAN, THE PLAN

While Millipore was setting up its server, the Internet was a moving target. New versions of Mosaic and other WWW browsers were coming out on a regular basis. Two thousand corporations a month were setting up Web servers. At the same time, Millipore was learning how to put documents up on the Internet, finding out what constituted an effective "home page," and researching and talking to customers. Within the company, there was skepticism as to whether customers would use an electronic medium to access information, and there was concern about security and catalog pricing information. There was also concern about Millipore's networking infrastructure and the resources needed to create and maintain a robust and reliable server. The Internet itself was viewed with skepticism. Would it last? Would it collapse?

Who owned it? What was the cost? Would Millipore increase its revenue through this channel?

A small team was created to address these external and internal issues and develop a working plan for putting Millipore on the Internet. The plan identified two business objectives, provided a business rationale, targeted certain Internet-savvy customer groups, outlined the information content of the Millipore server, and addressed various issues related to linkages between the outer Internet and the internal company computer networks. The plan covered technical and graphics issues and set measurement criteria. It provided for a training and education program and projected the personnel, capital, and operating costs of going forward.

Millipore's two basic objectives were to provide an information channel that would: (1) enable existing and potential customers to interact with Millipore for technical, application, product, news and ordering information, and (2) enable Millipore scientists and marketers to interact with strategic partners, regulatory agencies, and external databases.

The business rationale was simple: Millipore needed to be in a communication channel increasingly used by scientists and engineers; it needed to deliver information in the format that was most convenient and accessible for its customers. The plan targeted customer segments within each of Millipore's market-focused divisions as well as the company's financial community. A rationale and action plan was developed for each of the segments.

In the laboratory area, Millipore initially focused on the bioresearch customer. The bioresearch community was using the Internet, as evidenced by the large number of databases and hyperlinks related to bioresearch. Millipore had a great deal of technical information available for this audience, which was always looking for the latest applications and protocols. Millipore also targeted its microelectronics customers. Microelectronics companies had very deep and extensive Internet servers themselves. It was felt that they would respond to newsletters and catalogs on-line.

The immediate advantages of using the Internet to market to the pharmaceutical and biotechnology industry (outside of the research laboratory), to customers outside of the United States, and to the financial community were less clear when the plan was created. There were new initiatives in each of these areas, however, and the Internet was added to the marketing mix.

In the pharmaceutical and biotechnology industry, the Internet offered Millipore a means of interacting with process engineers and scientists on drug-validation and process-improvement services as well as on products. It was a means of delivering customer case studies, regulatory news, and hyperlinks.

Millipore has a strong global infrastructure, with more than two-thirds of its business coming from outside the United States. The Internet was seen as a way of furthering and strengthening that infrastructure, particularly in fast-growing areas such as Southeast Asia. An Internet-savvy Millipore customer in Singapore had been asked, via the Internet, by a scientist in Thailand, what company he would recommend for equipping a new three-story laboratory. The customer e-mailed back a ringing endorsement of Millipore. By being on-line itself, Millipore could better support both of those customers.

For Millipore's financial community, the Internet could improve the distribution of quarterly results and corporate news. It would also put that news in the context of our internal marketing efforts and external financial information resources. There was a specific initiative to get information to shareholders and investors faster than could be done by traditional mailings and newspaper reports. Distribution by new voice mail, fax on demand, and Internet channels would help achieve that objective.

In each of these customer areas, the Internet was seen as a means of disseminating and collecting marketing information. It would add speed and depth to that process. Fulfillment of a typical mail-in literature request from a potential customer responding to a journal advertisement might ordinarily take six weeks and several steps to be fulfilled. The customer query goes, in sequence, to the journal's mail house, to Millipore, and to Millipore's literature-fulfillment center. The Internet would speed up that six-week process to a six-second process. Moreover, instead of perusing one or two mailed brochures, the customer could search the entire document database for all information of interest, find additional information, and then leave a question for Millipore technical service. The financial analyst looking at Millipore would be able to see not only the financial press releases and corporate documents, but all the product information and the latest market-specific newsletter, stock quote, and 10K documents.

IMPLEMENTING THE PLAN

Millipore broke down the implementation of the plan into three phases of increasing complexity and functionality. Each phase would make available a richer database of documents and information than the preceding phase, allow more interactivity between the company and its customers, and widen the scope of the server. Millipore anticipated that as the quality and quantity of information on its server improved, there would be a corresponding increase in the quality and quantity of files accessed from the server. Exhibit 6-1 shows a summary of Millipore's three-year plan to move from a minimalist information server in 1994 to full interactive Internet presence by 1996.

Information Content

The Internet action plan helped to focus efforts and provided an ongoing benchmark of progress. The key to Millipore's successful implementation, however, was the relational database of its product catalogs developed just prior to the Internet marketing initiative. This database provides the depth of product content that customers find useful. It includes color photos and product specifications and provides search capabilities and easy linkages to other internal documents and services. Core data in the relational database, maintained in Oracle, are converted to Hyper/Text Markup Language (HTML) for Internet use. Film positives can be generated from the database for use in print and CD-ROM catalogs, on-demand catalogs, contract catalogs, and Internet catalogs.

Using the relational database to put up a catalog on the Internet is ten times faster and ten times less expensive than creating a print catalog, and four times faster and three times less expensive than creating a CD-ROM catalog. The first print catalogs created using this system cost 70 percent less than

	Phase 1	Phase 2	Phase 3
Customer access	Millipore catalog on Johns Hopkins server Millipore Web server (set up in July 1994)	Millipore catalog on Johns Hopkins server Millipore Web server	Millipore catalog on Johns Hopkins server Millipore Web server "Hot links" to and from customers' servers Possible multiple servers worldwide
Functionality	Interactive information source	Interactive information source E-mail delivery of HTML forms to Millipore technical service and webmaster E-mail delivery of market-specific information to customers on request Access to Usenet groups by marketers and scientists	Interactive information source E-mail delivery of HTML forms to Millipore technical service, order service, Millipore network, and webmaster E-mail delivery of market-specific information to customers on request Access to Usenet groups by marketers and scientists Order processing Interactive seminars
Content	Searchable catalogs: • Laboratory products • Microelectronics products Annual report	Searchable catalogs: • Laboratory products • Microelectronics products • Pharmaceutical products Applications information: • Articles • Tech briefs • Newsletters • Software demos Financial information: • Annual reports • Earnings releases • Forms 10K and 10Q • Stock quotes Customer case studies Customer "hyperfilters" with links to regulatory agencies, virtual libraries, and other customers	Searchable, multilingual catalogs: • Laboratory products • Microelectronics products • Pharmaceutical products Applications information: • Articles • Tech briefs • Newsletters • References Product literature: • Marketing brochures • Instruction manuals Financial information • Annual reports • Earnings releases • Forms 10K and 10Q • Stock quotes Customer case studies Customer "hyperfilters" with links to regulatory agencies, virtual libraries, and other customers

Exhibit 6-1   Millipore's Plan for Achieving Full Interactive Internet Presence

	Phase 1	Phase 2	Phase 3
Access from within Millipore	Core group of Internet marketers; scientists	Field marketing staff Headquarters marketing staff Scientists Technical service Investor relations	All employees on the network
Measurement criteria	Number of files accessed	Number of files accessed Number of computers accessing Number of customers accessing Number of participants in user groups Number of technical service inquiries Customer surveys Focus groups Content quality and quantity Cost savings	Number of files accessed Number of computers accessing Number of customers accessing Number of participants in user groups Number of technical service inquiries Number of orders Customer surveys Focus groups Content quality and quantity Cost savings

similar catalogs produced by traditional desktop graphics methods. The print savings alone justified the cost of the relational database.

The relational database also makes it easier and faster to update catalogs with new product information and to link customers to Millipore's technical service (just a fill-in form away). With its relational database and Internet server, Millipore finds it can put information in customers' hands faster than it can via the print method. Millipore envisions a new publishing process in which the electronic product comes first and the print product second, as opposed to the current situation in which the print product comes first and the electronic product second.

Design

For its Internet presence, Millipore had a vision and an architecture in mind. To make these accessible and tangible, one

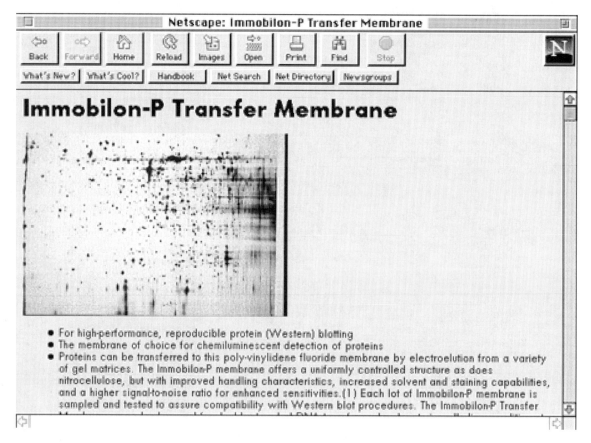

Figure 6-1 An Interactive Catalog Page

of the first things Millipore did was to commission its home page to a brilliant designer with whom the company had worked for years. Created in May 1994, the Millipore home page (see Appendix E) encapsulates the company's desktop architecture, using images from current communication tools. The home page is designed to filter out casual Internet users; it provides a brief description of the company and enough information to enable users to decide quickly whether they want to enter Millipore's technical world. Interactive buttons on the home page invite "deep reading" by customers and prospective customers who are truly interested in Millipore's technology offerings.

Millipore's home page has changed and will change again, but its first iteration helped get Millipore started on the Internet and made the Internet real for the company's management and customers. It also got Millipore attention from various Internet gurus and seminar leaders.

Design makes a difference. The look and feel of the HTML point-and-click protocol is the reason behind the quick ramp-up of Internet usage in late 1993 and 1994. Pictures, graphs, and relevant hyperlinks also make a difference. Information must be easy to get to, accessible, and fun. Millipore has found that combining outstanding design with outstanding content contributes to its progress on the Internet. Providing photos in the catalog of product applications, such as the photo of a protein Western blot on a Millipore membrane shown in Figure 6-1, makes catalog information useful and meaningful to Millipore's scientific and technical customer base.

Interactivity

Millipore's Internet action plan called for increasing levels of customer interaction. A search mechanism was included in each of the market-specific catalogs and in the server as a whole. Links to technical service and ordering information were provided on catalog pages. Technical service inquiries could be entered on a fill-in form and e-mailed to Millipore's technical service department. Comments about the server could also be made on a fill-in form. A "MilliGram" form was created to register people to receive e-mail updates of what is new on Millipore's server. Other means of interacting through "live" chats or seminars, targeted market research, and user groups and prototypes were also envisioned.

Internet Training and Education

The action plan provided for Internet training and education at all levels within the company. Because Internet technology was moving fast and Millipore was moving fast on the Internet, the implementation team had to ensure that it had (1) the support of the marketing and management information systems (MIS) people; (2) the buy-in, or at least the forbearance, of senior management; and (3) open channels of communication with Millipore's various business, divisional, and geographic entities. The Millipore Internet team found that there were various levels of understanding; not everyone was at the same point on the racetrack.

On a regular basis, the Internet team apprised Millipore's interdivisional and international marketing council about where the company stood on the Internet curve. It also presented its plans and results to a senior-level information systems council at six-month intervals. The team was in frequent contact with Millipore's network administrators and MIS people and was seeding interested parties with Internet-accessing capabilities. Standards were set for Internet catalogs that would facilitate the transfer and updating of information from Millipore's relational database. Selected people and agencies—including Millipore's annual report design firm, its catalog production house, and its internal graphics department—were trained in HTML conversion protocols. The Internet experiment prompted gains in Millipore's entire electronic document posture. Methods were developed to convert all printed documents into Internet-friendly formats.

A biweekly Internet update document was e-mailed to key sales and marketing and MIS people worldwide. It surfaced ideas and concerns, connected the Internet team to the field, and resulted in interest, progress, and support. These updates always included the server usage graph, customers' e-mailed comments, and information about various hyperlinks and databases that had been connected or added to the server. In addition, outside speakers were brought in to talk to various groups. Leading customers addressed their Internet strategies and suggested partnership activities. Training and communication were vital because Millipore is not a computer or software company. There was a sea of information, with great waves, but few Millipore surfers.

Technical and Financial Issues

The Internet action plan also identified the technical and financial requirements for Millipore's system. Ever optimistic, Millipore increased its bandwidth to ensure speed of graphic transmission, upping the company's annual line costs. A Sun workstation was reassigned to be the Internet server, so there were no initial equipment purchases. Millipore's internal computer marketing expert shifted his priorities toward the Internet and spent half of his available time on the implementation. To move the project forward, Millipore used a team approach in implementation and maintenance, with MIS, corporate, and divisional involvement. The company's first-year implementation costs were minimal, about the cost of one four-color marketing brochure. This level of investment was commensurate with the results Millipore expected to obtain initially and was made possible in part by Millipore's existing investment in marketing information technology infrastructure. A viable worldwide network, a relational database of products with product photos and graphs, computers, and personnel resources were already in place. The Internet implementation required realignment of existing resources rather than starting from scratch.

The Internet implementation plan also provided an impetus for aligning and combining Millipore's Internet activities with other marketing information technology systems and databases. It opened up gateways issues and compatibility issues. It prompted Millipore to set electronic standards and processes for key documents so that they could be moved to different platforms, based on need and urgency.

INITIAL RESULTS

Millipore's server was set up in May 1994. In its first 56 weeks of operation, over 105,000 files were accessed from about 9,500 different computers in about 14,500 different sessions. (Millipore defined a session as a sequence of accesses from the same computer with gaps of less than an hour). A similar number of files were accessed on Millipore's on-line catalog at Johns Hopkins. Figure 6-2 shows the growth in usage per week over a 69-week period, a pattern that mirrors that of other scientific Internet servers.

From the access log, Millipore was able to determine that important customers, including major microelectronics, biotechnology, and pharmaceutical companies, and university and government research centers, were using the service. Accesses were made from 50 countries. In addition, identifying the number of key word searches, the number of technical service inquiries, and the specific files pulled down provided useful benchmarks. The searchable product catalogs, as expected, got the most "deep reading." The "What's New"

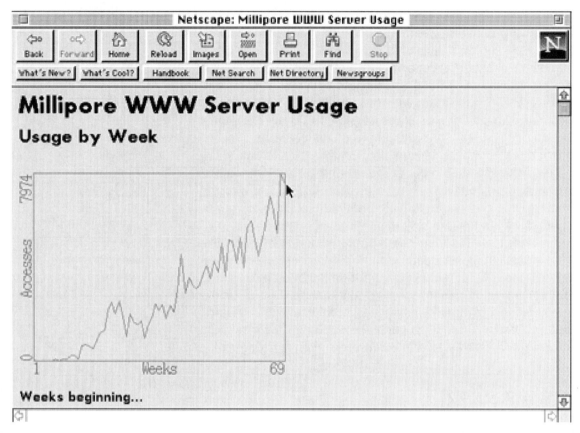

*Figure 6-2   Usage of
Millipore's World Wide
Web Server during Its
First 69 Weeks*

page was the most frequently downloaded file after the home page, and, surprisingly, Millipore's annual report was among the top 10 files accessed during the first year. A histogram of accesses indicated that Millipore's home page was filtering out casual users. The average number of files pulled down was 7.25, although as many as 300 files were accessed in some sessions.

Millipore's Internet address was promoted as a means of response for two new marketing campaigns during the first year. Demonstrations at scientific trade shows, as well as Millipore sales meetings and industry-specific technical articles, promoted interest.

BROADENING AND DEEPENING MILLIPORE'S INTERNET PRESENCE

The technical content and the interactivity of Millipore's Internet server grew along with the usage growth. Searchable color catalogs for all divisions were added as well as layers of applications and reference and product information. Newsletters were added for key markets, along with press releases, quarterly results, and Internet-designed annual reports. Customer case studies were also added. Marketing brochures went on-line as did employment opportunities. The interactivity of the server also increased during its first year of operation, with new search mechanisms and technical service and e-mail capabilities added as the year progressed.

Millipore's Internet presence was deepened and broadened through hyperlinking to major customers, regulatory agencies, publishers, and societies. Some linkages were spontaneous: webmasters excited about what they saw on Millipore's server added Millipore to their hyperlink files. Millipore requested other linkages to its leading customers, who responded positively. Millipore also hyperlinked to government servers relevant to its industry. In two key markets, Millipore created a "hyperfilter" that consolidated a complete market infrastructure of databases, regulatory agencies, research institutes, and companies.

One example of a spontaneous linkage involves the research vessel *Wecoma,* a ship owned by the United States National Science Foundation and run by Oregon State University. The *Wecoma* is basically a floating laboratory used by researchers from various universities and research institutions. Whenever the *Wecoma* docks, it hooks up to the Internet, connecting researchers to their home laboratories and to oceanographic databases worldwide. The ship is equipped with high-powered computers, a sophisticated computer network, a towing vehicle, and wet laboratories. Its laboratories contain equipment needed for doing first-rate research, including a Millipore water purification system that produces ultrapure water needed for scientific experiments.

The *Wecoma*'s Internet server provides information about the vessel's equipment and facilities, including information about the Millipore water-purification system. Scrolling down the *Wecoma*'s home page, the user sees a photo of the water-purification system, along with a brief product description. Clicking on the photo or on a highlighted phrase in the text brings the user to Millipore's product catalog, which contains a detailed description of the system and pertinent application information—information that is located on Millipore's Internet server in Bedford, Massachusetts.

The linkage was the idea of the *Wecoma*'s webmaster. It is good for the *Wecoma,* as it demonstrates the completeness and sophistication of the vessel's floating laboratory, and it is obviously good for Millipore. But the linkage is also useful for the researcher who may need immediate access to detailed specifications and technical service from Millipore. The linkage demonstrates the marketing reach of the Internet as well as the Net's ability to accelerate the flow of product information specified and selected by the customer, a flow that is vital to a knowledge-based, niche-marketing organization like Millipore.

Millipore also hyperlinked to major customers who responded positively to e-mail requests. Offered as a means of accelerating the flow of information, the links were sometimes made on internal WWW sites at customers and sometimes made publicly on the "hot list" or "what's cool list" on the customer's public site.

In addition, Millipore created "hyperfilters" for two key industries that it serves. These hyperfilters were seen as a convenient tool for customers, linking them to other customers, regulatory agencies, and technical databases. The pharmaceutical/biotechnology hyperfilter, for example, has links to the Food and Drug Administration (FDA), the National Institutes of Health (NIH), the Center for Disease Control (CDC), viral databases, protein databases, and biotechnology and pharmaceutical companies (see Figure 6-3). The microelectronics hyperfilter connects customers to major microelectronics companies and research centers worldwide.

The hyperfilters are seen as enhancing the Millipore server's value for its customers. They are modeled on other information sources on the Web, and they are connected to some of these. Providing the best jumping-off point for

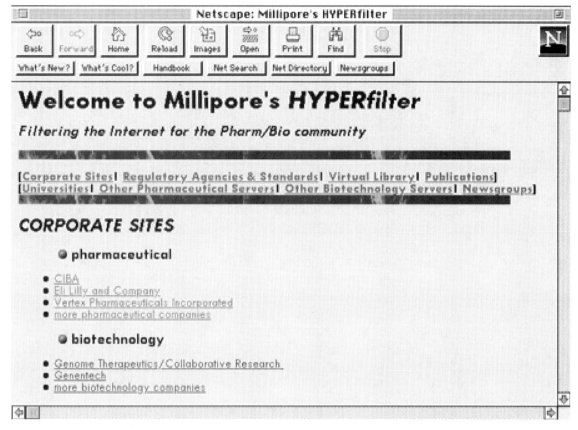

Figure 6-3 Millipore's "Hyperfilter" Links Customers, Regulatory Agencies, and Technical Databases

exploring Millipore's unique market infrastructure, the hyperfilters are useful to Millipore people as well as customers.

Millipore sees such linkages as the primary mode of increasing the right traffic on its server. Internet marketers need to have the information that people want where people traffic. The marketing model is McDonald's, not L.L. Bean. Scientists and engineers in particular want fast, accurate, and thorough information. They want it current and complete. The hyperlinking capability of the Web puts that information in context and makes each user, in a sense, his or her own publisher.

LESSONS IN MARKETING TO THE GLOBAL DESKTOP

Millipore's Internet experiment has met its key objectives and milestones at each phase of implementation. In addition to downloading of files and accelerated transfers of data to several thousand people, there have been e-mail technical service requests from all over the world. Links to leading customers have been strengthened. Ties to key parts of the company's marketing infrastructure—the trade press, consultants, agencies, and financial analysts—have been strengthened as well. Outgoing marketing activities have also grown through Millipore's Internet efforts. Product managers are working more with external Usenet groups and databases, and competitive research has been speeded up. Millipore is also measuring the e-mail usage of the Internet, both incoming and outgoing. It hopes, as other companies have shown, that the Internet can be a cost-saving tool as well as a sales-generating tool.

The experience of the past 14 months has taught Millipore some lessons about marketing on the Internet. Let's take a look first at what Millipore has learned, then at what remains to be done.

> ▶ *The Internet is a viable means of reaching key customers worldwide with information they need.* This was proved in phase 1 of the implementation program and reinforced in phase 2. The access log indicated that leading customers accessed Millipore's server and pulled down technical and product information. Usage of the form for requesting technical service indicates that customers will use the Internet to get help, register complaints, praise, and otherwise interact with the company. This gave Millipore a means of monitoring what customer segments were looking at on the server. Customers' comments to the webmaster have reinforced the design and content choices made for Millipore's server.
>
> Hyperlinks for four of the five targeted customer segments have been well received. The phar-

maceutical/biotechnology segment, in particular, has developed into an innovative resource for the business and the industry, with its hyperfilter, and customer case studies. The microelectronics, laboratory, and financial customer segments have also been well served. For example, Millipore's hyperlink to the EPA provides customers in the environmental area with information about regulatory approval of new products. Hyperlinks for the financial customer segment have developed more rapidly than expected; for investors, Millipore has provided hyperlinks to the company's earnings information, annual reports, Forms 10K and 10Q (through hyperlinks to the Securities and Exchange Commission [SEC]) and stock quotes (through another hyperlink).

▶ *The Internet is a means of cutting costs and accelerating information flow.* Millipore has eliminated printed quarterly reports in favor of distributing reports via the Internet, fax on demand, voice mail, and other electronic media. The Internet has proved to be a faster and more cost-effective means of publishing than either CD-ROM or print. As noted previously, the relational database allows Millipore to produce an Internet catalog faster and at lower cost than producing a print catalog, and such a catalog is more up to date and more easily updatable. There are also documented literature and mailing savings, if one assumes that data obtained electronically would have been requested through other channels.

▶ *The Internet is a means of accelerating competitive research.* With access to the Internet, Millipore's marketers and researchers are gathering more data more quickly than they previously did. They can track the competition, monitor relevant news, and dig into key agency archives at the FDA, CDC, EPA, and SEC. Research that might have taken several weeks can now be accomplished in several hours.

▶ *The Internet is a means of providing customer service.* On several occasions, Millipore's marketing opening to the Internet has alerted the company to what customers are saying about its products and services. In one case, learning that a customer had peppered a niche market with e-mail complaining that a particular type of research filter was on back order from Millipore, the marketing director for that area reached the customer via e-mail and arranged to ship the filter without delay. (Millipore's customer service now uses hyperlinks to Federal Express to track customer packages.) If a tree falls in the forest, a tree falls in the forest. Marketers on the Internet must have an ear to the market so they can monitor both negative and positive messages.

▶ *Growth of Internet marketing is a function of external awareness.* Millipore is in a race to build content on its server and let people know that its server exists. Promotion via traditional media is one way of building awareness of the new medium. Scientists in Millipore's technical service group, for example, have received queries via the Internet as a result of Millipore advertising in *Science* magazine. Millipore hopes to build awareness and traffic through ongoing reference to its Internet server in financial, product, and technical literature, coupled with sales aids, publicity, and partnerships.

There is a traffic issue, however. Millipore's catalog on the Johns Hopkins server gets as much downloading as the product catalog on Millipore's own server. This is because many of the scientists who access the Johns Hopkins server on a daily basis are simply looking for information, not for "product." Millipore is exploring various ways of partnering with its trade press and customers to build content. At the same time, Millipore is looking not so much to have the most-trafficked server as to have the most commercially viable server, with the information needed by Millipore's customers. The key to attracting the "right" traffic is having the right hyperlinks, and these are being steadily developed.

▶ *Internal communication is as important as external communication.* Rapid changes in Web browsers, in

Internet traffic, and in server content require a constant stream of internal information. This is particularly true of a niche-marketing, worldwide organization. Millipore's partnerships with customers and vendors facilitate internal communication. For example, seeing how Digital Equipment Corp. deals with improper use of the Internet helps Millipore determine how it will handle similar improper usage. Understanding Intel's multiple-server architecture assists Millipore in mapping its future. Seminars, demonstrations, biweekly newsletters, and the education of Internet "champions" have been used and will continue to be used to accomplish the change in marketing thinking prompted by the Internet.

Phase 2 of the plan calls for increased use of the Internet by Millipore's marketers. Education and example are the means for achieving that objective. The Internet's "live chat" capability is promising for knowledge-intensive companies like Millipore. This is just another way of delivering valuable information to Millipore customers. The technology is not quite there, but it should be during phase 3 of Millipore's implementation program.

To complete phase 2 of its program, Millipore needs to build additional content for the server, build traffic, and continue to build hyperlinks and customer partnerships. Ideally, Millipore's on-line catalogs would be on heavily trafficked servers worldwide. In addition, various experiments are under way to utilize the domain-specific power of the Internet and to use the multimedia capabilities of the Web.

One key question for Millipore, which it hopes to resolve in 1995, is whether customers on the Internet can securely place product orders and check their status. Customers who use Millipore's CD-ROM catalogs can view a product and then point-and-click and drag the product description to an order form, which is automatically faxed to Millipore's order service department. The same ease of ordering is needed for the Internet catalog. This functionality, however, will require advances in current security and payment protocols.

There are larger marketing lessons to be learned from Millipore's experience. First, the information needs of scientists, engineers, and health care professionals have always been high; these needs have traditionally been met by means of journals, word of mouth, and professional societies. The Internet is a channel for distributing journal information, for extending the range of word-of-mouth information. Easier access to databases, which has been shown to improve diagnosis and treatment by health care professionals, is making similar gains possible in other technical professions.

Second, access to a wider and deeper range of information can only help accelerate research. Of course, there is always the potential for propagating mistakes, but the democracy of this new sea of information would seem to bode well for the eventual dissemination of truth backed up with hard data.

Third, the Internet offers suppliers to the technical community a new mode of interacting with the customer. The customer selects only the information he or she needs, at the desired level, and with the desired backup. Hyperlinks to regulatory agencies, to published papers, or to databases that connect to a particular product help the customer put the information in context. Customers can see what a product does, who has used it, and what references exist, and can ask for a demonstration. A customer can "talk" to a colleague in Singapore as quickly as he or she can walk down the hallway to a colleague in the next laboratory—and the customer may have a greater chance of finding the colleague in Singapore at his or her desktop than of finding the colleague at the laboratory bench next door.

Fourth, the Internet is a mechanism of mass customization. A person accessing Millipore's home page may or may not be interested in seeing the latest regulation for a bacterial test published in the *Federal Register;* the Internet gives the person a choice. The Internet, with its domain access, offers real advantages in terms of customer specificity. French customers could see product descriptions in French, with the prices quoted in French francs; U.S. government agencies that purchase from Millipore could see a product catalog with General Services Administration (GSA) pricing. Millipore can set up "secure" areas for regulatory agency review, and even more secure areas for collaborative research and development programs.

Marketing on the Internet offers possibilities for customers and others to come into a company, but it also offers a company the opportunity to go outside and watch its competition, see what its customers are up to, locate useful databases, and send e-mail to the 100 people it needs to influence. What makes the Internet such a wonderful marketing tool is that it shows fairly quickly what works and what does not. Information can be changed, dropped, and created based on measurable data about what is being looked at and for how long by what type of company or institution.

The Internet was projected to collapse in March 1993, just before it entered the period of its most dramatic growth. There are risks in going on the Internet, but the Internet—or its replacement—is vital for success in today's increasingly interconnected, information-demanding world. Marketers can make things happen on the Internet.

Millipore's Internet action plan established various measurement criteria for each phase of implementation. By year-end 1995, Millipore expects to have an even more robust and rich server, at least 10,000 files a week downloaded from the server, meaningful hyperlinks to more than 300 databases and key customers, and measurable gains in various awareness studies and market research activities that are under way. The ultimate measurement is the number of products ordered over the Internet. Some consumer servers allow ordering products now, and a great deal of work is going on to ensure secure transactions. Some scientific servers on the Internet have limited ordering capability, and Millipore is watching this area of the Internet closely. A marketing test should be possible during phase 3 of Millipore's Internet action plan. In addition, Millipore expects to experiment with on-line software demonstrations and on-line chat/seminar sessions as that Internet technology evolves. Millipore also expects to move further ahead of its competition in server substance, usage, and aesthetics. The scientific, engineering, and medical communities have the Internet on their desktops and laptops; Millipore aims to be there as well with the information and interactivity they need.

SCHLUMBERGER

The Internet Advantage across the Corporation

SCOTT GUTHERY

Scientific Advisor, Schlumberger Ltd.

SCHLUMBERGER IS AN international corporation with operations in over 100 countries and employees of as many nationalities. Schlumberger's business is the acquisition, analysis, and delivery of data. The company is perhaps best known for its oil field services and its water, gas, and electric meters. Timely and accurate communication, both internally and with customers, is at the very foundation of Schlumberger's way of doing business. It has been so since the company logged its first well in 1927, and it is ever more so today.

The Internet is one of the many communication channels Schlumberger uses to gather data from remote locations and deliver data to its customers. This chapter focuses on three information technology applications that Schlumberger has implemented based on Internet protocols and programs—technology watch, employee self-serve directory updating, and employee recruitment.

The first application, technology watch, draws on internal and external network resources to provide Schlumberger's managers, researchers, and engineers with information about the state of the art in specific technical domains. The employee self-serve directory application is a purely internal application that provides a useful business function while helping to spread network-based work habits within the corporation. Employee recruitment is a purely external application that seeks to attract the interest of Internet travelers who are not currently Schlumberger employees.

These three applications have been chosen for discussion because they demonstrate the Internet's capacity for enhancing communications throughout the organization. It is this broadening of the communication paths between employees in different parts of the company and between employees and customers and suppliers that produces the Internet advantage. In other words, it is immediate access to the people on the Internet and not the Net itself that yields corporate and community value.

SCHLUMBERGER'S INTERNET INITIATIVE

Through its joint research connections, Schlumberger has been connected to the Internet since 1986. It was not until Transmission Control Protocol/Internet Protocol (TCP/IP) was adopted as the corporate communication standard in 1992, however, that Internet connectivity to employees' desktops started to become a reality. Fueled by senior management's commitment to worldwide network connectivity and Internet training, Schlumberger's use of Internet resources and technology has risen dramatically in the past three years.

While allocating resources to building a TCP/IP infrastructure and to training employees in the use of Internet access tools was part of management's deployment strategy, the active use of these tools by senior managers was the spark plug that energized Schlumberger's rapid adoption of Internet technology. The need to act on information from one's management chain is powerful motivation for acquiring and learning to use the tools necessary to access that information.

From the beginning, Schlumberger organizations were encouraged to use the network not only for gathering information but also for providing information to others. Thus, the dual roles of each employee as a consumer and a supplier of information have never been decoupled. Everyone is simultaneously an information client and an information server.

TECHNOLOGY WATCH

Schlumberger provides solutions to its customers' problems by integrating other people's ideas and technologies with those developed within the company. This strategy allows Schlumberger to focus its research and development (R&D) resources on its core competencies and partner with companies that are the best of their breed to deliver quality solutions to the customer.

The need both to benchmark the company's core competencies and to identify best-of-breed suppliers outside those core competencies requires that Schlumberger's corporate scientists and engineers be always alert to developments in the technology marketplace. In order to plan product research or product development, technology managers must know not only what technology is available but also what directions technology innovation is taking. At Schlumberger, the activity of monitoring the technology marketplace is called technology watch.

Of course, no scientist or engineer in the high-tech sector needs to be told to track his or her specialty. Rapid "knowledge rot" is a well-known property of the high-tech landscape, and staying current in one's field is energized by the desire to survive. Nevertheless, increasing project demands coupled with the proliferation of available sources of technological information have made the job of doing individual technology watch more difficult.

At the same time, in the continued search for increased internal efficiency, Schlumberger has found that it can ill afford duplicated development efforts, particularly in foundation technologies. Thus, on the one hand, it is important to connect foundation technology specialists directly to product developments, and on the other, it is important to ensure that these specialists not become isolated from each other.

Schlumberger's response to these twin problems—the need for more intense technology monitoring and the need for better internal communication among technical specialists—was to establish, in 1994, a technology watch coordination group at the company's Austin Research Center in Austin, Texas, and to identify technology watch specialists in each of the company's large R&D centers. Initially, the technology watch coordination group consisted of one full-time employee. Currently, the group consists of a manager and two engineer/scientists. Each member of the group has a Ph.D., over ten years of seniority at Schlumberger, and experience working on a wide range of research and engineering projects for the company.

The goals of the technology watch coordination group are to assist Schlumberger's project scientists and engineers in monitoring the technology in their respective specialties and to ensure that internal connections between technology specialists and specialties are made and strengthened. The group takes full advantage of Schlumberger's Internet initiative. Internet tools that have been and are used to achieve the group's goals include electronic mail (e-mail) distribution lists, newsgroups, distributed text databases and search engines, and World Wide Web (WWW) servers.

Schlumberger's Technical Communities

It was clear from the beginning of the technology watch effort that technology monitoring would best be performed on a specialty-by-specialty basis. For at least the first year, therefore, the technology watch coordination effort focused primarily, although not exclusively, on finding, building, and strengthening "technical communities of interest" within Schlumberger and identifying those that were core competencies. The definition of technical communities of interest, in addition to addressing the objective of improving internal communications, provided a framework for organizing technology monitoring. Since the way in which a company structures its approach to the vast amount of information available on the Internet is critical to its ability to turn that information into business value, it is perhaps worthwhile to say a few words about how the technology watch coordination group set about defining Schlumberger's technical communities of interest.

Schlumberger offers employees two career tracks—management and technical. The technical ladder consists of approximately 180 senior scientists and engineers working primarily in the company's oil field services division. Early in 1994, the technology watch coordination group surveyed these senior technologists to determine what they considered to be the company's foundation technologies, what communities of technical interest existed within the company (whether recognized as such or not), and which technologies should be the subject of organized technology monitoring. The 26 technical communities of interest identified as a result of the survey became the initial framework for organizing technology watch information.

These categories, which range from the very general (e.g., materials science) to the very particular (e.g., drilling), have been useful for reorganizing the information found in a "wide-spectrum" source, such as the Internet, into a form that is more readily applied by Schlumberger's scientists and engineers. This categorization will certainly be modified and adapted over time, both as a result of reconsideration and reanalysis and as a result of customers' changing requirements. Nevertheless, it was necessary to organize the technology watch effort in a way that connected to the company's business, and basing technology watch coordination on the technical communities within the firm—however imprecisely defined—seemed like a productive path down which to head.

Technology Watch Servers

From the very beginning, the technology watch coordination group recognized that Schlumberger's project scientists, engineers, and managers did not want or need just another information feed. Initially, therefore, the group concentrated on implementing information services that users had to engage deliberately (e.g., newsgroups and other WWW services), as opposed to interrupt-driven services (e.g., e-mail, which arrives uninvited and on the sender's schedule rather than the recipient's).

To be successful, the technology watch effort must provide the right information at the right time, in the right form, and with the right amount of effort. The large number of available Internet information technology tools, and the ease with which they can be combined and integrated into the user's day-to-day working environment, has helped the group meet this information delivery objective.

In 1994, Web clients were spreading rapidly on employee desktops as a result of a companywide education effort the year before, and Web protocols were gaining standing as the Internet information service platform. The technology watch coordination group therefore chose the Web as the vehicle for organizing, presenting, and distributing technology watch information.

While accessing information from a Web server is easy for the information consumer, this ease of use is purchased with extra efforts on the part of the information provider. Since the group viewed all of the company's technologists as simultaneously consumers and providers of technology watch information, it was forced to address the issue of how hard it was to set up and run a Web server and how the expense of doing so could be justified to the technologists' managers. Again, as at the time of initial deployment, it was senior management's use of the new tools that spurred adoption; the use of Web servers by senior managers, particularly the company's chief information technology officer, provided the spark needed to turn the question "Why do we need it?" into "How do we implement it?"

Over the course of 1994, approximately 20 domain-specific technology watch servers were constructed at Schlumberger. A few of the servers were aligned with the 26 technical communities identified within the company, but most were focused on subspecialties within these communities. Approximately half of the servers were simply information servers that had technology watch pages added to their existing offerings; the others were new stand-alone servers dedicated to the technology watch function.

Running a WWW Server

With a little forethought and planning, one day of training, some well-defined operating procedures, and a couple of good examples, running a WWW information server is not a difficult or time-consuming task. In fact, the experience of the technology watch coordination group with running approximately 20 internal servers supports the view that publishing and distributing information on a Web server is no more difficult or expensive than publishing and distributing information on paper.

The advantages of using the Web rather than paper as an information delivery medium, which account for the Web's popularity and rapid growth, include:

➤ Lower cost of distribution

➤ Greater speed of distribution

➤ Ease of cross-indexing information

➤ Ease of using and reusing information by "cutting and pasting" pieces of the information into other documents and/or analysis programs

➤ Ease of correcting and updating information because there is only one Web version that everybody accesses

➤ Ability to monitor who is interested in obtaining what information

There are, however, some disadvantages to using the Web for information distribution. They include:

➤ Less control over the distribution of information because anyone with a Web browser and network connectivity can access the information. (Recent Web servers have made some strides here, but the administrative overhead is still considerable.)

➤ Less control over the copying of information and therefore over the spread of information.

➤ Difficulty in searching for information across servers because there is as yet no satisfactory cataloging and indexing service for collections of Web servers.

➤ Greater fluidity of electronic documents, which can change and disappear and thus are less suitable for reference.

The use of the Web for information delivery is the subject of much active research and development and is one of the topics of Schlumberger's technology watch.

The Technology Watch Home Page

The role of the technology watch coordination group, besides stimulating and supporting the growth of the technology watch server population, is to merge information generated within the company with relevant external Internet-based information and to make the result readily accessible to project scientists, engineers, and managers. This has been accomplished with the Technology Watch home page.

Schlumberger's Technology Watch home page contains a number of sections, the most important of which are the Databases section, the Technology Communities section, and the Techology Watch Servers section.

The Databases section contains pointers to a number of databases that people seeking specific technical information can query, including three patent databases, an internal database of technical reports, and an internal database of university relations. This section also contains a selection of pointers to databases out on the Internet.

The Technical Communities section contains a pointer to additional pages—one for each of the 26 technical communities. On each page is found the following:

> ▸ The names of the members of the Senior Technical Community with significant expertise in the specialty

> ▸ The names of outside contacts that Schlumberger maintains within the specialty

> ▸ Pointers to internal resources, including internal technology watch servers that contain information relevant to the specialty

> ▸ Pointers to public Internet resources that contain information relevant to the specialty

> ▸ Direct pointers to any particularly useful on-line documents pertaining to the specialty

Finally, the Technology Watch Servers section lists all the technology servers within Schlumberger by their specialty and by the organization supplying the information. Figure 7-1 shows a page from the Technology Watch Servers section of Schlumberger's Technology Watch home page.

This presentation and organization of technology watch information, which can and will be improved, was designed to fix in users' minds that there is one place to go to when they want to quickly find all the corporate resources pertaining to a particular technology.

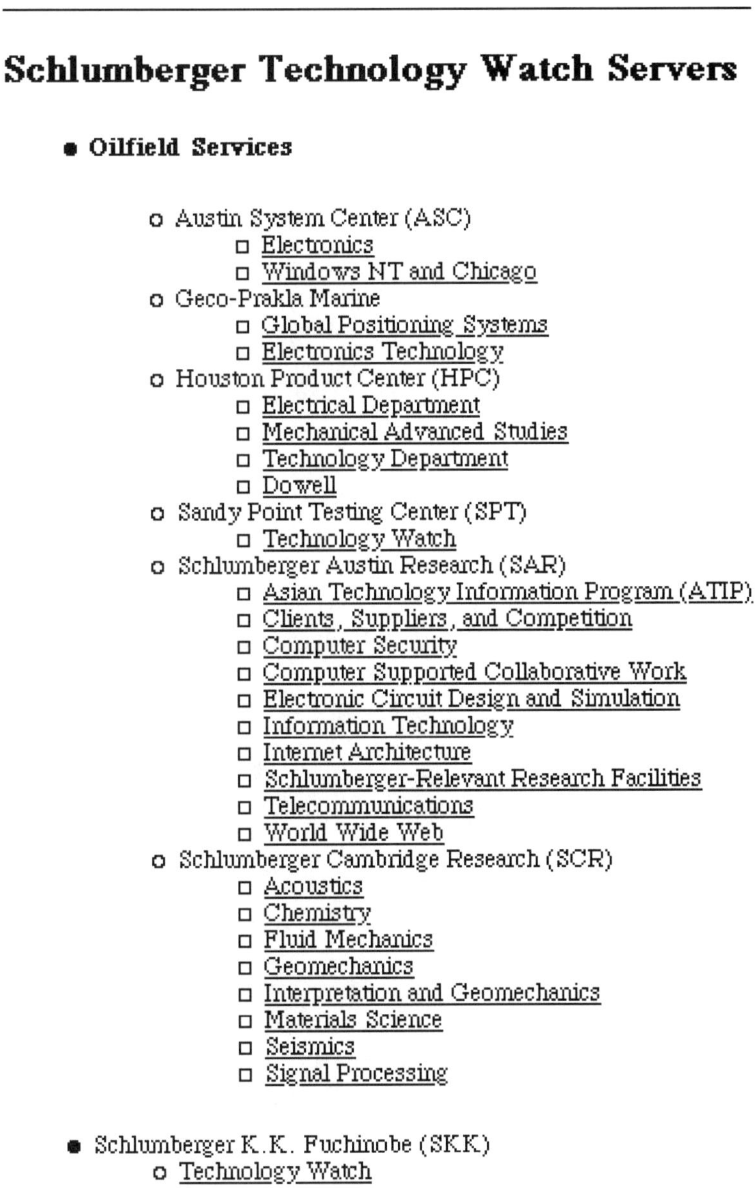

Schlumberger Technology Watch Servers

- **Oilfield Services**

    - Austin System Center (ASC)
        - Electronics
        - Windows NT and Chicago
    - Geco-Prakla Marine
        - Global Positioning Systems
        - Electronics Technology
    - Houston Product Center (HPC)
        - Electrical Department
        - Mechanical Advanced Studies
        - Technology Department
        - Dowell
    - Sandy Point Testing Center (SPT)
        - Technology Watch
    - Schlumberger Austin Research (SAR)
        - Asian Technology Information Program (ATIP)
        - Clients, Suppliers, and Competition
        - Computer Security
        - Computer Supported Collaborative Work
        - Electronic Circuit Design and Simulation
        - Information Technology
        - Internet Architecture
        - Schlumberger-Relevant Research Facilities
        - Telecommunications
        - World Wide Web
    - Schlumberger Cambridge Research (SCR)
        - Acoustics
        - Chemistry
        - Fluid Mechanics
        - Geomechanics
        - Interpretation and Geomechanics
        - Materials Science
        - Seismics
        - Signal Processing

- Schlumberger K.K. Fuchinobe (SKK)
    - Technology Watch

Figure 7-1   A Page from Schlumberger's Technology Watch Home Page

Network-Based Publishing

While it is not clear what network-based publishing is, it is very clear that network-based publishing differs substantially from publishing on paper. The first stage in network-based publishing is simply to make machine-readable copies of a paper document available on the network. There are a number of preprint servers on the Internet today that perform this useful function. However, anyone accessing one of these servers soon realizes that virtually no editing is performed on the content of these servers, either for veracity or for presentation. The lack of a peer review and an editorial pass is both the blessing and the curse of such servers.

In the second stage of network-based publishing, a hypertext veneer is laid over the files containing paper documents as an aid to finding documents on a particular topic of interest. After the hypertext cover is laid down, the paper documents acquire "live" links to other documents, collections of documents, and general information resources on the Internet. In other words, the documents become "Net-aware."

Once the physical boundary of paper has been breached, however, confusion about the identity and pedigree of the document begins to creep in. When, for example, does a document cease to be simply an annotated collection of referents and become a substantive addition to the discussion? Alternatively, can a composition that is nothing but an organized collection of referents be a substantive contribution?

The lack of a recognized set of review and editorial procedures and the fuzzy boundary between the document and its referents make it difficult to assess the quality and value of a network-published paper. In the near term, this difficulty may discourage scientists from publishing their papers on the Internet or from working as hard on Net-published papers as they now do on papers that are published in print format.

The sudden appearance of vast amounts of this new kind of unorganized, unedited, and unvetted information on employee desktops led to a desire to build individual- and project-specific filters to help users find relevant and valuable information in the infomorass. Even though the orientation of the technology watch coordination group was information servers, not alert services, the group made one foray into automatic information refining during the first year of technology watch. The group started with the premise that project team members, due to the pressures of the project, would monitor only the key, high-grade information sources for developments that could impact their project and not scan secondary and low-grade information sources.

Working with Professor Greg Newby of the Graduate School of Library and Information Science at the University of Illinois at Urbana-Champaign, the technology watch coordination group attempted to automatically derive filters that characterize a project's interests from the documents produced over the normal course by the project itself (requirements documents, marketing studies, specifications, designs, three-year plans, monthly reports, status reports, slide shows, and so forth). It then applied these project-specific filters to public-domain information sources and commercial sources (e.g., patents, NetNews, DIALOG) in an effort to produce high-grade "information pearls" from secondary sources of information relevant to the current interests of the project.

Newby's technique not only identified keywords in the project documents but also computed correlations among the keywords and analyzed the principal components of the correlations in order to derive some concepts that interested the project. These concepts were then sought in the items in low-grade information sources.

While the automatically produced filters did uncover some items of interest, they did not reject items of no interest that seemed to have a high enough level of relevance. Thus, although the information coming out of the filters was of a higher grade than what went in, it was not regarded as being of sufficient value to warrant the attention of project scientists, engineers, and managers. Subsequent discussions with commercial news-filtering services reinforced the group's conclusions that state-of-the-art text-analysis programs do not support the automatic creation of rapidly changing interest profiles such as those associated with a high-tech development project.

The technology watch coordination group repeated the experiment in 1995. The group picked two well-defined projects, read the project documents and talked to the project engineers, then built by hand the information filters for these projects. The group also analyzed what the filters produced in an attempt to understand why undesirable material was getting through. This understanding will inform the filter-tuning process.

Automatic information refining is of interest to this discussion because one of the issues that the technology watch coordination group faces in harnessing the power of the Internet is how to define the boundary between the network information user and the network information service. The ultimate goal is clear—to organize information and access to information in such a way that the user has to say very little in order to get a lot of information that is of keen interest and very little that is of no interest.

What Works and What Needs Improvement

The application of Internet technology to Schlumberger's technology watch shows signs of being worth additional effort for the following reasons:

- ▶ Much more corporate technical information is available because it is easier to publish on the Internet than to publish on paper.

- ▶ Corporate technical information is available to more people more easily and more quickly than when documents were printed, distributed, and stored on paper.

- ▶ New uses and new users of technical information have been discovered, as people who were not previously known to be interested in such information (and thus were not on the distribution lists for it) have made their interest known.

- ▶ Once a relatively short learning curve was traversed, it has become less expensive to publish on the Net than to print reports. Corrections and updates can be made more cheaply and in a more timely fashion—that is, instantaneously.

There are opportunities for improvement, however, in both the technology watch initiative and the electronic document initiative. Schlumberger is evaluating new products and working with vendors of network and text database tools to address several shortcomings.

One shortcoming is that there are no effective commercially available tools for mining low-grade information ore. Many of the text-analysis engines on the market function as worlds unto themselves and assume that the user is looking for a particular document in a collection of relatively homogeneous documents. They require the user to enter a sack of text feed, wait for the system to masticate it, and then ask questions of the resulting cud. This is the wrong model. What is needed is a text-analysis engine that is based on interest profiles and has the following properties:

> Point-and-click program for profile development, including editing, testing, and characterization

> Seamless integration with existing network clients such as newsreaders, e-mail programs, and Web browsers

Text analysis is not an independent, detached database. Text analysis fully informed by personal-interest profiles must be embedded in the constant ebb and flow of material through the tools used to handle text on the desktop. Encryption and decryption are special cases of this kind of embedded analysis. Some e-mail clients are starting to develop the ability to encrypt and decrypt on the fly. This model should be extended to general text analysis and automatic processing.

Another shortcoming is that the wall between personal information managers and public information servers is still far too high. While public information servers now support pointers and automatic access, most personal information management tools are not even Net-aware, let alone able to easily mix, match, and merge personal information with public information.

Meet the Author

One emerging property of network-based documents that this author believes will eventually surpass all the others in its impact is the property that Net-aware documents can be interactive. Interactive documents can directly connect the author with the reader and the reader with other readers. Initially, interaction may be nothing more complicated than a comment box on a form that a reader can fill in and send to the author via e-mail or append to the document itself. (A simple example of an interactive document is Schlumberger's employee recruitment feedback form, discussed later in this chapter.) However, even this modest first step can help to clarify, correct, elaborate, and generally improve network-based documents. It turns documents from frozen time capsules of information history into active information exchange points.

The coffeepot at the University of Cambridge Computer Laboratory (http://www.cl.cam.ac.uk/coffee/coffee.html), the Netscape Communications Fish Cam (http://home.mcom.com/fishcam/fishcam.html), and Studio 2000 (http://este.darmstadt.gmd.de:5000/cgi-bin/capture.pl) are where network-based publishing is going. In fact, Ted Nelson saw the future of networked literature over 20 years ago. The Xanadu system he described in the late 1960s foretold the World Wide Web and more. Unfortunately, computing's dawn of history always seems to be last month's *Byte* magazine.

Using the Internet for Technology Watch

First, much valuable technology watch information is available through an Internet connection, and a growing amount is unavailable without an Internet connection. All indications are that this trend will continue. Furthermore, Internet technology can be usefully deployed internally to disseminate proprietary technology watch information within Schlumberger. As with any other data-processing activity, these new information sources will yield business value only if their consideration is shaped by the interests of the firm.

Second, while network connectivity to the desktop can help employees discover commonalities of technical interest, network connectivity in and of itself cannot sustain these connections in the long run. Network connections still play a supporting role to one-on-one conversations, technical forums, conferences, workshops, and formal presentations and reports. A network should not be thought of as a substitute for direct human interaction.

Schlumberger participates in the sci.geo.petroleum newsgroup and posts that newsgroup's Frequently Asked Questions (FAQ) on its public Web server, at http:// www.slb.com. The reader is invited to follow some of the pointers found there to see what one industry is doing to build a shared network-based information base.

EMPLOYEE SELF-SERVE DIRECTORY

Like many other companies, Schlumberger has followed the growing popularity of employee self-serve (ESS) human re-source management systems (HRMS). While some compa-nies have had notable successes with such systems, Schlum-berger's experience with closed-shop mainframe personnel systems, together with war stories from the client-server front, convinced the company that it had better learn to walk before trying to run this race. As a modest first step, Schlum-berger decided to implement an on-line directory of employ-ees' e-mail addresses and phone numbers. Each network-connected employee would have a personal record in this directory and would be responsible for keeping this record up to date. The directory would not be an HRMS and yet would exhibit all the attributes of an ESS-HRMS—heavy use, daily changes, client-server computing, database availability, software installation, employee training, and distributed ad-ministration, to name just a few. Schlumberger intended to use the implementation of this directory as an experience base to draw on during the planning for a fully functional on-line HRMS.

For many years, Schlumberger had maintained on al-most all of its major computer systems a flat file containing the name, telephone number, and e-mail address of each employee who had an account on some computer in the company. Each local computer center was responsible for sending updates to this file at a central location once a month. Updates from some 350 computer centers around the world would be merged with the existing file and a new file then redistributed to all centers. Not only was this process time consuming, but information in the file was always at least 30 days out of date.

In early 1993, Schlumberger standardized on the Eudora e-mail program. Built into this program is the ability to access an on-line directory called the "ph directory." Since there was general dissatisfaction with the flat-file e-mail directory and since the company was looking for an opportunity to test the client-server waters, building a ph directory from the e-mail address file and offering it as a service to the Eudora community seemed like a natural.

The Directory Prototype

"Ph" is a piece of Internet "freeware" available from the University of Illinois Computing and Communications Services Office (CCSO) by file transfer protocol (FTP). The FTP address is vixen.cso.uiuc.edu. Ph—more properly, the CCSO Nameserver—is actually a suite of programs written in 1988 by Steve Dorner, the author of the Eudora e-mail program. The suite includes:

- ▶ ph—client programs to access the directory
- ▶ qi—the server for the on-line directory
- ▶ programs to build and administer the directory

The ph program suite is widely used in the academic community, and over 200 ph directories are available on the Internet. The directory working group reasoned that if ph was robust enough to be used on 200 college campuses, it was probably solid enough for some 350 Schlumberger computing sites and their 17,000 network-connected employees. (One of the myths about free Internet software is that it is not of industrial quality. This is true. It's often better.)

In April 1993, the directory flat file was loaded into the ph database, and the qi directory server was mounted on the company's internal network. To the data fields from the flat file—name, phone number, and e-mail address—were added 20 other fields, including location, fax number, reports to, home address, and home phone number. The directory working group left these 20 fields blank and let word of mouth spread the news of the availability of the server through the Eudora community.

Since the ph client in the Eudora e-mail program can query the directory but does not let the user update the information in the directory, within a week employees began asking how to update their own information. This led to the ph client programs' being made available on VAX/VMS, UNIX, Windows, and Macintosh systems to enable self-serve directory updating.

The Requirements Phase

Schlumberger has implemented a formalized process that guides any software project. The first step in this process is determining the project's feasibility, which the Eudora prototype had demonstrated. The second step is defining project requirements. During May and June 1993, the directory working group wrote, circulated for comment, and recirculated an employee directory requirements document. HR professionals, computer center managers, network technicians, and a wide range of end users from senior managers to clerks read the requirements documents and gave the group feedback on how they wanted to use the directory and what concerns they had about its contents and their responsibility for maintaining their own entry. As part of the requirements phase, the group also gathered information on the directory component of real on-line HRMS and visited a couple of other companies that were in the process of installing ESSs.

By mid-July 1993, the working group had a solid requirements document that covered the needs of a self-serve directory from both the end user's point of view and the system administrator's point of view. The requirements phase yielded the following design rules for the directory:

- ▹ The directory is about people finding people; only information that serves this purpose should be considered for inclusion.
- ▹ The directory must connect to other existing systems such as hard-copy directories and e-mail distribution systems.
- ▹ Almost all information in an employee's record is

optional and is provided at the discretion of the employee; the only required fields are name, business phone, and e-mail address.

A metarule that came out of the requirements process and will guide further planning for a self-serve HRMS is: enter it once, use it everywhere. When different departments are maintaining separate personnel systems, the overhead of entering the same information into many systems is hidden. When each employee is responsible for updating personal information in a combined personnel system, tolerance for entering the same information more than once quickly disappears.

Planning for Transition

During the fall and winter of 1993, the directory working group started to plan the transition from the old way of doing things to the new way. The transition would be cold turkey; there would be no attempt to run parallel systems. Each month from May 1993 on, the group had updated the ph directory from the new month's flat-file directory. This process had become increasingly time consuming and error prone and was frustrating for everybody involved.

The primary cause of this frustration was the fact that the flat-file directory and the ph directory had very different data models. The flat-file directory permitted multiple records per employee whereas the ph directory insisted that there be exactly one record per employee. Worse yet, there were no unique identifiers in the flat-file directory as there are in the ph directory, so if there were five entries for John Adams, there was no way to tell whether there was one employee named John Adams who moved around a lot or five employees named John Adams.

Finally, the lack of a unique identifier in the flat file forced the working group to use the employees' names to connect records in the flat-file directory to records in the ph directory. The working group discovered the hard way that people were dissatisfied with how their names were presented in the flat-file directory and took advantage of the self-serve feature of the ph directory to get their names right, thereby breaking the only link with the flat-file directory.

Surprisingly, the least involved part of transition planning was shifting from the use of a local file directory to a network-based client-server model of directory access. The network management people were already in the process of deploying the TCP/IP substrate in the company and providing local workarounds for situations in which it could not be deployed. The directory working group's task was just to make sure it could field ph clients for all the company's computing platforms.

The final part of the transition plan was identifying all the systems that connected to and relied on the flat-file directory. This proved to be more difficult than anticipated and, in retrospect, needed more attention than it was given. The problem, of course, is that people can connect a downstream system to a flat file (either by simply reading it or by making a copy of it) without the knowledge of the people providing the flat file. As a result, without simply deleting the file and waiting for people to complain, it was very difficult to identify all the systems that used the flat-file directory information. One of the less talked about advantages of client-server computing is that one sees one's users.

The plan for the transition from the flat-file directory to the on-line directory was presented to Schlumberger's international network management community at its semiannual meeting in March 1994. At the meeting, the directory working group described the plan, listened to concerns, and modified and extended the plan. This process continued until a consensus was reached.

While there was some discussion of the directory's contents and some concern about data quality, the primary contribution of the network managers was to clarify and firm up the directory's operating procedures. First, it was decided that only the central directory would accept directory updates but that there would be satellite read-only versions of the directory to respond to user queries in the event that connectivity to the central directory were interrupted. (Schlumberger's global network extends into areas of the world where network connectivity cannot be assumed to be continuous.)

Second, a clear division of responsibility between the local computer center and the HR department was enunciated: the local computer center would be responsible for providing ph clients on all local platforms, and the HR department would be responsible for providing the directory contents. In particular, the HR department would create a directory record for each new employee and delete the directory record of each terminating employee. The computer center and the HR department would, however, be jointly responsible for user education.

The Big Bang and Its Fallout

On May 1, 1994, the flat-file directory was "turned off," and the ph directory became Schlumberger's official corporate directory. What actually happened was that the on-line ph directory rather than the flat file became the only and the official entry point for directory data. In other words, the responsibility for the currency and accuracy of directory data shifted from the computer centers to the individual employees. This change was announced in a companywide posting.

Shortly after the directory was introduced, it became clear that it was necessary to provide the ability to query the database via e-mail as well as from a desktop client program for a number of reasons. First, remote locations that had e-mail connectivity to the rest of the corporation but had no plans to provide full TCP/IP connectivity could occasionally connect to a TCP/IP-connected computer to update directory entries but found this procedure too onerous for merely querying the database. Second, employees who wanted to load the result of a directory query into a desktop program, such as a spreadsheet, found the output provided by their ph client unsuitable for desktop use.

An e-mail query interface to the directory has now been implemented so that the result of a query can be returned in a number of formats, including forms that users can read and load into desktop programs. Figure 7-2 shows one such form.

Occasionally, directory updates apply to a relatively large group of employees; for example, when there is a change in a telephone exchange or in the address of a location. In these situations, it was deemed best not to badger the affected employees to update their own records but to make a batch change to every affected record. Unfortunately, because there are no client tools that support batch changes to the ph directory, this kind of mass update must be made

PH Query: *name=Scott Guthery*

```
[ Org Chart ] [  1 Level Up  ▼ ] [  2 Levels Down  ▼ ]


             alias: guthery
              name: Scott Guthery
          nickname: scottg, sguthery
             voice: 1 512 331 3774
         alternate: 1 512 331 3000
             pager: By email: guthery@airnote.net
                  : By phone: 1-512-604-2933
               fax: 1 512 331 3760
             email: guthery@austin.sar.slb.com
          X400mail: S=GUTHERY G=SCOTT
          HOSTmail: SAR::GUTHERY
         languages: English, German
        home_voice: 1 512 250 1526
          home_fax: 1 512 258 1342
            office: F2.110
          location: 8311 North FM 620 Road, Austin, TX 78726 USA
    postal_address: P.O. Box 200015, Austin, TX 78720-0015 USA
      home_address: 11100 Leafwood Lane, Austin, TX 78750 USA
  assigned_country: USA
       cost_center: 9525
       center_code: SAR
        department: Technology Watch Coordination
         job_title: Scientific Advisor
      job_category: Technical
        reports_to: denis3
           project: Technology Watch Coordination
       workstation: asterix.austin.sar.slb.com
           printer: lps07@bartles.austin.asc.slb.com (PostScript)
            family: Maria, Tyler
         expertise: software, databases, statistics, networks
          schedule: Mar. 30 ... Data Visualization Course, Austin, USA
                  : Apr. 20-28 ... SCR, Materials Workshop, Cambridge, UK
                  : May 17-19 ... SAR, IT Workshop, Austin, USA
                  :
       outside_SLB: YES
             other: Picture
                  : Vitae
            source: self
      last_updated: 95/3/16
        GIN_number: 0345835
             proxy: kjohnson
```

Figure 7-2 A Staff Directory Query

off-line by the directory administrator and then reloaded into the database.

The use of Schlumberger's employee on-line directory has grown to approximately 15,000 sessions from 2,500 separate users per day. As of the end of July 1995, roughly 70,000 connections were made per week from 6,000 separate users.

The main ph database and its qi server run on a SPARC-10/50 workstation with 64 megabytes of memory at Schlumberger's network operations center in Sedalia, Colorado.

Since procedures for automatic and robust updating of read-only satellites are still being worked out, there is currently only one read-only satellite, located in Austin, Texas.

20/20 Hindsight

What things went as well as or better than expected? Picking a popular but non–mission-critical application for an initial foray into client-server computing and self-serve HR databases was certainly a good idea. One can react to the inevitable bugs and surprises much more effectively than if there are ancillary pressures and concerns being brought to bear. Using Internet freeware was also a good idea since it had been thoroughly beaten on and lots of free consultants on the Usenet newsgroup info.ph were on immediate call for help.

Initially, the directory working group thought that data security and data sensitivity would be a big concern; however, this has not turned out to be the case. The data in the directory are almost by definition public so that nobody is particularly concerned who knows the information. Working out the details of on-line self-serve computing with insensitive data has allowed the group to decouple purely computing issues from data content issues. Obviously, the working group will have to address these issues as it moves toward a more fully functional HRMS.

The working group should have spent as much time working with HR people as it did with computer center and network management people. Probably more. The group concentrated on throwing the ball but did not fully prepare the catchers. In a highly decentralized global company such as Schlumberger, one is critically dependent on the people "on the ground." Slowly, over time, the working group has built up a cadre of about 100 local directory administrators who help the central directory administrator maintain the content of the directory. The working group should have identified these people earlier, determined what computing platforms they used, and made sure it could support them.

Follow-Ons

The ph directory is a useful desktop information resource and a good client-server training ground, but it was never intended to be either a full-fledged ESS-HRMS or a component of a global directory system. These latter systems are already in Schlumberger's development pipeline.

On the other hand, the notion of a companywide Rolodex has found other applications. For example, a ph database containing all the company's purchasing agreements has been built to allow employees considering a purchase to find out from their desktops whether the company has negotiated discount agreements with a specific vendor. Another ph directory contains descriptions of all the senior technologists in the company and their areas of expertise. This directory can be searched by Schlumberger managers seeking consultation or advice on a specific subject.

Besides its intrinsic usefulness, the directory project has provided an excellent introduction to the use of the Internet as an information resource. With a little help from a list of worldwide servers, employees quickly discovered that they could access name server directories at many universities around the world and look up friends and colleagues. The desire to solve a real problem, such as simply finding somebody's e-mail address, is a powerful motivator for learning.

EMPLOYEE RECRUITMENT

Recruiting employees on the Internet is the newest of the three Internet-based applications developed at Schlumberger, and it is still regarded as highly experimental. Historically, Schlumberger has recruited graduating students by sending teams of engineers and scientists to approximately 100 technical schools and universities around the world. About 70 percent of Schlumberger's annual new hires come through the recruiting activity of such teams.

A number of factors have tended to weaken the big-university model of recruiting. One factor is the Internet itself, which enables distance learning. This trend has reduced the number of students who are on campus to sign up for interviews or to be interviewed. Indeed, distance learning has begun to erode the need for a central campus at all.

Cost-effectiveness is a second factor that drives companies to look into alternatives to on-campus recruiting. Not only is there the real cost of sending teams of recruiters to campus, but because Schlumberger finds it most effective to use working project engineers and scientists rather than HR or recruiting professionals for on-campus interviewing, there is the hidden cost of the recruiters' lost work.

Finally, Schlumberger employs individuals with a wide range of talents, skills, and worldviews. This means that it must look in an ever-growing number of places for graduates and in places where it is simply uneconomical to send an on-campus recruiting team of even one person.

When Schlumberger decided to begin recruiting on the Net, it was natural to fit this new virtual campus into the existing recruiting organization by simply making a new team with a new team captain. Schlumberger's Web captain is a team of one recruiting at World Wide Web University.

The employee recruitment application appears on the Internet as a collection of Web pages on Schlumberger's public server at http://www.slb.com. In addition to the pages that describe the company using the FAQ format, there is a feedback form that anyone accessing the server can complete (see Figure 7-3). The form collects basic information about a candidate (e.g., name, postal address, e-mail address, name of school, degree, major area of study, type of position in which candidate is interested) and allows the candidate to choose the type of follow-up desired: "Send additional information," "Have a recruiter call," or "Contact me if you visit my campus." When the candidate clicks the "submit" button, the form is automatically e-mailed to Schlumberger's Web captain for reply and follow-up.

The recruiting pages, together with the feedback form, were added to Schlumberger's public server in January 1995. In the first three months, inquiries have come in at the rate of roughly one a day. Approximately 10 percent of the inquiries are from graduates of schools where Schlumberger sends recruiting teams. Requests for information from these individuals are forwarded to the on-campus recruiting team captains at the respective schools for follow-up, while inquiries from applicants at other schools are handled by Schlumberger's Web captain. Nobody has yet been hired through the Web, but the quality of the people who have sent in their applications via the Web is encouraging.

As an adjunct to the public recruiting pages, Schlumberger's Recruiting Coordination department has constructed an internal recruiting Web server that contains information

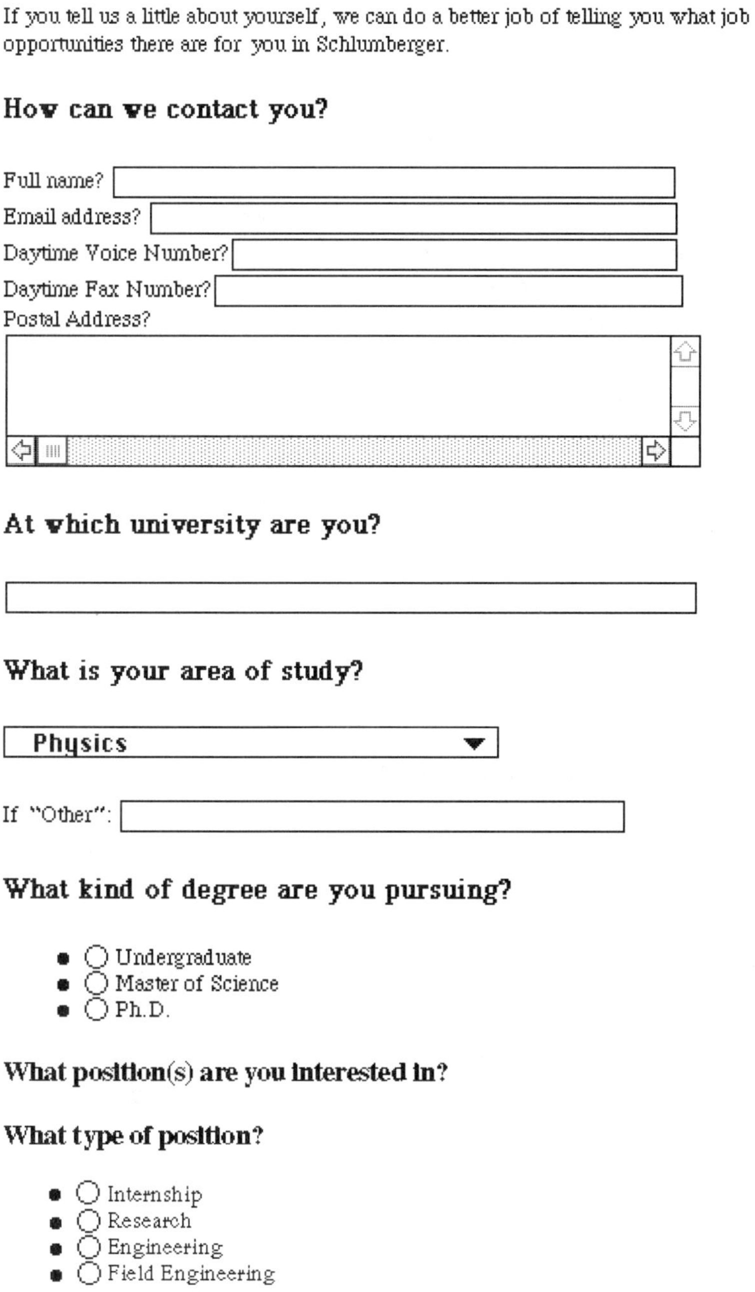

If you tell us a little about yourself, we can do a better job of telling you what job opportunities there are for you in Schlumberger.

How can we contact you?

Full name? [   ]
Email address? [   ]
Daytime Voice Number? [   ]
Daytime Fax Number? [   ]
Postal Address?

[   ]

At which university are you?

[   ]

What is your area of study?

[**Physics**   ▼]

If "Other": [   ]

What kind of degree are you pursuing?

- ○ Undergraduate
- ○ Master of Science
- ○ Ph.D.

What position(s) are you interested in?

What type of position?

- ○ Internship
- ○ Research
- ○ Engineering
- ○ Field Engineering

Figure 7-3   Employee Recruitment Feedback Form

about candidates gathered on campus as well as on the Internet. This server, which is available to everyone in Schlumberger, is a fast and efficient way of distributing candidate information to line managers. The server contains campus interviewer reports as well as scanned candidate résumés.

One of the very first responses received on the public server included the job applicant's uniform resource locator (URL), an Internet pointer to the appplicant's home page on his campus Web server. The URL was added to the student's entry on the the internal recruiting server, enabling interested Schlumberger managers to immediately access information that the student wanted to present about himself, including biographical information and published papers.

Anybody who has done any campus recruiting quickly realizes the amount of paperwork saved by this instant and high-bandwidth connection between Schlumberger departments looking for new hires and job candidates. The era of the multimedia, network-based résumé has arrived.

THE ESSENCE OF THE INTERNET ADVANTAGE ACROSS THE CORPORATION

None of the applications described in this chapter is particularly complex or technically challenging. Rather, they are characterized by being user-centered and adamant about regarding users both as sources of information and as consumers of information. The Internet advantage across the corporation is as much a matter of opening up previously nonexistent information flows as it is of moving existing flows to a new medium. It is by making available this previously inaccessible information and by making previously unmade connections—not simply by reformatting existing information—that the Internet advantage is achieved.

MEASURING THE VALUE OF THE INTERNET FOR BUSINESS

8

JOEL H. MALOFF

President, The Maloff Company

V IRTUALLY EVERY PHASE of business involves exchanging, managing, and acting on information. In today's competitive business environment, every company needs faster and more efficient means of accessing and processing information and more effective ways of communicating information internally across the organization as well as externally to customers, suppliers, and business partners. The Internet can improve the speed and efficacy of a company's information access as well as expand a company's communications abilities and is certainly a technology option worth consideration. Connection to the Internet, however, entails technical, security, and personnel requirements and costs, which may not make it a viable or an optimal solution for all companies.

This chapter presents a methodology for measuring the potential benefits and costs of connecting to the Internet, illustrated with examples, and includes a sample cost-justification worksheet for companies that are contemplating an Internet connection.

IMPACT OF THE INTERNET ON BUSINESS COMMUNICATIONS

The Internet provides a global standard for information exchange—whether that information is in the form of the text, graphics, speech, or numbers. It functions as a "network of networks," a worldwide mesh that permits a user in London, for example, to send a message to other users around the world with a single computer command. There is no need to have expensive "leased circuits" connecting a corporation's multiple facilities. There is no need to wait in line to fax a one-page memo. The "mesh" takes care of the information transfer instantly.

The Internet also provides a variety of international connectivity options for linking branch offices, customers, and suppliers to the same services. Thus, a company headquartered in Boston may use the Internet access services of BBN Planet, while its branch office in France is connected to Internet Way, and its Toronto branch uses services provided by UUNorth. Even with these varied and distant providers, the different sites can be linked by a "virtual private" data network.

The Internet, however, is more than just a vehicle for information exchange. It is a growing, vibrant community comprising more than 30 million people in all corners of the world. Its millions of interconnected computers offer a wealth of information and human resources. Unlike proprietary networks and computer systems, the Internet connects users directly to resources, regardless of the kind of system used to access it. It does not matter whether the system is a Macintosh computer, a Windows machine, or a UNIX workstation.

In addition, because the Internet embraces open standards, it offers more flexibility for growth and expansion of a company's communications activities than can a closed environment. In fact, many closed communications environments, such as CompuServe and Advantis, have found that interconnection with the Internet is essential. These closed environments have already become part of the Internet.

MEASURING POTENTIAL BENEFITS AND COSTS

A company's environment and the nature and scope of its business operations determine its specific communication needs. When seeking to measure the value of an Internet connection for business, it is important to take a step back from the technology of the global network. A company should first analyze its existing communications practices and costs, identify the practice or activity that needs improvement, and then examine alternatives for achieving the necessary improvement. In some instances, the solution may be better staff training or better cost management. In others, improvement may require the implementation of a new technology. The Internet is only one of the alternatives.

If the company concludes that connection to the Internet is warranted, it needs to evaluate different kinds of Internet services, their anticipated benefits, and the corresponding requirements and costs.

BENEFITS OF AN INTERNET CONNECTION

Three "measures" of the value of the Internet for business are discussed in this chapter: reduced communications expenses, increased revenues from existing and/or new sources, and "intangible" benefits (e.g., improved employee morale, customer satisfaction, and enhanced competitive position). As the examples in the following subsections illustrate, however, companies are discovering that tangible and intangible benefits are often intertwined.

Reduced Communications Expenses

Most companies today still rely on private-line networks, internal telephone systems, voice mail, faxes, and messenger and overnight courier services as the principal vehicles for internal and external communications. Internal communications include the transmission of organizational announcements, critical financial data for day-to-day operations, management reports, information to be used in preparing for corporate meetings, and so forth. External communications with customers, vendors, potential business partners, and others outside the organization include sending and receiving purchase orders, invoices, delivery notices, press releases, marketing literature, and requests for proposals.

There are many ways in which the Internet can reduce the costs and improve the efficiency of business communications as they are currently conducted.

Private-line networks. For voice communications, many corporations with major branch offices have private-line networks, which create dedicated links between each site. Private-line network services are leased from either long-distance carriers (e.g., AT&T, MCI, or Sprint) or local exchange telephone companies (e.g., a regional Bell Operating Company, General Telephone, or Metropolitan Fiber Systems). The costs of private-line circuits tend to be fixed rather than usage-sensitive, so the more traffic packed over these circuits, the better. Unfortunately, these circuits are billed on a mileage basis (i.e., the longer the circuit, the higher the charge). International private lines are even costlier. Because of the cost, few companies can afford to link together all of their smaller branches and more remote offices, even though there may be substantial interaction between the sites and between each site and corporate headquarters.

Implementation of Internet electronic mail (e-mail) service could lessen the need for voice communications, reducing long-distance telephone expenses. By connecting each location to the nearest Internet access provider, a company can supplement its private-line network for substantially less than it would cost to implement dedicated access. For example, instead of paying several thousand dollars per month for a 56-kilobits-per-second (Kbps) or 64-Kbps private line between the United States and France, a company would pay an Internet access provider an average of $550 per month for 56-Kbps Internet access in the United States and about $1,000 a month for 64-Kbps Internet access in France. Add a site in Australia for another $1,000 per month, and the company has suddenly created a "virtual private" network for less than $3,000 per month—one that would have cost ten times more were it a leased-line network. In addition, with the proper use of encryption tools for network security, each of the company's sites can reach many other sites via the Internet at no additional charge.

Internet e-mail service has other advantages over voice communications. Even with ubiquitous voice-mail services today, companies often find themselves playing "telephone tag." Voice communications also tend to take longer—abruptness over the telephone may seem rude—whereas written messages can be more to the point, helping to shorten the communication cycle.

In some cases, proper engineering and design can replace private-line network services. The Trane Company, a major manufacturer of air-conditioning systems in La Crosse, Wisconsin, has replaced large portions of its private network with secured Internet access, thus creating a "closed user group" across the public Internet. This solution has saved Trane money and increased the efficiency of its network management. It also gives Trane the ability to extend the network quickly to any new sites that may be established.

Fax transmissions. It is estimated that fax transmissions account for about 36 percent of the yearly long-distance telephone bill of the average *Fortune* 500 company. What is being faxed? To whom are the faxes going? Why is the material faxed rather than mailed? Was the material prepared on a word processor, faxed to the distant party, and either reworked further on the other end or used as is?

If the bulk of the company's outgoing faxes consist of corporate announcements, confirmations of delivery schedules, and notifications of price changes sent to the company's remote sites, one alternative to faxing is the use of Internet e-mail. With e-mail, the same information can be communicated to all the remote sites at one time, the transmissions can be scheduled to take place at any hour of the day or night rather than in "real time," and no staff time is lost standing by the fax machine.

If the company can reduce its long-distance telephone bill by 15 percent through diminished need for faxing, how much would it save per year? A company that spends $300 a month would save $540 a year. That's almost two free months of long-distance telephone service. For a company that spends $3,000 a month on fax transmissions, the cost savings would almost equal the salary of a full-time middle manager.

Overnight courier service. Use of e-mail can also reduce the need for overnight courier service (e.g., Federal Express or United Parcel Service), as illustrated in the following example.

Company A used to send out packages from corporate headquarters to 500 branch offices twice a month via overnight courier service at an average cost of $15 per package. The packages contained software updates for printing customized forms on laser printers. Since it was important that all sites use the same laser printer formats for consistency, all sites had to receive the updates within 24 hours. Each software update shipped by courier consisted, on average, of 2 megabytes (MB) of data. Occasionally, documents containing the equivalent of up to 1 MB of data were included in the packages. The courier costs for this activity alone came to $180,000 per year ($15 × 2 packages × 12 months × 500 sites). In addition, the company incurred clerical costs for assembling the packages, preparing them for shipment, and filling out the shipping forms. Preparation of each package took an average of five minutes. The activity was performed by five clerks, consuming an estimated 41.7 hours twice a month. At $10 per hour, clerical costs amounted to $10,008 per year ($10 × 41.7 hours × 2 × 12 months). Thus, the total costs associated with preparing and shipping software updates via courier service were $190,008 per year ($180,000 + $10,008).

A year ago, Company A calculated what it might save by switching to alternative delivery methods. The volume of data made fax transmissions impractical. Implementing Internet e-mail service would reduce costs marginally but would provide a number of intangible benefits. The calculation of costs and benefits was as follows:

Using a mathematical engineering model, the company determined that the installation of a 56-Kbps dedicated line at headquarters would be sufficient to support the level of traffic, assuming no other applications were running. Connecting each site to an Internet service provider would eliminate the need for a more expensive leased-line direct connection. To allow each of the 500 remote sites to access the

Internet, it was sufficient to equip each site with a 19.2-Kbps dial-up line to the host system. The cost of this solution—including the router and other required hardware, average "leased-line tail circuit" cost, and the service provider's fees—came to $20,000 per year. The cost of 500 dial-up accounts for "800" number service, with each account using an average of four hours per month billed at $6 per hour, came to $144,000 per year (500 accounts × 4 hours × $6 × 12 months).

The additional cost of securing a company's "intellectual property" can range from $2,000 to $25,000 per year. Depending on the nature of the business and the systems used, it may be sufficient to provide network security only at the company's main location, or it may be necessary to provide security at each remote site as well. In Company A's case, network security would be provided only at company headquarters for an estimated cost of $25,000 per year.

The total estimated cost of Company A's Internet connection is $189,000 ($20,000 + $144,000 + $25,000) a year. By expending $189,000 a year, Company A saves $1,008 ($190,000 − $189,000) a year on courier service costs for the targeted activity. Although the costs in this case are nearly a "wash," Company A gains the following intangible benefits:

- ▶ The five clerical personnel are freed to perform less tedious, more productive tasks, and their morale improves.

- ▶ E-mail service is available for immediate communication of company "happenings" to the branch offices, which will make employees at the remote sites feel more "in the loop."

- ▶ Many of the company's customers and prospects are pleased because they are already connected to the Internet and have expressed their preference for receiving sales and marketing information via Internet.

Note that not all courier service costs can or are likely to be displaced by an Internet connection. In addition, as discussed later in this chapter, connectivity may require modifications to the company's internal local area network

(LAN), additional internal network operations and monitoring, the establishment of a "help desk" function, and continued user training. Because these additional costs are specific to each organization, it is important to perform a detailed benefit-cost analysis before setting expectations.

Increased Revenues

The second measure of the value of the Internet for business focuses on the potential for generating revenue from new and existing sources. There are many ways in which the Internet can assist a company in obtaining new sources of revenue. One way is by boosting the visibility of the company and its products or services in the global electronic marketplace. Visibility can be enhanced by participating in Internet discussion groups or by creating a home page on the World Wide Web (WWW). A server may be established to respond automatically to a customer's request for company literature or product information (infobots), provide a sample of the company's product, or register a request that a sales rep contact the customer. It may provide an order form, and—if the company sells digitized text, music, or graphics—it may even provide the facility to accept payment and deliver the product while the customer is on-line.

Fidelity Investments, for example, uses a WWW server to offer information about customer accounts and to provide information about Fidelity's financial services to prospective customers. Smaller businesses that lack the technical expertise or financial resources to establish and maintain a Web server can achieve visibility by renting space on electronic "malls," such as the Branch Mall (http://branch.com), and paying to have customized storefronts created by the mall operators.

Another way in which the Internet assists a company in uncovering new revenue sources is by facilitating the finding of new business partners and supporting subsequent collaboration on joint ventures. Conducting a keyword search or posting a note to a bulletin board service can quickly find individuals and companies engaged in the same line of business or offering a related product or service. Using Internet e-mail, a company can start a dialogue with a potential business partner or a supplier anywhere in the world, negotiate the terms of an agreement, and exchange final documents. Except for the signatures on an agreement, everything required to do business can be accomplished or at least supplemented through the Internet.

Most businesses know that their current customers are the best source of new business. Reducing customer defections and turnover (or "churn") is therefore of utmost importance. One way in which a company can reduce churn is by maintaining high-quality contact with customers through regular e-mail notes or on-line newsletters. Contact with customers (known as "face time") may uncover little annoyances or service problems of which the company was unaware and which, if not detected and corrected, might result in lost business. By letting customers know of new products or new models of existing products before the products come on the market, a company may not only earn revenues through advance sales but also increase customer loyalty.

Intangible Benefits

The Internet can increase the efficiency and effectiveness of business communications in a variety of ways that are not always quantifiable in the short term but are significant for the company's image, its competitive positioning, and its success in the longer term.

All companies with distributed employees can benefit from the use of Internet e-mail. Rand Technologies, the Toronto-based developer of computer-aided design and manufacturing software, uses Internet e-mail to post announcements of company policies, new hires, and promotions to its many branches throughout North America. This reduces the amount of time that was previously required to get the word out and helps to make employees at branch offices feel more as if they are an integral part of the corporation.

Company B, which is based in San Francisco, maintains an Internet server at corporate headquarters to provide its overseas sales offices with the latest product updates, support for technical issues, and information about the competition. When the sales office in Milan, Italy, runs into a technical problem that needs an answer from the company's engineers in San Francisco, the sales office has two options. If the problem is not urgent, the Milan office sends an e-mail message across the Internet to the technical staff at headquarters. The engineers in California see the detailed description of the problem when they arrive in the morning and send their response via e-mail. If an answer is needed immediately, the sales office will first search the answers to Frequently Asked Questions stored on the server. If the answer is not available, a request for technical assistance is e-mailed to headquarters. The ability to access remote information resources quickly is a vital tool in this company's strategy for competing in today's global economy.

Company C has started using Internet services to distribute requests for proposals (RFPs) to vendors. Previously, the company would mail copies of an RFP to a list of vendors, wait two weeks for vendors to submit proposals, and follow up with a second mailing to the interested parties. Assuming the company received 120 proposals in response to one RFP, one-fifth of which are submitted by overseas vendors, and then sent each vendor a 20-page specification document, the costs would be as follows:

- ► Duplicating 120 copies of a 20-page document, at approximately $7 per copy, equals $840.
- ► Postage for 120 packages (a minimum of $2.95 each for domestic delivery and $18.00 each for international expedited delivery) equals approximately $715.
- ► Salary and benefits for clerical personnel who spend one day making photocopies and preparing and mailing 120 packages equal approximately $1,000.

The cost of this one-time activity is $2,555, and it takes two days from the time the proposals are received to the time the specifications are mailed.

After Company C connected to the Internet, it posted an announcement regarding each RFP to Internet discussion groups that pertain to the specific topic of interest, asked vendors to submit indication of interest, and sent specifications via e-mail to those that responded. One employee was designated the primary recipient of all incoming vendor responses. This employee forwarded the responses electronically to all parties within the company involved in evaluating the proposals and sent out follow-up documents via e-mail—a task that takes less than an hour.

By using the Internet to solicit and receive vendor proposals, Company C now saves thousands of dollars in copying, mailing, and personnel costs. Distribution of its RFPs over the Internet also enables Company C to reach many more vendors than might otherwise have been possible, netting a larger number of proposals for consideration, allowing for more competitive bids, and ultimately saving the company more money. There is no doubt that the process would be substantially less comprehensive and less efficient without the Internet.

Companies need to know what their customers are thinking so they can quickly modify a sales or marketing approach that is not working or, alternatively, enhance one that is working. Marketing departments have found that Internet services, such as chat rooms and newsgroups, allow them to conduct cyberspace "focus groups" and obtain instant feedback on new marketing approaches and comments on product quality and service.

Companies are also discovering the value of electronic distribution of press releases to those newspapers and radio and television stations that now accept press releases via e-mail. Sending a press release electronically to the news media not only saves time and money, it makes it more likely (although it does not guarantee) that: (1) the press release will be read and used by the reporter or editor rather than lost in a stack of paper mail, and (2) the company's message will remain intact—because the portions of the press release that the reporter or editor wants to use can be "cut and pasted" directly into the news story, without the need for rekeying or scanning.

Currently, any business that is involved in any way with the movement of information needs to be "on" the Internet. Within a few years, any company that does not have an Internet address will find itself at a disadvantage and will be seen as not ready to do business in the "information age." Companies that have a home page on the Web and have an e-mail information number and other infobot sites listed on their brochures and in their advertisements will have a decided advantage.

INTERNET CONNECTIVITY REQUIREMENTS AND COSTS

Connectivity requirements and costs vary with the size of the company and the type of activity for which Internet services are to be used. Some companies may only want the ability to exchange e-mail. Others may want to set up a Web server and offer users access to their services via a graphical browser such as Mosaic or Netscape Navigator. Until a company has determined what it intends to do on the Internet, it is almost impossible to identify the costs and measure the value of an Internet connection for its business.

This section examines the basic requirements and costs in four areas: hardware and software, Internet access services, technical support, and network security.

Hardware and Software

For a one-person office or a very small company, the hardware and software requirements are relatively straightforward. Connection to the Internet requires a computer, a modem, and a telephone line. As previously noted, it does not matter whether the computer is a Macintosh, a Windows machine, or a UNIX workstation. The modem does matter. A modem transmitting at 14.4 Kbps or 28.8 Kbps is the standard for most Internet services. A slower modem will work but will take a long time to send or receive large files, especially files containing graphics. A company should invest in the fastest modem that it can afford.

To access some Internet accounts, standard communications software (such as Procomm or Microphone) is required. Many Internet service providers are now including software as a part of their services, so it is a good idea to obtain information about software requirements up front before making any software purchases exclusively for this purpose.

Last, a telephone line is required. Most larger corporations will use a dedicated connection to an Internet service provider to accommodate transmission of large amounts of information generated by many users. To ensure that an Internet access session is not interrupted when using a dial-up connection, call waiting and other voice communication services must be disabled. This means that incoming voice callers will receive a busy signal. As this is undesirable for a business, an additional line, separate from the line used for voice communication, is an appropriate investment.

Internet Access Services

Once the company has identified a specific business application that warrants connection to the Internet, it should address the following questions:

> ▶ What is the size of the typical data file or the typical number of pages that will be transmitted?
>
> ▶ To how many destinations will the information be sent, and where are they located?
>
> ▶ What is the frequency of information transmissions?
>
> ▶ To what extent is the information "mission-critical" or time-sensitive?

The answers to these questions will help to determine the kind of Internet connection needed to handle the information flow, or the communication bandwidth. The following example should help to clarify this point.

Company D and its branch office need to transmit approximately 75 pages of text (the equivalent of 240 kilobytes [KB] of data) back and forth twice a day for comment. Data storage is measured in bytes, but communication bandwidth is measured in bits per second (bps). There are 8 bits per byte. In this case, taking into account additional text (headers, addresses, and so forth), assume that the conversion factor is 10 rather than 8. Thus, 240 KB become 2.4 megabits. Since the material is time-sensitive, each site will need a modem transmitting at 14.4 Kbps to allow the transmission of 2.4

megabits over the Internet in less than three minutes over a simple dial-up connection.

Once bandwidth needs are known, the proper type of Internet access can be selected. This depends on the functions to be performed and on the number of people at each site wanting to access the Internet at any given time.

A dial-up connection costs between $10 and $35 per month. Some Internet access providers impose an additional usage charge of between $1 and $5 per hour. For "800" number service, the usage charge can be as high as $9.50 per hour. The advantage of a dial-up connection is that it requires minimal site rewiring and setup and is therefore relatively inexpensive to install. Dial-up connections are recommended for companies that are testing the waters before committing themselves to the substantial investment required for full dedicated-line Internet service.

One alternative to individual dial-up accounts for a site with more than three or four users is a "host" (or LAN) access account. A host/LAN access account permits users to "share" a single dial-up connection to an Internet access provider. Sharing is accomplished either through the use of the LAN or by giving each user access to the host computer. In any organization where four or more people will be using Internet services with regularity, a host/LAN access account cuts down on the number of telephone lines needed as well as on monthly Internet access provider fees.

When the number of Internet users within the company grows, a dial-up connection—limited by the speed of modems and the number of users on-line at any one time—may become congested. At that point, dedicated access service should be considered. Dedicated access service (also known as "leased-line" service) is provided by installing a leased line from the nearest location of the selected Internet access provider to the company's offices. Leased lines are commonly referred to by their bandwidth:

- DS-O line: a 56-Kbps or 64-Kbps line
- Fractional T-1 line: a 128-Kbps or 512-Kbps line
- T-1 (also known as DS-1) line: a 1.5-Mbps line
- 10-Mbps line
- T-3 (also known as DS-3) line: a 44.74-Mbps line

The cost of leased-line service typically includes the following:

- ▹ *Internet access provider's fee:* In the United States, the average monthly fee is $550 for a DS-O line and $1,324 for a T-1 line.

- ▹ *"Tail circuit" costs:* The leased line from the company's location to the Internet access provider's site is normally furnished by the local telephone company, although a long-distance telephone company may furnish the connection for a more distant site. The costs of connection are determined by mileage and bandwidth and vary by region. Typical tail circuit costs range from $100 per month for a DS-O line serving a company located at a short distance from the service provider to several thousand dollars per month for a T-1 line serving a remote site.

Internet access service providers are listed in a number of reference books. Because the landscape is changing so rapidly, with new providers emerging, older ones being acquired, and large companies like IBM and Microsoft jumping into the fray, the best way to identify access providers in the area is to ask other companies for referrals. There are also discussion groups on the Internet concerning access providers, and a company should be able to obtain a list of potential vendors in its area by conducting a keyword search. Companies that have access to Mosaic, Netscape Navigator, or some other Web browser may find a local access provider through ElNet Galaxy or Yahoo, by entering the keyword *Internet* and then the state, city, or country.

Technical Support

A company that uses dedicated-line Internet services needs technical personnel to assign e-mail addresses to employees, monitor the status of internal network functionality, and implement new software as required. A "help desk" is also needed. The help desk serves as an "institutional memory." When a better method of communicating via the Internet is discovered, the help desk ensures that all other groups within the organization know about it as well. To maximize the value of the Internet connection, a company with dedicated access must seriously consider creating a help desk function. This can cost as much as a half-time person or considerably more for larger organizations.

Network Security

Companies that are considering an Internet connection frequently overlook or fail to address adequately the issue of network security. If a company has telephones, fax machines, and modems, it should already have formulated a policy regarding their use. For what purposes are employees permitted to use these tools? Are there certain times when they should be used and other times when use is not permitted? What about authorization codes? Are access codes for modems required to have both alpha and numeric characters? How often should access codes be changed? Are there explicit rules against using commonplace or easily identified passwords?

Before implementing Internet (especially dedicated-line services), management must give serious consideration to the company's existing network security measures and policies. In addition, management should start thinking about which individuals or groups in the company should have access to Internet services and for what purposes. Thinking about how employees use even basic services, such as e-mail, is important for a variety of reasons, yet a recent survey of companies with Internet services revealed that 43.5 percent of the respondents had no written policies regarding the use of e-mail, while 38.7 percent assumed, but were not certain, that they had formal guidelines. Because communications networks are company assets, the company can be held liable for employee misuse of the Internet connection. Examples of misuse include circulating defamatory statements in e-mail messages, using the company's Internet connection to operate a sideline business, downloading and distributing files unrelated to the business, and surfing the Net for personal purposes. Hallmark Cards, a participant in the survey cited above, has established guidelines based on interviews with experienced Internet users and warns its employees: "Assume the message you send will never be destroyed."

Developing a written security policy is a worthwhile

investment of time and effort. Without a clearly worded policy, distributed throughout the organization, employees may knowingly or unknowingly use company resources inefficiently and thus cost the organization substantially more in the longer term.

When evaluating the security risks of an Internet connection, the following questions should be asked:

- ▸ What is to be protected?
- ▸ From whom is it to be protected?
- ▸ What will protection cost?

Once the questions have been answered, a comprehensive security plan can be developed. From that base, the combinations of tools that are needed to implement the plan can be identified. The following steps could prove quite useful:

1. Determine whether there are any existing plans regarding network usage within the organization.
2. Collect all written documentation concerning those plans.
3. Identify all individuals to whom the plans have been distributed.
4. Review the existing plans to determine whether they are adequate.
5. Examine minutely the potential threats posed by implementing the Internet.
6. Specify clearly which individuals or groups should have access to Internet resources, both incoming and outgoing, and any restrictions on access that apply.
7. Develop a written plan that covers the issues previously considered.
8. Explore the available "tools" that will permit the organization to implement the plan.
9. Acquire and implement the tools.
10. Ensure that all affected personnel are thoroughly briefed on the plan and subsequent updates.

The choice of Internet security tools can be made effectively only after the company has developed its network security plan. Internet security tools range from modifications in routers (the devices that connect the internal network to the Internet access provider's network)—called "route filtering" or "packet filtering"—to "fire walls" that provide a buffer between the corporate network and the Internet access provider, to encryption systems and "smart cards."

Route/packet filtering is fine for organizations that have experienced technical personnel, but not for smaller organizations that lack the necessary resources. In addition, route/packet filtering does not protect the network against "spoofing," attempts to gain access from outside the system that give the appearance of coming from an authorized site. By itself, route/packet filtering is a modest deterrent at best—akin to a putting a hook and eye on an outside door. Whether the system needs a more robust security device—something closer to a deadbolt—is a decision to be made in the security-planning process.

A "fire wall" is a system that can prevent intruders from breaking into a corporate network or company personnel from using network resources without authorization. Fire walls come in two basic models. The standard fire wall system consists of a UNIX workstation buffered on either side by a router. One router interfaces with the external world; the other connects to the company's internal network. Standard fire wall systems use specialized software, require a reasonably high level of administrative sophistication, and transmit information with a certain delay. The delay is due to the workstation's "storing" the information for a short period of time and examining the originating addresses to ensure that each incoming packet is acceptable. Although this delay may not seem like much, it can become onerous at a high-volume site. Adding a fire wall also means that users need to go through another authentication step. The additional authentication requirement may be annoying—like having to disarm an alarm system before entering a secured office—but it is the price that must be paid for security.

The second type of fire wall is called the Bastion Host, or Applications Layer Gateway. The Bastion Host is a single self-contained unit that performs all the functions performed by the workstation buffered by routers. However, because the

Bastion Host establishes a through session, rather than storing incoming information, it normally performs faster than a standard fire wall.

Encryption systems and smart cards are other security devices that can be used in conjunction with route/packet filtering and fire walls. An encryption system encodes data sent over the Internet so that only another system that has the "keys" to unlock the particular encryption algorithm used can read the data. Encryption systems rely on algorithms ("something the system knows"). A smart card relies on a unique pass code generated by a credit card–sized device issued to each authorized user ("something the user has in his or her possession"). This pass code is synchronized with the company's server. When combined with passwords and identifiers, smart cards can be very effective.

Evaluating and selecting network security tools is an important part of implementing a security plan. To ensure the best selection of tools, a company should develop a detailed RFP and circulate it to as wide a group of prospective vendors as is manageable. This will provide a range of proposals and a variety of choices. The following questions should be considered in preparing an RFP for network security vendors:

- Will Internet connectivity be limited to a single host that is not connected with any other internal network systems, or will connectivity extend to the entire network with potential access from any system?

- What type of internal network does the company have (e.g., Novell, SNA, DECNET, Ethernet, or some other variety)? (This information will affect the choice of interface used in implementing the security plan.)

- What kind of Internet connection is desired? Will connection be via a dial-up line, a 56-Kbps line, a T-1 line, or a T-3 line? (Systems differ in their ability to handle bandwidth. Some work well with a dial-up connection, whereas others cannot handle traffic beyond 56 Kbps.)

- Will the company provide Internet access to all

corporate users, or will it establish a "virtual private" network and limit access to selected sites? (The security tools for a virtual private network are different from those designed for wider access.)

▶ Will the Internet connection be accessed primarily from stationary sites, or will there be significant access by mobile users, such as sales personnel and field technicians? (Companies that have a large number of mobile users find that smart cards work quite well when used in conjunction with standard fire walls and Bastion Hosts.)

▶ Is encryption required? (If encryption is required, the company must specify the nature of the requirement (domestic, international, etc.) so that security system vendors can respond properly.)

Many companies find that they need outside expertise when they start to create or evaluate their network security plans and policies. The number of consultants that specialize in network security planning and implementation for business clients is growing. Some of the companies that offer comprehensive Internet security services are:

▶ Trusted Information Systems: netsec@tis.com or (301) 854-6889

▶ Livermore Software Labs: portusinfo@gw.lsli.com or (800) 240-5754

▶ ANS CO+RE: info@ans.net or (703) 758-8700

▶ CheckPoint Software: info@checkpoint.com or (800) 429-4391

▶ NetPartners: sales@netpart.com or (714) 759-1641

▶ Hughes Information Security Products: netlock@mls.hac.com or (714) 732-1637

Costs associated with network security vary widely, ranging from $200 a week for a few hours of personnel time to more than $25,000 per year for maintaining a fully fortified Bastion Host. Each type of security system comes with a different set of features and functionality. Some are delivered only as software to be run on a UNIX workstation.

Others are complete systems that include all the required hardware and software.

Since the choice of security tools can only be effectively made after the company has developed its security plan, the more effort a company invests early on in the process, the more secure its facilities are likely to be.

CONDUCTING A COST-JUSTIFICATION EXERCISE

After identifying the potential expense displacement or revenue enhancement of an Internet connection and the types and costs of Internet services that might be needed, it is time to weigh the benefits and costs and make a decision. There are times when it may not be practical to conduct a detailed cost-justification exercise or when the evidence for change is so overwhelming that there is no need to perform a cost justification. In these cases, it is still important that the company analyze carefully which groups in the company will be impacted by Internet implementation and how.

The Maloff Company has developed a four-part cost-justification worksheet designed to help companies work through the evaluation of alternative solutions and arrive at a decision. Exhibit 8-1 shows a sample worksheet on which typical connectivity costs, additional fees, and the estimated tangible value that a company might expect from an Internet solution are filled in.

Justifying the costs of implementing a new technology requires a clear understanding of existing costs, possible new sources of income, and potential alternatives. The benefit-cost ratio is calculated by dividing the total value of the anticipated benefits to be derived from the solution under consideration by the expected costs of implementing the solution. Performing an objective cost-benefit analysis for Internet connectivity is essential for the preparation of a sound business case to be presented to senior management and for clarity in the planning process.

The ratio would be 1:1 if the anticipated value of the solution were equal to the investment required. There may be instances in which the value of intangible benefits is sufficiently great that a 1:1 ratio is acceptable. Often, the implementation of additional applications, at minimal cost, may improve the ratio. Moreover, the ratio obtained for the first year may rise in subsequent years. In Exhibit 8-1, note that the first-year ratio of 4.13:1 is expected to rise to 4.84:1 in subsequent years. A business that can achieve a better than 4:1 return on its investment should certainly consider the investment favorably.

The Maloff Company
Internet Consultants
joel@maloff.com

Try to answer all the questions in this worksheet as accurately as possible, but do not hesitate to enter "guesstimates" where needed.

Part One: Status Quo

1. What is the business activity to be improved? (Examples: reducing costs of courier service or fax transmissions, reducing "telephone tag" between company employees, finding a better method of distributing software to outlying branches or customers, or gaining greater access to customer prospects.)

   Reduce the costs associated with distributing software updates to 4,000 customers.

2. What is the current cost of this activity per year? (Examples: postage costs, fax costs, courier service costs.) How much revenue can the company conservatively expect to gain with a small percentage increase in efficiency? What are the intangible benefits, if any? (Examples: enhanced employee morale, customer loyalty.)

   Distribution via U.S. postal service costs $50 per unit. Total cost of distributing 4,000 units
   3 times a year = $600,000 per year. Switching to distribution over the Internet could save the
   company $300,000 a year. Currently, 25 percent of the customers never unwrap the software;
   another 25 percent want software updates distributed over the Internet.

3. How frequently does this activity occur?

   3 times per year

4. What is the volume of information transmitted/exchanged? (Examples: number of pages, number of bytes.)

   Estimated 5 megabytes per unit

5. To what extent is this activity "mission-critical" or time-sensitive? (Check one.)

   ____ High   _X_ Moderately high   ____ Moderate   ____ Not at all

6. What other alternatives (besides the Internet) have been considered? Why were those alternatives not implemented?

   Distribution via Federal Express. Too costly.
   Distribution via fax transmission over direct dial-up line. Inconvenient for customers.

Exhibit 8-1   Sample Cost-Justification Worksheet

Part Two: Internet Alternatives

7. Which Internet access service is most likely to meet your requirements? Specify the cost of the one you select.)

Low-end dial-up (local access number) ($240–$1,200/year)   _____

Host/LAN dial-up (local access number) ($2,300–$4,600/year)   _____

Host/LAN dial-up ("800" number access) (add $700–$1,300/year)   _____

56-Kbps dedicated access ($7,000/year) $7,000/year

T-1 (1.5 Mbps) dedicated access ($18,000–$47,000/year)   _____

8. What additional fees are required? (Specify the cost of all that apply.)

Local telephone company charges:
- Message unit or timed unit charges ($50/year)   _____
- "Tail circuit" cost for leased line:
  - 56 Kbps ($2,000–$10,000/year) $5,000/year
  - T-1 ($4,000–$30,000/year)   N/A

Hardware (not included by access provider):
- Router ($3,000–$8,000, one-time) $8,000 (one-time)
- CSU/DSU ($500–$2,500, one-time)   Included

Software (e.g., TCP/IP, Gopher) $2,500 (one-time)

9. What are your estimated internal management costs?

Additional network operations center costs $20,000 (personnel)

"Help desk" function   Included above

Continuing user-training program   N/A

10. What are your estimated network security costs?

Development of security plan (personnel) $10,000

Security tools:
- Route/packet filtering ($2,000/year, human resources)   N/A
- "Fire wall" ($10,000, one-time)   N/A
  - ($5,000+ human resources)   N/A
- Applications Layer Gateway ($10,000–$25,000/year) $20,000/year

11. What are the total estimated costs? (Add 7 through 10.) $72,500

Part Three: Evaluation and Analysis

12. What is the likely quantifiable impact of the solution on the status quo?

    $300,000

13. What are the potential intangible benefits of the solution?

    Increased customer loyalty

    Enhanced responsiveness to customer requests

    Appearance of technological proficiency

14. What is (are) the downside(s) if the status quo remains unchanged?

    Continued high expenses

    Depressed ROI

    Loss of customers to more responsive organizations

15. What is the potential cost of an Internet solution?

First year	$72,500
Subsequent years	$62,000

16. What is the benefit-cost ratio of an Internet solution?

First year	4.13:1
Subsequent years	4.84:1

Part Four: Additional Applications

Note: The ratio calculated above is for *one* application. The investment required for additional applications may be minimal.

17. What is the quantifiable value of additional applications?

Application	Value
None at this time	

18. What incremental costs will be incurred by these additional applications?

Application	Value

19. What is the revised benefit-cost ratio?

First year	N/A
Subsequent years	N/A

PRODUCTIVITY, POLICY, AND INTERNET TRAINING ISSUES

MARIAN BREMER

Senior Information Specialist, BBN Systems and Technologies

THE INTERNET IS perhaps the most important new tool for today's "learning organization," but it does itself represent a substantial learning challenge. As U.S. and international corporations rush to connect to the Internet, their employees confront a new technical infrastructure that will have an impact on the management infrastructure, their systems, and their interaction with customers. In addition, the Internet brings with it an array of new equipment, software, and sources of information that must somehow be integrated into work processes and, therefore, must be learned and understood.

U.S. corporations are already aware that their employees require continual training and retraining in the tools, resources, and processes that underpin their companies' operations. As those operations change more rapidly, investment in training to manage the learning curve has increased as well. In 1994, U.S. corporations invested more than $50 billion in formal employee training.[1] Today, 88 percent of all organizations sponsor training in computer skills versus 75 percent five years ago. Ken Hansen, director of strategic information for Motorola University, predicts that the "future will be about whether a company can constantly renew itself in the face of continual change."[2] Indeed, one article predicts that "[o]ver the next few decades, the private sector will eclipse the public sector as our predominant educational institution."[3]

Organizations planning to connect to the Internet or to extend their existing Internet connection to employee desktops are confronting new software, new resources, and a new environment that will not only enable continual change but also deliver (using changing tools) everything that anyone could possibly want to know about change. With this in mind, *Internet training* is at best only an indicative term. Since the introduction of the Internet has revolutionized existing processes, using new tools that require new underlying technical support systems, training about the Internet mixes aspects of management, technical, and basic end-user computer training. From deciding to connect to the Internet to deploying the Internet to employees, each step of the way raises new and challenging policy and rollout issues and requires decisions that must be informed by the best-quality information.

This chapter discusses why an Internet training plan is necessary and how it can and should be used to give employees the skills they need in order to achieve the organization's strategic Internet goals. It includes a discussion of the types of training required to support objectives at each stage of Internet rollout, a description of a training implementation strategy to deliver Internet training to employee desktops, and a discussion of policy decisions that must be communicated to employees through a successful training program. The chapter also describes how a training plan might support corporate policy in regard to the Internet.

THE CASE FOR INTERNET TRAINING

Which companies need access to all the tools and resources provided by the global network to decrease operating costs, improve customer relations, gain access to critical technical and competitive information, and create new sales and marketing demands? Arguably, all of them. However, no one individual or group could possibly explore, much less master, all the tools and resources now available on the Internet. The

Internet has many faces, and not all of them are fit to grace the halls of America's corporations. This Information Highway provides access to a multitude of tools and resources, including:

- Repositories of proven and unproven software of all kinds for all platforms for all purposes
- Electronic marketplaces for a wide variety of companies selling everything from flowers to pizzas to vintage clothing to computers
- A high-speed two-way connection to customers, partners, and suppliers
- A functioning Better Business Bureau/*Consumer Reports* capacity with product reports from millions of customers
- Just about every piece of information available electronically at the most economical price—sometimes "free"—delivered right to the employee desktop

To use the Internet for competitive advantage, it is critical for an organization to decide in advance *which* types of Internet applications and resources are necessary to achieve its strategic goals and how they fit with existing tools and processes. The total quality management concept of identifying the "vital few" (versus "all possible") changes that could be introduced is a useful one here.[4] Each Internet software program introduced within an organization brings with it all the attendant requirements of support, upgrade paths, hardware requirements, and training.

Ironically, it is still a rarity for organizations to articulate, quantify, or measure what would constitute a "successful" Internet implementation. Even more rarely does the typical organization plan in advance how training will be mobilized to ensure that employees have the skills they need to achieve that success. Companies that have used the Internet to maximum advantage will testify that they achieved these results through trial and error, and teaching themselves what they needed to know as they went along.

Perhaps because the Internet connection typically represents a minor expense in comparison to investment in a corporate information system or manufacturing automation system, the skills necessary to manage the connection and master the tools that it makes available are somehow taken for granted. In addition, the media's continued use of recreational verbs like *surf* and *cruise* implies that Internet software tools need not be learned—that the employee can "pick them up" playing at home or during lunch hour. On the contrary, the road to using the Internet and its tools for competitive advantage is as time consuming as mastering any other business tool and requires the acquisition of a large number of expert skills.

Fortunately, from the experience of Internet pioneers, there has come a body of information that companies can use to design an achievable and measurable plan for Internet implementation—one that includes training as a critical element of the plan.

ANALYZING INTERNET TRAINING NEEDS

An Internet training plan cannot be designed in isolation from a clearly articulated statement of how the organization plans to use the Internet. Crafting that statement of purpose is not a trivial task. Different constituencies within the corporation may have diverse and even incompatible Internet requirements. For example, engineers and programmers, who may have been responsible for pushing the organization to connect, may want the most open Internet environment possible, with access to every conceivable tool and resource. In addition, they probably will not understand why training is necessary to achieve the desired results. Financial managers, on the other hand, who typically have strong concerns about the security of corporate assets, may lobby for a very restrictive Internet environment. They will almost certainly want the technical staff trained to safeguard the corporate network and want all Internet-connected employees to understand both the Net's potential and its dangers.

One of the major challenges for management in planning for Internet implementation is understanding how these diverse groups intend to use the Internet, whether these objectives are feasible, and what each group will need to know in order to use the Internet effectively. Strategic goals and policies and Internet training should ideally be developed as an integrated plan.

Articulating Internet strategic goals also addresses one of the most frequently asked questions of senior managers evaluating the Internet as a business tool: will it make their employees more or less productive. There is no greater information delivery vehicle than the Internet. One can extrapolate from a growing body of literature on knowledge-based business that in accelerating information gathering, the Internet delivers competitive advantage by giving employees more information on which to base their decisions. How can the Internet make an individual employee more productive? To cite just one common example, many companies currently publish the latest information about their products, services, and even their acquisitions and mergers on the World Wide Web, while continuing to distribute paper memoranda and flyers about these products and plans to their employees. A salesperson with direct Internet access can use the on-line product information during sales calls, access it to keep up with new announcements while traveling, and more easily compare product features to those of competitors. Such access is faster and far more efficient than continually filing and retrieving paper. The most successful Internet roll-out will have designed an Internet interface for both internal and external information distribution. Lack of such planning can lead to employee frustration and decreased productivity.

One approach to an integrated plan is to create a corporate Internet implementation team with specific responsibility for drawing up the plan, identifying the necessary resources, and evaluating the progress made at each stage. Ideally, this team should be informed by input from the organization's early Internet adopters (technical and research staff), computer operations/data-processing staff, and information scientists.[5]

The Internet implementation team's composition will vary depending on company goals. To the extent that the organization intends to use the Internet to gather information about the competition and deliver it to employees' desktops, staff librarians should be tapped to contribute their information expertise and familiarity with employee needs to this enterprise. If the company's primary goal for its Internet connection is to establish a new sales and marketing vehicle, then sales and marketing managers must be represented on the team.

Whether or not a formal team tasked with Internet implementation exists, outsourcing is always a possibility. For example, if the company lacks the technical resources to manage the Internet connection and enabling security technology, it may decide to contract with its Internet access provider to provide managed connectivity services. If a company finds that its competitors are gaining advantage by selling goods and services over the Internet, it may decide that outsourcing development and maintenance of a corporate Internet service for electronic commerce is faster than having the in-house team do it.

In the case of training, either internal or external resources can be effective in delivering desired results. If a company plans to develop its own training program using internal staff, its computer operations and library staff should work with the trainers to design the curriculum for end users. If internal resources are not adequate, the company may engage one of the many firms that now provide Internet training via seminars, conferences, and hands-on training sessions, both on-site and off-site.

For an effective rollout, each business unit should be interviewed to provide input to the Internet plan. Some departments may need significant training to support their goals. Generally, sales and marketing staff will have heard about the extraordinary power of the World Wide Web (WWW) to advertise the complete panoply of a company's goods and services, gather marketing data, and even permit customers to order on-line. Although they may never have "touched" the Internet, the staff in these departments will be highly motivated to learn what they need to know as soon as possible to be able to accomplish their objectives.

This point bears repeating: no matter what the task, the more closely the curriculum supports the specific tasks that each employee must accomplish to achieve objectives, the more successful the training! Introducing Internet tools is no exception. Similarly, it is important to coordinate the timing of training with rollout. The most extraordinary trainer will contribute very little to the implementation if the employee returns to an "Internet-less" office with no opportunity for directed practice.

TRAINING TO SUPPORT THE STAGES OF INTERNET IMPLEMENTATION

Focused training is critical at each step of the Internet implementation. Once the decision has been made to connect to the Internet or to upgrade existing Internet functionality, senior managers must understand the Internet and its capabilities well enough to prioritize and make available resources to support the company's strategic plan. Representatives from the business units that are expected to achieve measurable results from the Internet implementation must understand in some detail what the medium will deliver and how to map these new functions onto existing processes. The early Internet enthusiasts who spearheaded the Internet implementation must learn how to balance their goals with the priorities of the company as a whole. System administrators need to support the Internet connection and to design and maintain systems to protect the company's proprietary electronic assets from unauthorized intrusion.

Typically, companies introduce the Internet in stages, as shown in Figure 9-1. Once the connection is secure and the WWW advertising vehicle is launched, the decision follows to deliver the Internet to employees. At this point, the technical staff must configure the local area network (LAN) to deliver Transmission Control Protocol/Internet Protocol (TCP/IP) to the desktop and support end-user applications. Diverse software applications and utilities (sometimes on diverse platforms) must be installed to support these diverse groups of end users. End users must know what they are supposed to do with these tools and how to do it. Customization and research are necessary for maximum end-user satisfaction and productivity.

Each of these stages in the implementation process will require a different type of training. The implementation curve

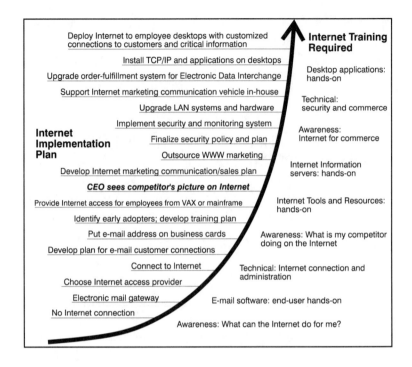

Deploy Internet to employee desktops with customized connections to customers and critical information — **Internet Training Required**

Install TCP/IP and applications on desktops

Upgrade order-fulfillment system for Electronic Data Interchange — Desktop applications: hands-on

Support Internet marketing communication vehicle in-house

Upgrade LAN systems and hardware — Technical: security and commerce

Implement security and monitoring system

Internet Implementation Plan — Finalize security policy and plan — Awareness: Internet for commerce

Outsource WWW marketing

Develop Internet marketing communication/sales plan — Internet Information servers: hands-on

CEO sees competitor's picture on Internet

Provide Internet access for employees from VAX or mainframe — Internet Tools and Resources: hands-on

Identify early adopters; develop training plan

Put e-mail address on business cards — Awareness: What is my competitor doing on the Internet

Develop plan for e-mail customer connections

Connect to Internet — Technical: Internet connection and administration

Choose Internet access provider

Electronic mail gateway — E-mail software: end-user hands-on

No Internet connection

Awareness: What can the Internet do for me?

Figure 9-1 Internet Implementation/Training Coordination

shown in Figure 9-1 depicts how Company X, a medium-sized company, coordinated its training needs with the phases of Internet implementation.

TRAINING METHOD AND CONTENT

Training to use the Internet comes in a variety of flavors and depends on the task to be accomplished. To guarantee success, the training method must be matched to the task. The three principal training methods are: awareness training (via lecture-demonstrations and case studies), technical training, and hands-on end-user training.

Awareness Training

A new spreadsheet software program typically does not require any form of "awareness training" in order to demonstrate its benefits to the end user. The Internet, however, is an extremely complex system with both major opportunities and major risks that are not easily understood or evaluated. Lecture-demonstrations of Internet capabilities are a good way of helping employees to understand what the Internet can do and what resources will need to be devoted to implementation in order to obtain desired results. Senior and midlevel managers who will be responsible for the Internet implementation and the heads of functional organizations who will have an influence on how Internet tools and services will be used within the organization are the best candidates for awareness training because the benefits of such training will spread through the organization. These early attendees of awareness training often become the internal marketers of the Internet for companies not yet connected.

In the previously mentioned Company X, for example, the sales and marketing departments became committed to using the Internet as a new marketing communication vehicle after undergoing awareness training. They chose to outsource the publication of their Web server in order to get it on the Net as quickly as possible. Later in the implementation plan, these departments will provide their staff with the necessary hands-on training to take over management of the server in-house.

In fact, it is important for companies to integrate training into their Internet marketing plans. Apocryphal tales abound of how companies entering the Internet marketplace inadvertently offended millions of their potential customers through inadequate understanding of "netiquette" and landed on "Worst of the Web" lists. Understanding the marketing promise of the Web alone requires background on Internet culture and customers' technical requirements as well as a grounding in concepts of hypermedia and distributed systems in general.[6]

There are many ways to find out about the Internet. Approximately 40 articles per day about the Internet were published in 1994, and almost every professional society's annual conference has its Internet track. Publications and conferences are useful ways for managers to understand the potential uses of the Internet in a specific profession or vertical market. Internet training classes, which have proliferated in the past several years, range from low-cost evening courses at adult education centers to highly technical hands-on training seminars costing several thousand dollars. Talks and seminars are scheduled in all the major metropolitan areas, and trainers are available to deliver classes on-site.

The variety of courses available has made the choice of training more confusing, but the best Internet awareness training should:

- Target the narrowest possible audience, preferably individuals with the same level of experience, in the same industry, and with similar work responsibilities
- Be developed by, and preferably delivered in partnership with, recognized industry experts
- Include live demonstrations of advanced (relevant) Internet applications
- Include case studies of companies (in the same industry) that are using the Internet to advantage
- Not attempt to cover every aspect of the Internet in one day
- Be clearly a training event, not a sales event (if delivered by a vendor of other Internet products and services)

Awareness training will continue to be useful throughout the implementation plan as the Internet is rolled out to other functional units with specialized needs such as sales, human resources, finance, and purchasing. In each case, the more specific the training is to the needs of the group, the more successful it will be.

Another important consideration in developing an Internet training plan is how to keep up with the rapid advances in Internet technology. Continued awareness training and seminars on Internet developments are critical to competitive use of this new technology. The expert Internet trainer should be able to provide recommendations for using the Internet to keep up to date on new technical developments, for example, by monitoring specific mailing lists and newsgroups, tracking the activities of Internet organizations responsible for standards, and consulting the Web publications of those companies introducing products that provide Internet business solutions.

Technical Training

The original Internet community of system administrators and programmers is a highly technical group with specialized expertise in UNIX, TCP/IP, and all the related Internet utilities. In many cases, companies new to the Internet are faced with the challenge of bringing their technical staff and Internet administrators up to speed. The availability or lack of in-house technical services will inform the company's choice of an Internet access provider. Some Internet access providers include training packaged with the access service and may offer more specialized training as needed.

Training for technical staff must cover such topics as the TCP/IP reference model, interconnectivity of local area networks and wide area networks, the Domain Name System, the Simple Mail Transfer Protocol, IP routing basics, and implementing an IP internetwork. Time should be allocated for discussion of network management problem solving and site-specific issues.

One of the most important technical topics of Internet training relates to security. Implementing and monitoring Internet site security is a course in itself. Management should know how to develop a network security policy, the design of which will inform the technical implementation of the policy. Technical staff must understand the process and content of risk assessment and know how to select appropriate site-security technical solutions. Even more important, the technical staff must know how to establish a process for monitoring and evaluating the solutions once installed.

Security technology, or technology that enables privacy in communications and commercial transactions on the Internet, is increasingly important to the achievement of corporate Internet goals. End-to-end encryption and secure systems that support Internet commerce—like CommerceNet—have become the hottest new topic on the Internet. Because of the high expectations raised by the trade press, some companies have made training on secure systems the top priority for their technical staff.

Hands-On End-User Training

In a knowledge-based, market-driven business model, companies cannot afford *not* to deliver the Internet and its associated resources to the desktop, where employees can make the most use of them. However, these tools and resources can and should be delivered to employees in a format that directly reinforces their work. The planning required to design a customized electronic workspace, and the training required to help employees feel confident about using the tools provided, cannot be minimized. For increased productivity, training must be designed to enable employees to use the Internet to do their jobs, not merely to master the Internet itself.

This subsection examines the twin tasks of designing customized electronic workspaces and then training employees in their use.

Creating customized electronic workspaces. Data is the "unorganized sludge" of the information age,[7] and the Internet indeed provides an unprecedented direct line to massive quantities of data. Action verbs such as *surf, navigate,* and (as used in the title of an Internet conference sponsored by the Special Libraries Association) *plunder* describe the effort necessary to yield a return on an Internet research investment. Unfortunately, the popular misconception that the Internet is "free"[8] sometimes leads individual employees to conduct lengthy wild-goose chases in search of information that is readily (and immediately) available from more conventional and reliable sources.

Surfing, navigating, plundering, and conducting wild-goose chases are the antithesis of an efficiently designed business process. Identifying the gems of "information" and "knowledge" available via the Internet must not be left to individual employees. The company can substantially improve employee productivity and satisfaction in using the Internet by investing in the development and delivery of customized *electronic workspaces* in which the data are selected and organized in a way that supports and facilitates job performance. Such workspaces include, but are not limited to, the Internet.

Newer Internet tools can "hide" the Internet itself and

can enable data from internal information systems to be integrated with external Internet-based data sources. Using Web technology and careful planning, the company can design a variety of such electronic workspaces (or "home pages") to support the goals of different business units or even of individuals within the same business unit. Each electronic workspace can combine point-and-click access to applications and resources with instructions on how and when to use specific resources. (Designing such workspaces is a worthy hands-on training investment for Internet trainers!) Since planning will have reduced the number of possible user problems, technical support for such systems is also simplified.

The customized electronic workspace for the sales account representative will not resemble that for the purchasing agent. The former might include direct access to information about company products, qualified leads, and current accounts. The latter might provide tools for sending orders electronically, performing credit checks, and accessing government regulatory information. The "marketspace"[9] for the marketing staff might provide access to competitors' product catalogs, government data, and customers' interactive responses to marketing surveys.

What would a customized electronic workspace look like? The workspace shown in Exhibit 9-1, a home page designed using the WWW, was created to support an investment analyst, and the workspace shown in Exhibit 9-2 was designed for a researcher in a pharmaceutical company. Workspaces such as these provide point-and-click access to all the resources listed (such as real-time stock quotes, financial reports, current information about drugs, and useful contacts within the pharmaceutical industry) and include simple descriptions of the resources as well as guidelines on how to use them. They might also include advice on what employees should do when they cannot find the answer to a particular question by using the Internet.

Training employees to use customized electronic workspaces. The advantages of training employees to use customized electronic workspaces can be more fully appreciated if we first contrast such job-specific training with two popular

---

Internet information system to track your investment portfolio

- **SEC EDGAR Database**
  Current public company financial reports to the Security & Exchange Commission. For historical data, contact the Corporate Information Center.
  IBM reports
  Silicon Graphics reports

- **Security APL Quote Server** 15-minute delayed access to stock prices [query by ticket symbol]
  Standard & Poor's 500 Index
  Dow Jones Industrial Average
  Note: real-time data is available from the Corporate Investment stock price feed. Contact Shirley.

- **Stock performance: closing price and volume historical data**
  an experimental project at MIT
  IBM
  Silicon Graphics

- **Quote Com:** delayed stock quotations and other financial services (requires account). Note that free service is limited to 5 queries per day.

- **Nestegg Personal Investment Services:** Tradeline Performance Leaders for Current Week

Copyright 1994. BBN Internet Services Corp.

Exhibit 9-1   Investment Resources on the Desktop

Pharmaceutical Manufacturers Association
Gives the state of pharmaceutical drug testing for various drugs.

Pharmaceutical Information Association—"provides comprehensive scientific, medical and regulatory writing services for the pharmaceutical industry."

PharmInfoNet—"devoted to delivering useful, up-to-date, and accurate pharmaceutical information to pharmacists, physicians, and patients." Interesting parts include:

- Drug DB—Use this database to access information about drugs on PharmInfoNet, including Medical Sciences Bulletin review articles, DrugFAQs, and threads archived from the sci.med.pharmacy newsgroup;
- DrugFAQs—Frequently Asked Questions about drugs with answers from pharmaceutical manufacturers and other approved sources;
- PharmMall—An area for companies—pharmaceutical manufacturers, publishers, software developers, etc.—to place their home pages, catalogs, and product information.

Exhibit 9-2   Pharmaceutical Resources

---

alternatives, which might be termed the "generic," or "vanilla," approach to training and the user-hostile approach.

The generic approach to Internet training can best be described via an analogy to the introduction of telephones. Imagine that telephones are being rolled out for the first time in the business environment. The trainer would begin the training session for end users by describing the history of the telephone, how it works, and who uses it all over the world.

A diagram of the corporate telephone network would be shown—several times—to illustrate how a call gets routed. The concept of a telephone number would be discussed and some examples presented. Rotary and Touch-Tone dialing would be demonstrated in a multimedia environment. An hour would be devoted to explaining the concept of area codes, and a session on international dialing would climax with a demonstration of a real-time connection to a telephone user in Japan. The trainer would display a pile of telephone directories and show slides of sample pages to illustrate how to find a number and when to use the yellow pages or the white pages. More advanced classes might include a demonstration of how to search a lot of directories simultaneously using a database of telephone numbers on a CD-ROM. Although it sounds ridiculous, most Internet training today closely resembles this scenario.

The implementation curve for Company X (shown earlier in Figure 9-1) provides an example of the user-hostile approach. At Company X, the Internet was initially delivered to employees on the networked VAX, or mainframe, computer. Each employee was required to master (1) the steps necessary to connect in terminal mode to the mainframe and (2) how to use each installed Internet application. The "workspace" in that scenario might look like this:

```
The following commands exist:
archie date dig ftp gopher help mail man nslookup ping snap
{get, get next, walk} swais telnet traceroute whois www
For more information about any given command, type
"man <command>."
You have mail.
TERM = (unknown) vt 100
```

Possible frustrations with this system can be illustrated by the following attempt to use the simplest command—to disconnect:

```
1: logo
logo: Command not found.
2: logoff
logoff: Command not found.
3: logout
```

The goal of the Internet rollout should be to eliminate hurdles like this insofar as possible by designing an effective Internet information system.

The point is that recent advances in Internet software permit the creation of easy-to-use graphical interfaces and enable infinite customization to match individual employee requirements, making either the generic approach or the user-hostile approach to Internet training a poor investment in time and money for Internet end users.

The planning and preparation that go into the creation of a customized electronic workspace make it both immediately usable by employees and highly useful for training purposes because employees can be trained to use such a workspace in a relatively short hands-on session. In fact, hands-on workspace training goes a long way toward allaying the terror of neophytes, who will be surprised and relieved to recognize familiar landmarks and reliable resources among the completely new sources of information on the Internet. To the extent that new users realize that they already understand some of the material, the learning challenge will appear less daunting.

Training employees in the effective use of customized workspaces such as those that were shown in Exhibits 9-1 and 9-2 is a relatively straightforward task. They might need to learn to use at most two or three different Internet software applications and learn the organization of about half a dozen different Internet resources. Although employees would have to be informed about the volatility of the Internet environment, if the workspaces are created and managed carefully, any necessary explanations and changes can be built into the workspaces as Internet resources appear, disappear, and evolve. The employees would also need training in how to recognize and diagnose problems and when to report problems to system administrators.

Given that the Internet provides access to a limitless sea of resources, the customized electronic workspaces described earlier in this chapter may seem unduly restrictive. Exhibit 9-3 shows a portion of a less restrictive but still well-planned Internet workspace. It is designed to meet the needs of researchers, explorers, and the Internet implementation team by supporting and encouraging productive exploration of the Internet. Although a home page such as this will require more extensive skills training than the simpler workspaces shown earlier, it provides a useful structure that can be used over and over again for practice at the desktop.

Training employees individually or in small groups to use customized electronic workspaces requires significantly less investment in time and achieves significantly better results than hiring the most famous Internet trainer to deliver a "vanilla" presentation on "what the Internet can do for you" or setting employees adrift in an "unorganized sludge" of data. Providing a focused workspace—one that supports results-oriented Internet transactions—makes it less likely that the company's Internet users will be forced to become "surfers" to find the information they need.

The size of the training investment will vary, depending on the existing expertise of employees and on the company's strategic goals. Training a skilled system administrator to assume the additional responsibility of Internet administration, including the security monitoring and maintenance, may take as little as a week, whereas training a new computer user to search the text effectively for competitive information might be handled in weekly training classes over several months. If the immediate goal of connecting to the Internet is to implement a vehicle for Internet sales and electronic commerce, the training and consulting costs can be quite high. If Internet tools are to be integrated into a new corporate information infrastructure for all employees, the cost will be considerable. On the other hand, the cost of *not* training employees to use the Internet to achieve company

---

Directory of Internet Directories

This directory of Internet directories is compiled from several sources, including the default directories that can be downloaded with several popular World Wide Web browser applications.

Subject Approaches to Internet Resources

- Clearinghouse for Subject-Oriented Internet Information Services
- Gopher Jewels
- Hytelnet
- The WWW Virtual Library

Exhibit 9-3 Internet Training and Search Resources

goals is substantially higher in terms of reduced productivity and delayed results.

INTEGRATING CORPORATE POLICY INTO THE TRAINING PLAN

The Internet and its many tools and resources are a challenge to master. In addition, they create policy issues that must be addressed by senior management before problems occur. Here are some policy issues that could become problems:

> ▸ Employees can access text and images that are in questionable taste right at their desktops or play chess over the Internet with other chess enthusiasts worldwide.

> ▸ By law, employees' electronic mail (e-mail) is private unless stated otherwise.

> ▸ Employees can send e-mail—and even broadcast messages to customers—that appear to represent company policy.

> ▸ Most instances of security violations involve disgruntled employees rather than intrusion by anonymous hackers.

To avoid potential problems, corporate policy can be introduced and integrated into Internet rollout and training. Using the focused workspace approach, corporate policy can be restated and reinforced every time an employee accesses the Internet. For example, at one computer manufacturing company, employees inside the corporate network must access the Internet via one companywide home page, which has been designed to provide pathways to the resources most appropriate to support business activities. The company's Internet policy is posted on that page. Employees are also informed that their activity on the Internet—each destination that they contact—is automatically logged and that, although that activity is not routinely monitored, it does remain available in the event that abuse is suspected.

Using Internet functionality and training to support policy and productivity will enable the company to reap the greatest rewards in the long term.

THE ULTIMATE GOAL OF INTERNET TRAINING

The Internet currently represents a substantial learning curve. However, a well-managed Internet rollout will limit the steepest learning curve to technical staff, decision makers, and those who are responsible for customizing and introducing the Internet. Focused awareness training, technical training, and hands-on user training are all appropriate approaches to learning what the team needs to know in order to implement Internet connectivity and keep up to date on critical Internet developments. In contrast, individual employees may just need to learn how to use the targeted useful bits of the Internet that are appropriate to support their work, through a combination of focused awareness training and hands-on computer-skills training using a customized Internet interface.

In organizations where the Internet becomes a solution to everyday business problems, it is completely and transparently integrated into other systems. "My" Internet is my desktop device, with planned and organized access to the tools and resources that I need. This is the goal.

NOTES

1. Data from "1994 Industry Report: An Overview of Employee Training in America," *Training Magazine,* October 1994, 29 ff.
2. Bob Filipczak, "Looking Past the Numbers," *Training Magazine,* October 1994, 74.
3. Stan Davis, "The Coming of Knowledge-Based Business," *Harvard Business Review,* September–December 1994, 170.
4. Patricia Lankford, "The 'Vital Few' Save Costs," *Management Accounting* 68 (August 1986): 54 ff.
5. S. Kalin, "Collaboration: A Key to Internet Training," *Bulletin of the American Society for Information Science* 20 (February–March 1994): 20–21.
6. Donna L. Hoffman and Thomas P. Novak, "Marketing in Hypermedia Computer-Mediated Environments: Conceptual Foundations." This interesting paper (with bibliography) is available from Vanderbilt University, URL: http://colette.ogsm.vanderbilt.edu/cme.conceptual.foundations.html.

7. Robert Lucky, AT&T Bell Laboratories, quoted in Davis, "The Coming of Knowledge-Based Business," 166.

8. John Makulovich, "The Beauty of Consensual Anarchy," *Washington Technology,* February 24, 1994, 21 ff.

9. Jeffrey F. Rayport, "Managing in the Marketspace," *Harvard Business Review,* November—December 1994, 141 ff.

10

EMERGING PLATFORMS FOR COMMERCE OVER THE INTERNET

GAIL GRANT

Vice President for Business Development, Open Market, Inc.

THE INTERNET HAS grown dramatically in the past 10 years, going from about 1,000 systems in 1984 to over 6.6 million systems in July of 1995.[1] Much of this growth has occurred in the last two years, as firms rushed to connect to the Internet to communicate with their customers and suppliers, put up World Wide Web (WWW) servers to disseminate product and marketing information, and hook into the burgeoning amount of free information available to anyone with an Internet account. In October 1994, the number of U.S. commercial hosts on the Internet climbed to 1.054 million, surpassing the number of educational hosts. Even more significant than the 1.054 million figure was the rate of growth in the number of commercial hosts over the previous year: 103 percent.

By 1996, the Internet will have changed the way companies do business, just as surely as it has changed the way America communicates. However, the infrastructure to support commerce over the Internet is still lacking, and the problems that must be surmounted are legion. Once the challenges have been addressed and the infrastructure has been developed, commerce over the Internet will grow rap-

Miss Grant is writing as an individual, and her opinions do not necessarily reflect the views of Open Market, Inc.

211

idly, and new opportunities and different ways of doing business will develop.

This chapter discusses the challenges that must be addressed to make the Internet safe for electronic commerce and the available systems and technologies that offer potential solutions to the problems. It also highlights some of the new and not-so-new players in this emerging market.

COMMERCE AND THE ROLE OF TRUST

Commerce is more than just the buying and selling of goods or services; it includes customer service, buyer and merchant authentication, fraud detection mechanisms, and billing. In a transaction's most basic form, a customer goes to the store, selects what he or she wants to buy, pays the merchant, obtains a receipt, and carries away the item. In this simple cash-and-carry transaction, a number of things are largely taken for granted:

- The merchant has the right to sell the item purchased.
- The buyer is "qualified" (e.g., meets minimum age restrictions) to make the purchase.
- The currency given for the item is valid.
- The receipt given transfers ownership of the item to the buyer.
- The item purchased is worth the price paid.

Most people do not think about trust when they engage in a transaction. Yet these assumptions, which are critical for commerce to take place, are based on trust, on the belief in the authenticity of the parties to the transaction, the validity of the monetary instrument used to pay for the purchase, and the value of the item purchased: the merchant is who he or she purports to be; the buyer is who the merchant surmises; the cash is good; the receipt is valid; and the goods are as perceived/advertised.

If the purchase is charged to a credit card, additional assumptions are made:

- The buyer is using a valid credit card.
- The buyer is authorized to use the valid credit card.
- The bank that authorized the merchant to accept the credit card will pay the merchant.
- The bank that issued the credit card will pay the merchant's bank.
- The buyer will repay the bank for the credit extended.

The further that commerce departs from a simple cash-and-carry transaction, however, the greater the need for trust and the higher the risk that trust may be misplaced. The buyer might have exceeded the credit limit on the card or might be using a stolen credit card. The merchant selling over the telephone might be selling defective goods or might simply take the customer's money and deliver nothing. To be sure, a merchant or a bank can easily validate a credit card number and the credit limit, and check that other forms of ID match those that the buyer gave when he or she applied for the card. Credit card companies also afford buyers a certain measure of protection, by allowing them to "charge back," or refuse to pay for defective goods or for purchases charged by someone not authorized to use the card. Thus, when commerce is conducted between parties at a distance who have had no prior business relations with each other, assumptions must be bolstered by mechanisms that offer protection to both the buyer and the seller.

REQUIREMENTS FOR ELECTRONIC COMMERCE

When commerce is conducted over the Internet, a network open to millions of potentially prying eyes, the need for mechanisms to verify the identity of the party at the other end of an anonymous bit stream and to ensure the privacy of financial or other sensitive data becomes even more critical. If commerce over the Internet is to flourish, the following requirements must be satisfied:

- *Authentication:* The parties to the transaction are who they claim to be.

> ▸ *Privacy:* Transaction data are protected against snooping.

> ▸ *Integrity:* The message sent is the message received.

> ▸ *Guaranteed Delivery:* The message sent is received by the party for whom it is intended.

> ▸ *Nonrepudiability:* The sender cannot deny having sent the message.

Authentication

Authentication is one of the most difficult challenges to be overcome in order for commerce to thrive on the Internet. Generally, authentication involves checking:

> ▸ Something a person has, such as a key, a credit card, or some other physical device

> ▸ Something a person knows, such as a user name and/or a password

> ▸ Something unique to a person that can be compared to a known and trusted record of this information, such as a fingerprint, a signature, or a picture ID

The more valuable the transaction, the more important it is that the authentication system be robust. Physical devices are easily misplaced, lost, or stolen. Knowledge-based challenges, such as user name and password, are easy to implement and are the basis for most authentication systems currently in common use. Unfortunately, most people choose their passwords poorly, and software programs that compare encrypted versions of dictionary words against encrypted passwords are readily available on the Internet, making it easy for hackers to crack users' passwords and log in to users' accounts.[2]

Another approach to authentication involves the use of a challenge/response device, which looks like a calculator and requires proof that the user has possession of the device and knows the personal identification number or password to the device. Although challenge/response devices provide a higher degree of confidence in user authentication, the hardware devices are expensive to deploy and cumbersome to use. There are software versions of challenge/response devices—most notably, S/KEY, which provides for a software version of one-time passwords.[3] Software versions of challenge/response devices are readily integrated into applications, but they are also vulnerable to system compromise.

In addition to authenticating the user, it is also necessary to authenticate the system that is being accessed. The Domain Name System (DNS)[4] is generally used to translate the "name" of a system on the Internet (e.g., www.dec.com) into a numeric address that Transmission Control Protocol/Internet Protocol (TCP/IP) can use to communicate with that system. However, the DNS is not sufficiently robust for high-level business transactions unless there is some way to validate the authenticity of the name-to-address translation. A hacker can break into a system's primary name server or replace the server's valid address with an address of his or her choice.

Cryptography, using public key technology and digital signatures, offers a potential solution to the problems of authentication and nonrepudiability. Public key technology is a form of encryption that involves the use of a "key pair"—a private key and a public key. The private key is always kept confidential, while the public key is made widely available. A digital signature is a piece of data that is encrypted using the sender's private key and decrypted by the recipient using the sender's public key. Since the signature could only have been generated by the sender, the recipient can be assured that the message came from the sender and the sender cannot deny having sent it.[5]

Currently, public key technology does not provide for verification that a public key really is the key of the party in question. A public key system requires that there be a third party, trusted by both sender and recipient, to vouch for the validity of the sender's public key. This third party, commonly called a "certification authority," or CA, would produce a "public key certificate" that the CA must sign with a private key, stating that the sender is who he or she claims to be.

A certification authority is critical to commerce over the Internet, for without it, there is no guarantee that the buyer and the seller are who they say they are. Public key certificates will become an important component of business transaction systems, but the infrastructure necessary to deploy digital signatures and public key certification is still to be developed.

Privacy

The Internet is a public network, with traffic passing "in the clear." It is quite simple to "listen in" to a message as it travels over the network from the sender's system to the recipient's system, as the listener need only break into one of the systems. As more companies do business on the Internet, it will become more lucrative to listen in to the traffic over the Internet, and the potential for break-ins will increase. While Joe Citizen might not care whether someone listening in knows what he purchased and how much was paid, no large corporation would risk paying its bills over the Internet without some assurance that the transactions are safe from prying eyes. Privacy is a major issue that must be addressed to make the Internet safe for business.

There are four views regarding the seriousness of threats to privacy of commercial transactions over the Internet. The first view, at one end of the spectrum, is that no serious threat exists, so there is no problem with passing credit card numbers over the Internet. Those who hold this view note that theft of credit card numbers over the Internet requires a break-in at a system and that such attempts will be rare. This view is held by Jon Zeeff, one of the pioneers of Internet malls. Zeeff contends that using a credit card for purchases over the Internet is no more risky than using the card at a restaurant, where a dishonest waiter could make a duplicate imprint, save the carbon, or jot down the card number.[6]

The second view is that a problem does exist, but there are simple ways to solve it. One solution, for example, is to assign a credit card holder a user name or password or an account ID, which maps to a charge number that is not passed over the Internet. Those who hold this view—including Internet Shopping Network (ISN) and First Virtual Holdings, Inc. (FV)—believe that buyers do need protection but that account IDs are sufficient, if only because the infrastructure necessary to support the use of more sophisticated and more secure systems, such as cryptography, does not exist.

Most companies hold the third view, which is that, since

the frequency of break-ins will increase as the volume of commerce over the Internet increases, and since it cannot be determined when the threshold will be crossed, the problem should be addressed now, before the burgeoning growth of commerce on the Internet is stopped dead by a sensational break-in that frightens businesses away. Among those that hold this view are CommerceNet, NetMarket, and Netscape Communications Corporation, to name just a few. In response to the concern about break-ins, Secure HyperText Transfer Protocol (S-HTTP)[7] and Secure Sockets Layer (SSL)[8] have been developed. In addition, a number of companies, including CyberCash, Inc., and Visa International in partnership with MasterCard and Microsoft, are working separately to develop payment-specific protocols.

The fourth view is that the security mechanisms available today do not go far enough to protect buyers, and that since it cannot be assumed that the systems used by buyers are secure, it is important to have external devices (e.g., smart cards) to hold the "keys" to account usage. Companies that subscribe to this view include CyberCash; Digicash, Inc.; Open Market, Inc. (OMI); Spyglass; and Terisa Systems.

In a sense, all four views are correct. Privacy of transaction data is not currently a problem. The volume of commerce on the Internet is not yet large enough to warrant concerted attempts to break into systems for the purpose of stealing credit card numbers. Also, with the exception of computer systems and software, goods sold over the Internet today tend to be low-cost consumer items. The second view is correct in that because the potential for theft exists, firms that accept credit card numbers over the Internet should use available mechanisms to deter theft. The third view is also correct in warning that the frequency of break-ins will increase and additional authentication methods will be needed at some future point to counter the increased risks of Internet theft through spoofing, break-ins, and redirection of electronic mail (e-mail). Those who hold this view recognize that the software that enables easy encryption is available in limited quantities today and that, as the market matures, the number of cryptography-based solutions will increase and the choice of available solutions will grow. The fourth view, which may be regarded as overkill today, anticipates the time when a combination of hardware (e.g., smart cards) and security protocols (e.g., S-HTTP) will be needed to provide the most robust solution possible.

Integrity

The third requirement for electronic commerce over the Internet is assurance for both buyer and seller that transaction data sent from one party to the other cannot be diverted to or altered by an unauthorized third party. In a cash-and-carry purchase, it is possible to guarantee the integrity of the transaction by simply watching the merchant, checking the change, and verifying the amount on the receipt. In the case of a transaction over the Internet, it is not possible to guarantee integrity with the infrastructure available today.

Guaranteed Delivery

Another requirement of commercial transactions over the Internet is the assurance that the order or message sent is received by the intended party. Without this guarantee, the Internet cannot be used for business-to-business transactions. A company must be able to demonstrate that a critical transaction was indeed received by the intended recipient through some form of signed digital receipt.

Nonrepudiability

The final requirement is reliable identification of both the sender and the receiver of on-line transactions. Nonsecure electronic mail can be altered to change the apparent sender. Building in nonrepudiability means that the identity of the sender and the receiver can be attested to by a trusted third party who holds the identity certificates.

COMPONENTS OF A NECESSARY INFRASTRUCTURE

An infrastructure that enables the authentication of individuals and corporations must have four key components: (1) certification authorities that are trusted by the parties to the transaction; (2) services that allow retrieval of public key certificates for validation; (3) software that must be easy to use; and (4) the capability of being easily integrated into business transaction systems.

Certification Authorities

At least six companies are working on developing certification authorities, but their efforts are still in the planning stage. In addition, the U.S. Postal Service has announced plans to become a certification authority, and CommerceNet is fielding pilots to test the use of certification authorities. (See the discussion of CommerceNet in the section titled "Standards versus Proprietary Solutions" later in this chapter.)

As previously indicated, a certification authority must be an entity that companies are willing to trust. There has been a great deal of discussion about whether certification authorities should be commercial entities or governmental entities, or both. There is also the question of individual certification versus corporate certification and the question of guarantees. What level of confidence can you put in the certificate that is retrieved? Is there a liability guarantee? For what amount?

Certificate Validation and Retrieval

There is also the question of "revocation lists," which are lists of certificates that have been withdrawn before their expiration date. If an employee leaves a job, the company that issued the certificate to him or her as a company employee would want to revoke the certificate. Similarly, an organization that certifies small businesses would want to revoke the certificate of a merchant that goes out of business. The same would be true if a bank issued a certificate with a bank account that was closed before the expiration date. There are no answers at this point, but understanding the questions can help in crafting the answers.

How does one find a certificate? How can one check that it is valid? Currently, there is no central directory service from which a company can retrieve a public key. Although S-HTTP supplies certificates invisibly inside multimedia documents, other protocols and solutions do not provide such a mechanism. How will individuals and businesses find these keys? An Internet draft prepared in November 1994 proposes to add server certificates to the DNS.[9] This would help companies retrieve public key certificates using their own systems, but it does not help individuals.

Ease of Use

Incorporation of security mechanisms into easy-to-use applications is key. Until solutions that mask the underlying mechanisms are available, deployment of Internet commerce will be slow.

Integration with Existing Systems

An internal infrastructure is as important as an external one. Internal infrastructure in this instance means the ability of existing business systems to track, manage, and check on customer certificates. A digital certificate will be an integral part of customer information in the next few years. As the industry at large needs to develop mechanisms for exchanging certificates, these capabilities need to be built into the existing systems for tracking customer account information, including providing internal company infrastructure with the capability of validating a certificate as part of routine planning.

TECHNOLOGY CANDIDATES FOR DEPLOYING ELECTRONIC COMMERCE OVER THE INTERNET

Once the security problems have been solved, there still remains the task of matching the right technology for business transaction systems to the problem of paying for items over the Internet. Currently, there are two primary candidates for the technology used to deploy business transaction systems over the Internet: electronic data interchange (EDI) and the Web.

Electronic Data Interchange

EDI, a technology introduced by the transportation industry in the late 1960s, has been deployed for years as a platform for electronic commerce. The 1970s saw the adoption of the

EDI concept by other industries and the formation of the American National Standards Institute X12 Committee to establish an EDI standard. Since the 1980s, systems utilizing EDI have been deployed to automate ordering, tracking, shipping, and billing of goods. Initially, the focus of EDI was automated order entry and fulfillment rather than automated payment. More recently, the EDI standard has been expanded to cover automated payment.

EDI is used in business-to-business transactions, not consumer transactions. The technology does not specify what network should be used for communicating data or EDI forms, so some companies use modems, whereas others use value-added networks (VANs), which can store messages and forward them to the appropriate party.[10] Many smaller firms, however, cannot afford the high cost of using VANs. The Internet offers lower-cost entry into the use of EDI and would provide smaller firms with the opportunity to do business with companies that have implemented EDI for order processing.

World Wide Web

The Web is a wide area hypermedia information retrieval technology that gives easy access to information sources worldwide via hypertext servers. Web technology was developed primarily at the Centre Européen de Recherches Nucléaires (CERN), the European Particle Physics Laboratory located in Geneva, Switzerland, and is behind most of the potential platforms for Internet commerce today.[11] Payment systems or mechanisms based on Web technology are being built or deployed by Branch Information Services (BIS), CyberCash, FV, Microsoft, NetMarket, Netscape Communications Corporation, and OMI.

Hypertext is an information presentation medium that uses highlighted words (or links) to point to other hypertext documents. From a personal computer (PC) or a workstation, the user can access the documents by using a mouse to point to a link and click on it or by using the terminal cursor keys.

The Web is implemented by hypertext servers and browsers (or clients), which communicate via the hypertext transport protocol (HTTP). Servers send the documents that users request and record where the documents are sent.

Browsers are used both for requesting documents from servers and for displaying or presenting the requested documents, which are generally formatted using hypertext markup language (HTML). Documents formatted using HTML may contain text, images, video, and audio. Generally, access to a document over the Web begins through a "home page" that is created either by or for the user. To access a document, the user must specify the information provider's uniform resource locator, which identifies the type of server, the location of the server, and the place on that server where the requested document is to be found. Some browsers have ancillary "viewers" that allow the user to access more complex images, as well as video and audio.

A simple-to-use interface and a rich field of browsers allow anyone with Internet connectivity easy access to information on the Web. The explosive growth in Web usage can be traced to the availability of Mosaic, the browser developed at the National Center for Supercomputing Applications (NCSA) at the University of Illinois in Urbana-Champaign. In January 1993, there were approximately 50 known HTTP servers. By March 1993, Web traffic represented .1 percent of the traffic on the National Science Foundation (NSF) backbone. In September 1993, when versions of NCSA Mosaic were made available on most common platforms (i.e., Windows, Macintosh, and UNIX systems running the X Window System), Web traffic grew to 1 percent of NSF backbone traffic.[12] By the end of 1994, there were over 10,000 Web "sites,"[13] and Web traffic represented 8.5 percent of NSF backbone traffic.[14] These numbers include servers deployed by governmental and educational organizations, but the number of commercial Web servers has grown rapidly. The Commercial Sites Index, a popular registration site for commercial companies on the Web (at http://www.directory.net), listed close to 10,000 commercial Web sites in the summer of 1995 and boasted that the number of sites was growing at the rate of 5 to 10 percent per week.

Although most companies that have implemented Web servers are using them to provide free marketing literature and technical papers, not as platforms for commercial transactions, the fact that Web servers are proliferating at an incredible rate argues for using the Web as the presentation vehicle for electronic commerce. The drawback is that the

Web currently does not satisfy the security requirements for electronic commerce over the Internet. However, there are two candidates for standardization of security on the Web that may remedy this situation: S-HTTP, from Enterprise Integration Technologies (EIT)/Terisa Systems; and SSL, from Netscape Communications Corporation.

Secure HyperText Transport Protocol. S-HTTP is a protocol written specifically for the Web. It was developed in 1993 by Allan Schiffman, chief technical officer of EIT and CEO of Terisa Systems, a new company formed by EIT and RSA Data Security, Inc. S-HTTP has been submitted to the Internet Engineering Task Force (IETF) as an Internet Draft titled "The Secure HyperText Transport Protocol." The following description of S-HTTP is excerpted from that draft:

> Secure HTTP (S-HTTP) provides secure communication mechanisms between an HTTP client-server pair in order to enable spontaneous commercial transactions for a wide range of applications. Our design intent is to provide a flexible protocol that supports multiple orthogonal operation modes, key management mechanisms, trust models, cryptographic algorithms and encapsulation formats through option negotiation between parties for each transaction.[15]

The advantage of S-HTTP is that it incorporates the ability for a client and a server to negotiate for the type of encryption used, enabling a server to deal with multiple methods of encryption. The protocol allows for the embedding of a server's public key into the header of a document, which facilitates the passing of the key to the client. It also includes the ability to check the server's public key certificate.

The reference version of Secure Mosaic includes the concept of a "key ring," which allows an individual or a company to hold multiple keys for different purposes. For example, a college professor might use one key when acting on behalf of the university, another key when communicating with his or her publisher, and yet another key for making changes to a personal checking account. The reference version of Secure Mosaic has been given to the NCSA to distribute without charge for noncommercial use, and versions of the S-HTTP server are currently being tested by CommerceNet members. S-HTTP is also the basis for the security specification of the World Wide Web Consortium (W3C). (See the discussion of W3C in the section titled "Standards versus Proprietary Solutions" later in this chapter.)

Terisa Systems develops, markets, and supports a set of client and server tools called the SecureWeb Toolkit that addresses the issues of privacy and authentication. Terisa's S-HTTP technology has been licensed by CyberCash; OMI; O'Reilly & Associates; Spry, Inc.; Spyglass; and Verity.

Secure Sockets Layer.   Netscape Communications Corporation, based in Mountain View, California, was formed by Jim Clark, former CEO of Silicon Graphics, and Marc Andreessen, one of the originators of NCSA Mosaic. Netscape designed SSL to layer between TCP/IP, the communications protocol of the Internet, and application protocols such as HTTP and FTP. The advantage of separating data security concerns from the application protocols is that multiple applications can be supported with SSL. The following description of SSL is from the Netscape Web server:

> Netscape Communications has designed and specified a protocol for providing data security layered between application protocols (such as HTTP, SMTP, NNTP, and FTP) and TCP/IP. This security protocol, called Secure Sockets Layer (SSL), provides data encryption, server authentication, message integrity, and optional client authentication for a TCP/IP connection. SSL uses technology licensed from RSA Data Security Inc.[16]

The SSL protocol is freely available, but it is currently implemented only in Netscape's excellent browser, Netscape Navigator, and in the Netsite Commerce Server.

SSL's usefulness within the business setting has been questioned because the protocol does not provide nonrepudiability on the message level—a critical requirement for business transactions. Nonrepudiability cannot be ensured because the data stream, not the message, is encrypted, so a buyer cannot "sign" a particular message. SSL's current inability to support client certificates is another impediment to its adoption for business-to-business transactions, where authentication of both parties is critical. Netscape announced in February 1995 its commitment to support S-HTTP.

SSL does provide a reasonable solution for the encryption of a credit card number, but the solution is probably not robust enough for business-to-business transactions. One strong advantage of SSL is that it has already been approved for export, in a reduced-strength version, which would allow overseas buyers to charge their purchases to credit cards.

Marrying EDI and the Web

EDI provides a solution that addresses primarily business-to-business transactions, whereas the Web offers a solution that tends to focus on the consumer, which may or may not represent a business entity. Since early incarnations of EDI concentrated on the automation of product orders, while current Web-based solutions have moved toward the automation of the payment function, the best possible solution would integrate these two platforms and use each for the function for which it is most appropriate. The Web could readily provide the presentation mechanism for commerce, EDI could be used to track orders, and either could be used for payment. The solution that can bring together disparate functions into a single interface will offer the greatest competitive advantage.

STANDARDS VERSUS PROPRIETARY SOLUTIONS

If commerce over the Internet is to proliferate, the different solutions that have been proposed must interoperate. In order for this to happen, the development of standards is critical. History has shown, however, that standards-setting bodies move slowly and often simply ratify the de facto standards that are already in broad use. In the Internet market, as in any emerging market, there are many candidates for potential solutions and/or standards. The question is: which solution will dominate, and will the solution that dominates truly constitute a standard or will it merely be the victor in this potentially lucrative market?

It is possible to develop a proprietary system, using technology unique to a particular company—a point well proved by Microsoft Windows—but the difference between the Internet and a stand-alone PC is profound. It is not possible even to connect to the Internet without all the underlying standards, such as TCP/IP, and navigational solutions such as the Web. Because interoperability is a key requirement for Internet acceptance, the emergence of a purely proprietary solution is less likely than the emergence of a standards-based solution. Where will the standard originate? The potential sources are: the IETF, CommerceNet, and W3C.

Internet Engineering Task Force

The IETF, an arm of the Internet Architecture Board, was founded in 1986 as a forum to enable coordination between the organizations working on the development of the Internet. It has since grown from a U.S. government–funded entity to a worldwide cooperative organization with the charter to ensure "the evolution of the Internet architecture and the smooth operation of the Internet."[17] The IETF sponsors over 70 active working groups, many of which are addressing security and authentication issues. Both SSL and S-HTTP have been submitted to the IETF. Unfortunately, drafts submitted to the IETF tend to take a long time to become standards.

CommerceNet

CommerceNet was founded as a nonprofit corporation in April 1994 with a three-year $6 million grant from the U.S. Technology Reinvestment Program and matching funds from its members. The well over 100 members of CommerceNet include banks, computer companies, on-line services, VANs, software firms, research organizations, universities, federal and state government agencies, semiconductor houses, and credit card companies. Corporate members of CommerceNet range from Fortune 100 firms to fledgling start-ups.

CommerceNet's goal is to help companies connect to the Internet and find information once on-line, and to promote collaborative efforts among companies in addressing the basic problems of ease of access, ease of use, and security. The belief is that if an infrastructure that addresses these problems can be built, the cost of doing business over the Internet could be lowered and new opportunities for growth would emerge. The ultimate goal is "spontaneous commerce" in an environment in which buying and selling are simple and security and interoperability are assured. The hopes of the organizers are well expressed in the CommerceNet literature, which is available on-line over the Internet:

> CommerceNet's founders and supporters believe that the new Internet electronic marketplace will dramatically improve the productivity and competitiveness of its participants. The Internet provides access to an online global marketplace with millions of customers and thousands of products and services. It also provides companies with new, more cost- and time-efficient means for working with customers, suppliers and development partners. Internet-based electronic commerce will enable companies to:
>
> —Shorten procurement cycles through online catalogs, ordering and payment;
>
> —Cut costs on both stock and manufactured parts through competitive bidding; and
>
> —Shrink development cycles and accelerate time-to-market through collaborative engineering and product implementation.[18]

CommerceNet has formed working groups to test potential solutions to the above-mentioned problems, including the problem of building an infrastructure to speed the deployment of commerce over the Internet. Current working groups include:

- ▸ *Network Services:* working on issues of security, interoperability, and authentication
- ▸ *Payment Services:* working on payment mechanisms over the Internet
- ▸ *Collaborative Engineering:* working on transfer of engineering data and design-to-manufacturing integration
- ▸ *Electronic Catalogs and Directories:* working on on-line access, ordering, and directories; messaging; searching/indexing services; and information directories
- ▸ *Electronic Data Interchange:* working on EDI messaging on the Internet and VANs
- ▸ *Collaborative Tools:* working on bulletin board sys-

tems and shared chalkboards to enable interactive collaboration over the Internet

Members of CommerceNet enjoy a number of advantages. Through collaboration, companies can quickly identify potential solutions to the problems that face their industry as a whole. Small vendors can reach most of the key players in Internet commerce through CommerceNet's sponsorship of technology presentations by any company to the appropriate working groups. Members have open access to the technologies developed under the aegis of CommerceNet and to results of pilots undertaken by the organization, allowing them to deploy solutions faster and ensure interoperability of their solutions. When results of the pilots are made available to the general public, the information is used by the industry at large in setting directions and standards.

Given its membership and funding, CommerceNet could play a key role in the development of a national information infrastructure and the standards needed for deployment of commerce over the Internet. A CommerceNet-like infrastructure could potentially support efforts to create national information infrastructures in other areas such as education, health care, and digital libraries.

World Wide Web Consortium

The W3C is a joint initiative of CERN and MIT's Laboratory for Computer Science. The consortium, funded by membership fees, was formed in July 1994 to foster the evolution of WWW protocols into a comprehensive information infrastructure that addresses the needs of the Internet community worldwide. Members include most of the major computer, software, and service companies that offer Internet products.

The W3C is completely focused on Web-related technology. It has fielded a staff of seven to work on development of protocols, prototypes, and standards in the following areas:

- ▶ *Automatability:* automatic generation of pages from alternate sources
- ▶ *Extensibility:* incorporation of new/additional functionality without alteration of the protocol

> ► *Scalability and robustness:* graceful scaling to allow rapid growth
>
> ► *Privacy:* incorporation of authentication, privacy, and data integrity

In addition to the development of protocols, prototypes, and standards in the areas noted, W3C plans to develop validating/testing suites to help companies with compliance.[19]

The consortium's single-minded focus on Web technology should help to accelerate the standardization of protocols and mechanisms required to build the necessary information infrastructure. W3C is working closely with both the IETF and CommerceNet in this effort. W3C Director Tim Berners-Lee is also the cochair of IETF's Hypertext Markup Language Working Group, and many W3C members are also CommerceNet members.

Cooperative Efforts or Cross-Purposes?

Multiple groups working on the same problem could either speed or delay the adoption of the standards needed for commerce over the Internet to become a reality. In this instance, the three groups seem to be working cooperatively, rather than at cross purposes, with each adding value to the situation. The IETF has acted proactively in asking for a draft of S-HTTP, which it will fine-tune and issue as a standards-based Request for Comments (RFC). CommerceNet is actively implementing S-HTTP, testing its robustness and usability, and working to build the infrastructure necessary for its deployment. W3C is providing test suites, reference implementations, and valuable input. Since S-HTTP is the basis for W3C's privacy/authentication standard, the hope is that the IETF and W3C will enhance the effort through cooperation rather than delay it by setting incompatible standards.

Hopeful Signs

In April 1995, IBM (which owns 50 percent of Prodigy), CompuServe, America Online, and Netscape purchased a major portion of Terisa Systems. The stated goal of that purchase was to create a unified security solution, in the form of a toolkit that supports both Secure HTTP and SSL. This toolkit will enable software developers writing browsers and servers to support S-HTTP, SSL, or both in their servers. The trend is toward dual support in servers: all of the vendors that have announced secure versions of their server have also announced that they will support both S-HTTP and SSL.[20]

OPTIONS FOR INTERNET COMMERCE

Despite the lack of standardization, there has been no lack of products to meet the growing demand of companies that want to do business over the Internet. Most of the new products and announced offerings focus on solutions for consumer transactions paid by credit card rather than solutions for business-to-business transactions. The majority provide mechanisms for handling payment, but none provides a system for tracking transactions. Instead, transaction tracking is left to the banks that issue the credit cards. Although most of the new systems use the Web as the vehicle for presenting data, none of them uses the same software for settlement (i.e., transferring payment from the customer to the merchant).

Virtually all the vendors have claimed to be the "first" to offer a product for settlement over the Internet, and many have claimed victory for producing "the" solution for the future. Yet many of the vendors making such claims have been in business for less than a year or have been working on these issues for less than a year. Few of the current solutions address the problems of customer service, inventory control, and integration with a company's existing accounting systems. None of the solutions has been in production for a year, and none has a measurable market share. This suggests caution to any firm looking for a viable, functional, and cost-effective system to support business transactions over the Internet. Any solution provider claiming victory before the battle has even begun should be approached with caution, and any corporation looking to exploit a particular solution should make sure that the solution chosen not only meets its needs but also has a reasonable chance of survival.

The solutions announced or available today fall into three categories:

1. *Custom solutions:* contracting with a vendor to build a "storefront" for selling over the Internet
2. *Packaged tools:* purchasing a commercial software/service to be used in building (usually only a piece of) the company's own solution
3. *Combination solutions:* purchasing both a software product and a vendor's services, which may be paid for on a monthly basis

Each type of solution appeals to a different type of company. A custom solution is an attractive option for a company that does not have the financial resources and/or technical expertise required to set up and maintain its own server. A build-your-own approach might make sense for a large corporation with in-house expertise. A combination solution offers the most flexibility, allowing a company to choose how much of the system development effort to outsource and how much to manage in-house. The following subsections profile the leading vendors of products/services for Internet commerce and their offerings.

Custom Solutions

Custom solutions are available from over 114 vendors, or Web consultants, that provide "space for rent" and consulting services to companies that want to do business on the Internet. Fewer than 5 percent of these Web consultants, however, offer on-line ordering as part of a custom solution. Of those that do offer the ability to take orders and handle purchases over the Internet, BIS and ISN stand out for being pioneers in their field and for the large number of items they offer for sale.

Branch Information Services. BIS was one of the earliest malls on the Internet to provide a mechanism for direct ordering. Branch Mall opened its doors for business in January 1994 (at http://branch.com) with three electronic storefronts; today it boasts over 75 storefronts and is still growing. Each Branch Mall store is individually designed, with its own special on-line order forms. When customers find an item to purchase, they enter the item number on the store's order form, along with their address and credit card information, and send the form via e-mail or fax to the appropriate merchant for fulfillment.

Grant's Flowers, a Branch Mall store that was featured in *The New York Times* in June 1994, was taking more orders over the Internet than through FTD. Since then, Grant's sales have gone down a bit due to competition: at last count, there were more than 17 storefronts selling or advertising the sale of flowers over the Internet.

Jon Zeeff is the owner and founder of BIS. When Zeeff was asked about the risks of taking customers' credit card numbers in the clear over the Internet, he replied: "If someone does break in and steal a credit card number, the customer's liability is only about $50. The risk to the customer is small. Using the Internet is just like using a card-swipe machine; both of them send data over the phone lines." Zeeff holds the view that additional privacy mechanisms are not needed now and that, in any case, there are no viable solutions today. He believes that the barrier to the rapid adoption of Internet commerce is inertia. "Doing business over the Internet is a whole different way of thinking than people are used to. I believe that it [Internet commerce] will make companies more efficient and will act as an equalizer, since it will be easier to comparison shop."[21]

Internet Shopping Network. While BIS customizes the look and feel of each storefront, ISN takes a different approach. ISN (at http://shop.internet.net) looks like one large store with hundreds of departments. Founded in June 1993 by Randy Adams and Bill Rollinson, ISN opened its doors for business in April 1994 with 500 storefronts offering over 14,000 products. A year later, it was offering 20,000 products from 600 vendors. ISN has done so well that it was purchased by Home Shopping Network in October 1994.

Two things make ISN unique: its joining of the Web and EDI and its pricing model. ISN uses EDI to transfer orders to distributors and for customer service. It screens potential vendors to make sure that they can accept EDI orders and will commit to ship orders quickly. Vendors are also screened to make sure that their products match with ISN's offerings of brand-name merchandise. ISN does not charge vendors for placing their products on its Web server; instead, it makes its money by charging vendors a commission or a percentage of every sale made through the network.

To make a purchase from ISN, a customer must first fill out an application form and fax it to ISN or, alternatively, call up ISN to establish an account over the phone. ISN assigns the customer an account ID, which is sent via e-mail and which the customer uses to order goods on-line. The customer selects the desired items from the stores on the mall and specifies the number of products and the method of shipment when placing the order. The customer's order is put into an EDI order form that is sent to a VAN, which transmits the order to the appropriate vendor(s). When the goods are shipped, the customer receives confirmation of shipment. The status of each order and the inventory information for each item are batch-updated on a daily basis.

When Bill Rollinson was asked about ISN's position on taking credit card numbers in the clear over the Internet, his answer was emphatic:

> We don't even think that it is a good idea to give a customer the *option* to enter a credit card number on-line. There are two liabilities. When we signed for our merchant account, we promised to take reasonable measures to protect our customers' card numbers. I don't think that a credit card in the clear over the Internet qualifies as a reasonable measure. The second liability is bad publicity; if a credit card number were stolen and the theft was related to a purchase from us, it would ruin our image."[22]

ISN recently began offering secure mechanisms for entering credit card numbers and plans to offer additional payment mechanisms and real-time inventory/order tracking in 1995. On ISN's goal to let customers get information about their orders on-line, Rollinson said: "This lets the customer feel like he is in control, and this is good for both sides."

Packaged Tools

A company that wants to build its own solution has a choice between packaged tools and combination solutions. Packaged tools typically provide only a piece of the solution as opposed to a cohesive whole. They also require a fair amount of custom work and a direct Internet connection. However, they offer the advantage of being very focused. Two major vendors of Internet commerce tools are Netscape Communications Corporation and CyberCash, Inc.

Netscape Communications Corporation. Netscape Communications Corporation (at http://mcom.com) was founded in April 1994 by Dr. James H. Clark, founder of Silicon Graphics, Inc., and Marc Andreessen, one of the creators of NCSA Mosaic. Netscape offers an excellent browser, Netscape Navigator; Netsite, a commercial-grade HTTP server; and the Netsite Commerce Server. The company's stated goal is to become the premier supplier of software for both information transfer and commerce over the Internet.

In the fall of 1994, Netscape offered Netscape Navigator free of charge for noncommercial use for all major platforms. The software has been downloaded by thousands of users, and most reviews have been quite favorable. Netscape Navigator displays the document as it is being downloaded, instead of waiting until the download is completed, which is common with other browsers, and it is superior to other browsers in quality, performance, and ease of use.

The Netsite Communications Server is fully compatible with other HTTP servers and offers configuration/management tools that are not available in public-domain versions. The primary difference between the Netsite Communications Server and the Netsite Commerce Server is that the latter incorporates a security mechanism in the form of SSL. Netscape Communications has an impressive list of customers and partners, including Bank of America, MCI Communications, First Data Corporation, First Interstate Bank, the *San Jose Mercury News,* and Digital Equipment Corporation.

Using Netscape products, a company can build a server with the mechanism for accepting credit cards. Although Netscape does not currently have a product that is capable of validating credit card numbers for processing orders, its partnership with First Data Corporation, an outsourcer that processes credit card data for banks and other issuers, suggests that such a product may be forthcoming.

CyberCash, Inc. CyberCash, a company based in Reston, Virginia, was founded in 1994 by Bill Melton, Dan Lynch,

Bruce Wilson, and Steve Crocker to develop a secure payment system that works over the Internet. Bill Melton is also a founder of VeriFone, the company that produces the boxlike device used for processing credit card transactions at the point of sale. Dan Lynch is the founder and chairman of InterOp, the trade show company that produces the popular NetWorld and InterOp networking show and exhibition. Bruce Wilson has extensive experience in the area of electronic funds transfer, and Steve Crocker is one of the "fathers" of the Internet.

CyberCash (at http://www.cybercash.com) offers a package that includes buyer software, merchant software, and the CyberCash server. The software is used to implement a peer-to-peer system for transferring payment from the customer to the merchant over the Internet—safely, efficiently, and inexpensively. Buyers receive free client software that directly communicates with CyberCash servers. Merchants receive their software for free, but pay CyberCash a per-transaction fee. Financial instruments supported by the CyberCash system include credit cards, debit cards, electronic cash, and micropayments. The system works as follows:

1. The customer browses in the stores that are using the CyberCash package, such as Virtual Vinyards (http://www.virtualvin.com/), selecting items to purchase, and clicks on the "PAY" button when ready to make the purchase.

2. The merchant sends the customer an invoice on-line.

3. The customer fills in his or her name, credit card number, and card expiration date or uses electronic cash.

4. The completed invoice is encrypted and sent to the merchant, which adds its identification information and forwards the invoice to the CyberCash server.

5. The CyberCash server checks the private cryptographic signature for errors, then sends it to the customer's bank for processing.

6. Once payment is processed, the CyberCash server sends notification to the merchant to ship the order.

Note that CyberCash provides solely the service of moving funds. It does not perform the functions of a seller (e.g., marketing and fulfillment) or those of a bank (e.g., extending credit). Those functions remain in the hands of the traditional parties. Thus, the CyberCash system is neutral with respect to merchants, banks, platforms, and browser and server tools.

The CyberCash system can be deployed by all merchants that wish to do business on the Internet—merchants selling information services for delivery over the Internet and merchants selling hard goods for delivery by traditional shippers. The CyberCash system also allows third parties to build and operate services such as bill payment and currency conversion for international trading. The disadvantages of the system are: (1) the buyer must enter name, credit card number, and card expiration date for each purchase, and (2) the integration of the "PAY" button, which requires editing of the files or the creation of programs to generate the "PAY" buttons, must be done by the merchant or a consultant.[23]

Combination Solutions

Combination solutions offer a company the flexibility of choosing how much system development work will be done in-house and how much of the work will be outsourced. This is extremely advantageous if the company is uncertain whether it can or wants to commit the considerable resources needed to develop its own Internet commerce solution. Vendors offer differing degrees of freedom with respect to the split between in-house development and outsourcing, but the choice remains with the company. Two of the leading vendors of combination solutions are FV and OMI.

First Virtual Holdings, Inc. FV (at http://www.fv.com) was founded in 1994 by Lee H. Stein, Einar A. Stefferud, Nathaniel S. Borenstein, and Marshall T. Rose. Stein is an attorney and businessman with extensive experience in the entertainment, real estate, and infomercial industries. Stefferud is another one of the "fathers" of the Internet. Borenstein is the principal author of Multipurpose Internet Mail Extensions (MIME), the Internet standard format for multimedia data, and the author of a number of widely used software packages, including metamail and the Andrew Message System. Rose is the principal author of the Simple Network Management Protocol (SNMP) and has played a key role in the development of Internet standards for over a decade. FV's goal is "to make it easy for everyone to buy and sell information over the Internet."[24]

In October 1994, FV announced a payment system for the selling of information over the Internet. This was the first true "system" for processing transactions over the Internet, albeit only for transactions involving information products. The system has a number of interesting attributes:

- ▶ FV sets up accounts linked to credit card accounts for buyers and checking accounts for sellers.
- ▶ Buyers receive the products ordered *before* payment (in most instances).
- ▶ Sellers assume the risk of nonpayment.
- ▶ The buyer's credit card number is passed once over the telephone, without encryption, at the time the account is set up.
- ▶ All interactions between the buyer and the seller regarding the account are conducted via e-mail.
- ▶ The system is based entirely on standards and uses no proprietary software.
- ▶ Payment is made to the seller's checking account.
- ▶ FV created a complete specification for a MIME Content-type[25] for handling the negotiation of a transaction.

FV's try-before-you-buy approach for information products is unique in the industry. The company's founders believe that since the cost of reproducing information products is virtually nil when the products are sold over the Internet, the seller only stands to gain by allowing the customer to download the document prior to purchase. Another interesting aspect of FV's system is that it can deliver information using various methods, including the Web, file transfer protocol (FTP), and e-mail. This aspect of the system allows for selling information in a number of contexts—for example, selling photographs via a Web server, selling software programs via FTP, and selling subscriptions to mailing lists via e-mail. Regardless of the delivery mechanism, the payment process always works as follows:

1. The buyer downloads a copy of the desired information (or requests the information via e-mail and receives the information/subscription via e-mail) and gives his or her FV account ID.
2. The seller sends information about the purchase to FV.
3. FV requests payment from the buyer via e-mail.
4. The buyer responds by clicking on one of three buttons: "YES," "NO," or "FRAUD."
5. The buyer and the seller settle the account periodically.
6. If the buyer declines to pay, the seller absorbs the loss.

Nathaniel Borenstein describes FV's system as follows:

> Rather than try to simultaneously solve the problems of payment, cryptographic standards, and certification authorities, we designed a payment mechanism that could safely be used without cryptography for certain kinds of transactions. Over time, as the Internet begins to standardize mechanisms for cryptographic authentication, we expect our payment system to evolve along with those standards to facilitate a wider range of transaction types.
>
> The First Virtual approach has been to accept the Internet as it is, and to try to work from that starting point to enable commerce. As a result, First Virtual was able to begin safely processing third party payments over the Internet before anyone else, and within a few months there were entrepreneurs who had created profitable new businesses based entirely on First Virtual's payment system.[26]

The FV system is a very economical way of selling information products on-line. The company is now actively working on enhancements that would permit its system to process payment for purchases of hard goods as well.

Open Market, Inc. OMI was founded in early 1994 by David Gifford and Shikhar Ghosh to develop an end-to-end solution for electronic commerce over the Internet. Ghosh was a former partner at Boston Consulting Group and then the CEO of Appex, Inc., a firm that provides call-tracking and billing services for cellular phone companies. Gifford, a computer science professor and the head of MIT's Programming Systems Research Group, is a leading authority on payment systems and information systems, as well as an adviser to U.S. government agencies involved in building a national information infrastructure.

OMI (at http://www.openmarket.com) offers a suite of products and services that enable merchants to set up store-fronts on the Internet, sell goods, accept and fulfill orders, and receive payment in a secure environment. OMI services include store creation, account management and reporting, credit card authorization, authentication, and payment processing. OMI products include WebServer, Secure WebServer, Transaction Link, Merchant Server, Transaction Server, Desktop StoreBuilder, and Personal StoreBuilder.

Like FV and ISN, OMI requires a buyer to first register for an account using an on-line application form. The customer can send a credit card number to OMI using S-HTTP, Pretty Good Privacy (PGP), PEM, Interactive Voice Response System, PGP Mail, telephone, or fax. Once the account has been established, the buyer can purchase items either directly from a merchant's own server or through OMI's Merchant Server. The steps in making a direct purchase are as follows:

1. The buyer browses through the merchant's store-front until he or she finds an item to purchase.

2. The buyer clicks on the hypertext link that indicates the price of the item.

3. OMI's Payment Switch identifies and authenticates the buyer.

4. The buyer is notified of the completion of the purchase either through delivery of the item (if the item is an information product) or through confirmation of the order (if the item is a hard good).

5. OMI's Payment Switch settles the transaction with the buyer's bank or through the automated clearinghouse.

When shopping from OMI's Merchant Server, the buyer wanders from store to store selecting desired items and placing them in a "shopping cart." If the buyer changes his or her mind after placing an item in the cart, the item can be removed. When shopping is completed, the buyer may either purchase all the items in the cart or leave the cart and return to it at a later time.

OMI's WebServer product provides a fast, reliable HTTP server with easy-to-use management and configuration tools. OMI also offers Secure WebServer, which supports the proposed S-HTTP standard and enables merchants to authenticate buyers and ensure privacy for critical business transactions. Both server products can be used to sell information products, services, and hard goods on-line. OMI's Merchant Server builds on the strengths of the Web Server by adding StoreBuilder, a tool that enables a merchant to create a storefront on any remote server, simply by filling out a form using any forms-capable browser. Storefronts built with Store-Builder are searchable and revisable and, if the goods in the stores are assigned prices, automatically include payment-processing services.

For a company or a bank that wants to do its own payment processing, OMI offers Transaction Server, a product that implements authentication, transaction tracking, reporting, account management, and payment processing. By purchasing both Transaction Server and Merchant Server, a company can conduct electronic commerce on any IP-capable network, such as the Internet or a private network, or for tracking internal purchases. Payment mechanisms supported by the system include credit cards, EDI 820 forms, automated clearinghouse, corporate accounts, "demo" dollars (play money to let people try out the system), debit cards, and aggregated charges for the purchase of low-cost information products. Support is also available for transmission and tracking of orders via EDI.

For a merchant without an Internet connection, OMI offers a shrink-wrapped product called Desktop StoreBuilder that enables the merchant to create a storefront on a PC using Windows or on a Macintosh system and send the output to any organization that maintains an OMI Merchant Server. OMI also offers Personal StoreBuilder, a software program that can be used to create a small kiosk, an advertisement, or a "business card" that can be sent to any merchant server for hosting.

OMI believes in providing companies with a growth path for deployment of Internet commerce. A small company that wants to test the viability of Internet commerce might begin by building its storefront on OMI's server, paying a monthly fee for rental of the space—which costs about the same as creating a single advertisement—and using OMI Transaction Server for payment processing. A company that wants to set up and maintain its own Web server but does not want to do its own transaction processing might use OMI's payment services, which allow a remote server to refer the company's transactions to OMI Transaction Server, off-loading not only payment processing but also the first-line support for customers' questions about their purchases. Payment Switch can fulfill on-line orders for information products and can "finger-print" an information product so that the seller can trace the product back to the buyer.

OMI's combination solution offers the advantage of flexibility: a company can start with a storefront on OMI's server, go on to build its own server and use OMI for payment processing, then proceed to bring the entire process in-house. However, OMI's solution does not offer non-Web purchase mechanisms. Also, some customers might find OMI's standardized dialogue for authentication restrictive.

Solutions from Additional Players

There are a number of vendors that provide non-Web solutions for companies wishing to engage in Internet commerce. Premenos (at http://www.premenos.com) has been selling EDI software for years. In the fall of 1994, Premenos announced a pilot for EDI over the Internet that is similar to the EDI pilot proposed by CommerceNet. The foundation of Premenos's solution is encapsulation of EDI forms into encrypted mail messages that can be sent securely over the Internet. This solution would enable businesses that have implemented EDI to use EDI in transactions with their smaller suppliers. However, this solution still fails to provide a simple user interface, which the Web does provide.

With the exception of FV's solution, which does not use cryptography, all the solutions discussed in the preceding subsections use encryption software licensed from RSA Data Security, the leading U.S. supplier of cryptographic libraries and software. RSA was established in 1982, but the company owes its visibility to the recent concerns about security of transactions over the Internet and the subsequent increase in use of cryptography in systems development.

Another group of players that cannot be ignored is Microsoft, MasterCard, and Visa International. In January 1995, Visa and Microsoft announced that they will be creating "the" mechanism for secure transmission of credit card information across the Internet, and in July 1995, MasterCard joined the effort. Specifications will be available in late 1995. Although this could have a serious impact on the eventual standards established, this has not slowed the deployment of solutions, as witnessed by the solutions just reviewed.[27]

SELECTING THE RIGHT SOLUTION

The selection of an appropriate solution depends on each company's business needs and its goals and objectives in using the Internet as a sales channel. The following set of questions is designed to help determine those needs and objectives:

> ► What percentage of sales does the company expect to achieve through the Internet?

> ► Is the goal market awareness or actual sales?

> ► Who is the audience? Existing customers or new customers? Domestic customers or international customers? Consumers or businesses?

> ► Is the intent to develop a solution in-house or to outsource the development effort?

> ► What type of products or services will be sold via this channel?

> ► What type of payment instruments will be used? Credit cards? Electronic funds transfers? Procurement cards?

The answers to this first set of questions will make it clearer which type of solution best suits the company's needs. The next set of questions is designed to help the company evaluate various potential solutions.

> ► *What product or service does the vendor offer today? Who is using it? What is the experience of current users of the vendor's product or service?* Some vendors have made impressive announcements but have little in the way of working software. It is important to try to locate and talk to companies that are currently using the vendor's software or service in a manner similar to that which is planned.

> ► *How easy to use is the system?* Since end users typically try to use a system without reading the documentation, the best way to evaluate the ease of use of a potential solution is to test-use the system without documentation.

> ► *How easy is it to configure/program/manage the system?* It is important to have the company's programmer/system manager assess the difficulty of implementing the system or integrating any new mechanism into the company's existing systems. Simply looking at the documentation will not give the technical staff a sense of the practical difficulties of implementing the technology, maintaining the system, and training end users.

> ► *How does the proposed system deal with the issues of privacy, data integrity, and authentication?* If business-to-business transactions are planned, it is important to ensure that the functionality offered meets the needs of the most rigorous transaction the company has planned for the future.

> ► *What are the vendor's plans for incorporating standards as they become available?* Since no one knows who will win the standards debate, it is critical to choose a vendor that plans to incorporate new standards as they become available.

> ► *What payment instruments are currently supported*

by the vendor, and what instruments does the vendor plan to support in the future? Numerous proposals are under consideration regarding forms of digital cash, electronic checks, and other instruments for settlement over the Internet. The company should make sure that the vendor has plans to expand functionality in the areas that are critical to the company.

▶ *Does the vendor's system require the use of special buyer software? If so, what does the buyer software cost? On what platforms does it run?* Some solutions require deployment of custom browsers or other custom software. If special buyer software is required, it is important that the vendor make the buyer software available without charge to the company's customers. If the proposed solution requires a special browser, the company should be comfortable with locking itself and its customers in to that particular browser. At least four—possibly six—vendors have plans to release new browsers in 1995. The best way to avoid this problem is to insist on a standards-based solution.

▶ *What will the system require in terms of customer service?* To minimize the demands on customer support, the company should make sure that it chooses a solution that provides for on-line customer service interfaces.

▶ *How does the proposed solution integrate with existing systems?* A strategy for integrating the proposed solution with the company's existing systems and business operations is essential. If integration with existing systems is not possible, the benefits of implementing Internet commerce will be minimized and some of the cost savings unrealized.

▶ *Does the company participate in an industry group or organization that supports standards setting for electronic commerce over the Internet?* Membership in an industry group or a standards-setting body, such as CommerceNet, where companies facing similar concerns cooperate in finding solutions, can help a company that is starting out in Internet commerce establish priorities and avoid costly mistakes.

INTERNET COMMERCE: BEYOND PAYMENT

Most of the systems and technologies discussed in this chapter focus on the issue of secure payment over the Internet, but there are certain issues beyond payment that also must be addressed if commerce over the Internet is to provide the hoped-for competitive advantage. Those issues include technology exports, on-line transaction tracking and customer service support, velocity checking, and account management.

The U.S. Department of Commerce prohibits U.S. corporations from doing business with countries subject to trade restrictions or embargoes, as well as with certain groups of individuals and corporations that traffic in arms or that are involved in terrorism. In addition, export administration regulations provide for restrictions on the export of certain hardware and software. Business transaction systems on the Internet must be flexible enough to recognize the country of origin of requests and to respond selectively to customers in different areas of the world.[28]

Use of the Internet for commerce can either increase or decrease by more than 50 percent a company's customer service costs, depending on the solution selected. If the solution that best meets the company's needs is difficult to implement, the company should plan to hire additional support staff. For example, the more control a payment system maintains over customer accounts, the higher the number of service calls to update account information. In this case, implementing the following measures can both save on customer service costs and increase customer satisfaction:

- ▶ Give customers as much control as possible over their account information.
- ▶ Provide customers with on-line account information and transaction processing.

- ► Provide customers with e-mail access to customer service.
- ► Keep the interface as simple as possible and provide good documentation.
- ► Tag transactions in a unique and identifiable manner.

Providing customers with direct access to the record of their on-line purchases can reduce the customer service costs typically associated with on-line purchases. The flip side of providing customers with records of their on-line purchases is transaction tracking.

One of the benefits of commerce over the Internet is also one of its potential dangers: automation. The mechanisms that support automated purchases are also available to the thief. The only way to ensure that an Internet thief does not go on a spending spree with a purloined credit card or other financial instrument is to implement velocity checking—that is, monitoring transactions by account and ensuring that the buying pattern of any given account is reasonable.

WHAT THE FUTURE HOLDS

The future will most likely bring a whole new host of companies offering solutions for Internet commerce, each with its advantages and disadvantages. Given the trends in standards setting, S-HTTP will most likely emerge as the standard for security over the Web. As the number of laptops with PCMCIA capability increases and the price of smart cards decreases, the use of smart cards to enhance security will become more prevalent.

Over the next few years, the issue of certification authorities will need to be resolved. Just as an e-mail address is considered a must today, a certified public key will be a must-have tomorrow. It is too early to tell which of the players in this area will dominate. RSA Data Security is expected to play a major role, as it holds patents to a number of key technologies; however, many of those patents will expire in

1997. It is unclear what impact this will have on the development of the necessary infrastructure.

Another development will be the integration of inventory control, order tracking, accounting, and automatic refreshing of on-line catalogs into the full life cycle of a purchase. The marriage of EDI and the Web seems inevitable, with the Web providing the interface and part of the transport mechanism and EDI providing the format standard.

As the security concerns about commerce over the Internet subside, the spotlight will move to the issue of finding information on the Web. Given the exponential growth of Web sites, the ability to quickly locate an item of desired information or a particular vendor or a particular product will become critical.

The question is not *if* commerce over the Internet will become a critical sales channel for businesses, but *when*. The market is still new, and each company must decide in light of its needs and its resources whether it wants to risk being a pioneer and grapple with new standards and new software as they emerge or whether it would rather wait and risk being left behind.

NOTES

1. Mark Lottor, "Internet Domain Survey," October 1994. This report is available every three months from Network Wizards at http://www.nw.com or from ftp.nw.com.

2. Those interested in exploring this topic in more depth should read William R. Cheswick and Steven M. Bellovin, *Firewalls and Internet Security* (Reading, Mass.: Addison-Wesley, 1994). Chapters 1, 9, and 10 discuss passwords and authentication, and chapter 1 provides an example of an actual attack on a computer system's security.

3. Neil Haller, "The S/KEY One-Time Password System," RFC 1760, February 1995, is available from ftp://nis.nsf.net/documents/rfc.

4. Paul Mockapetris, "Domain Names—Concepts and Facilities," RFC 1034, November 1987, and "Domain Names—Implementation and Specification," RFC 1035, November 1987. Both are available from ftp://nis.nsf.net/documents/rfc.

5. Additional information can be obtained from RSA Data Security Corp. at http://www.rsa.com and Cheswick and Bellovin, *Firewalls and Internet Security*, p. 220. For more information on cryptography, refer to http://draco.centerline.com:8080/ ~ franl/crypto/cryptography.html.

6. Interview with Jon Zeeff, December 1994.

7. See either http://www.terisa.com or the draft from nis.nsf.net/internet/documents/internet-drafts/draft-rescorla-shttp-00.txt.

8. For more information about SSL, see http://mcom.com.

9. D. Eastlake and C. Kaufman, "Domain Name System Protocol Security Extensions," November 21, 1994, < draft-ietf-dnssec-secext-02.txt >, available via FTP from nis.nsf.net in internet/documents/internet-drafts.

10. Margaret A. Emmelhainz, *EDI: A Total Management Guide* (Reading, Mass.: Addison-Wesley, 1993).

11. For more information, see http://info.cern.ch.

12. For more information about the Mosaic browser, see http://www.ncsa.uiuc.edu/SDG/Software/Mosaic/NCSAMosaicHome.html.

13. See Matthew Gray's "Wow, That's Big!" page of automatically collected Web servers at http://www.netgen.com/cgi/comprehensive.

14. Merit Graphs of NSF backbone usage are available from http://www.cc.gatech.edu/gvu/stats/NSF/merit.html.

15. See note 7.

16. For details, refer to http://mcom.com/info/security-overview.html.

17. For more information about the IETF, see ftp://nis.nsf.net/documents/ietf/1ietf-description.txt.

18. For more information about CommerceNet, refer to http://www.commerce.net/ or call (415) 617-8790.

19. For more information, refer to http://www.w3.org.

20. See http://www.terisa.com/pr/apr10.html for details.

21. Interview with Jon Zeeff, December 1994, and http://branch.com/info.

22. Interview with Bill Rollinson, December 1994.

23. Communications with Steve Crocker.

24. Discussions with Nathaniel S. Borenstein, December 1994; and L. H. Stein, E. A. Stefferud, N. S. Borenstein, and M. T. Rose, "The Green Commerce Model," First Virtual Holdings, Inc., October 1994.

25. N. S. Borenstein and N. Freed, "MIME (Multipurpose Internet Mail Extensions) Part One: Mechanisms for Specifying and Describing the Format of Internet Message Bodies," RFC 1521, Bellcore, Innosoft, September 1993.

26. N. S. Borenstein and M. T. Rose, "The Application/Green-Commerce MIME Content-Type," First Virtual Holdings, Inc., October 1994.

27. See http://www.mastercard.com/Press/press.htm for the latest releases.

28. For an excellent compendium of export issues and regulations, see http://www.cygnus.com/ ~ gnu/export.html.

Appendix A

HISTORY AND GROWTH OF THE INTERNET_____

This outline of significant events in the evolution of the Internet has been adapted, with permission, from Hobbes' Internet Timeline, which is compiled and maintained by Robert H[obbes] Zakon. The most up-to-date version of the Hobbes' Internet Timeline can be found on the World Wide Web at the following address: http://info.isoc.org/guest/zakon/ Internet/History/HIT.html. Comments and additional information about Internet milestones may be sent via e-mail to hobbes@hobbes.mitre.org.

Year	Milestone
1957	The Union of Soviet Socialist Republics launches *Sputnik,* first artificial earth satellite. In response, the United States forms the Advanced Research Projects Agency (ARPA) within the Department of Defense (DoD) to establish U.S. lead in science and technology applicable to the military.
1962	Paul Baran at RAND Corporation authors "On Distributed Communications Networks" and sponsors packet-switching (PS) networks. In a PS network, the message is broken down into units of equal size (packets), routed along the most functional path, then reassembled at the destination.
1965	ARPA sponsors study on "cooperative network of time-sharing computers." TX-2 at Massachusetts Institute of Technology's Lincoln Lab in Lexington, Massachusetts, and Q-32 at Systems Development Corporation in Santa Monica, California, are directly linked (i.e., without packet switches).
1967	Plan for a PS network is presented at the Association of Computing Machinery Symposium on Operating Principles. First design paper on ARPANET (Advanced Research Projects Agency Network) is published by Lawrence G. Roberts
1968	PS network presented to the ARPA.
1969	DoD commissions ARPANET to do research into networking.

Year	Milestone
	First node connected to ARPANET at University of California at Los Angeles is soon followed by other nodes at Stanford Research Institute, the University of California at Santa Barbara, and the University of Utah.
	Bolt Beranek and Newman, Inc. (BBN), develops the Information Message Processors (IMP), a Honeywell 516 minicomputer with 12 kilobits of memory.
	First Request for Comments (RFC): "Host Software."
early 1970s	Store-and-forward networks begin to use electronic mail (e-mail) technology.
1971	Fifteen nodes (23 hosts) connected to ARPANET.
	ARPANET hosts start using Network Control Protocol (NCP).
1972	International Conference on Computer Communications features demonstration of ARPANET operation between 40 machines and the Terminal Interface Processor (TIP).
	InterNetworking Working Group (INWG) is created to address need for establishing agreed-upon protocols.
	BBN invents e-mail program for sending messages across a distributed network.
	Telnet specification (RFC 318) issued.
1973	First international connections to the ARPANET established at University College of London (England) and Royal Radar Establishment (Norway).
	Basic concepts for Ethernet, Internet, and gateway architecture developed and presented.
	File Transfer specification (RFC 454) issued.
1974	Vinton Cerf and Bob Kahn publish "A Protocol for Packet Network Internetworking," specifying in detail the design of a Transmission Control Program (TCP).
	BBN opens Telenet, the first public packet-data service (a commercial version of ARPANET).
1975	Operational management of Internet transferred to DCA (now DISA).
1976	AT&T Bell Labs develops Unix-to-Unix CoPy (UUCP) and distributes it with Unix one year later.
1977	THEORYNET is created at University of Wisconsin to provide e-mail (using UUCP) to over 100 researchers in computer science.
	Mail specification (RFC 733) issued.
	Tymshare launches Tymnet.
	First demonstration of ARPANET/Packet Radio Network/SATNET operation of Internet protocols with BBN-supplied gateways (July).
1979	Computer scientists from University of Wisconsin, DARPA (in 1972, ARPA became the Defense Advanced Research Projects Agency), and the National Science Foundation (NSF) meet and establish a Computer Science Department research computer network.
	Usenet is established between Duke University and University of North Carolina using UUCP to provide e-mail, file transfer, and electronic discussion groups (called newsgroups).
	First Multi-User Domain, MUD1, is established.
	ARPA establishes the Internet Configuration Control Board (ICCB) as an advisory group to provide technical help in managing the Internet.
	Packet Radio Network (PRNet) experiment starts with DARPA funding to develop mobile network links.

Year	Milestone
1981	City University of New York starts a cooperative network, BITNET, ("Because It's Time NETwork"), with the first connection to Yale University. BITNET originally stood for "Because It's There NETwork," in reference to the free protocols provided with IBM systems. BITNET provides e-mail and Listserv servers for distributing information as well as for transferring files. UCAR (University Corporation for Atmospheric Research) and BBN, with seed money granted by the NSF, build Computer Science NETwork (CSNET) to provide networking services (especially e-mail) to scientists at universities with no access to ARPANET. CSNET later becomes known as the Computer Science Network. Minitel (Teletel) is deployed across France by France Telecom.
1982	Transmission Control Protocol (TCP) and Internet Protocol (IP), which form the protocol suite commonly known as TCP/IP, is adopted as standard for ARPANET. This leads to one of the first definitions of an "internet" as a connected set of networks, specifically those using TCP/IP, and of the "Internet" as TCP/IP connected internets. Department of Defense declares TCP/IP to be the standard for DoD. European UNIX Network (EUnet) is created to provide e-mail and Usenet services. Countries originally connected via EUnet are Netherlands, Denmark, Sweden, and the United Kingdom. External Gateway Protocol specification (RFC 827) issued. EGP is used for gateways between networks.
1983	Name server developed at University of Wisconsin; network users no longer have to know the exact path to other systems. Cutover from NCP to TCP/IP begins (January 1). CSNET/ARPANET gateway put in place. ARPANET split into ARPANET for research and MILNET for military and defense applications. Desktop workstations come into being, many using the Berkeley UNIX operating system, which includes IP networking software. User focus shifts from having a single, large time-sharing computer per site connected to Internet to having an entire local network connected. Internet Activities Board (IAB) established by network participants. European Academic and Research Network (EARN) established. EARN works much the same way as BITNET works, with a gateway funded by IBM. FidoNet, a worldwide network of personal computers connected via modem and telephone lines, is developed by Tom Jennings.
1984	Number of Internet hosts surpasses 1,000 Domain Name System (DNS) is introduced. This distributed database system can translate computer names into numeric Internet addresses and vice versa, eliminating the need for users to remember long lists of numbers. Japan Unix Network (JUNET) is established using UUCP. Joint Academic Network (JANET) is established in the United Kingdom. Moderated newsgroups introduced on Usenet. William Gibson publishes *Neuromancer*.
1985	Whole Earth 'Lectronic Link (WELL) is established.
1986	NSF creates NSFNET backbone (with speed of 56 kilobits per second) and establishes five supercomputing centers (JVNC@Princeton, PSC@Pittsburgh, SDSC@UCSD, NCSA@UIUC, and Theory Center@Cornell) to provide researchers access to high-speed computing power via the Internet. This allows an explosion of connections, especially at universities.

Year	Milestone
	Cleveland Freenet comes on-line, marking the start of the National Public Telecomputing Network.
	Network News Transfer Protocol (NNTP) is designed to enhance Usenet news performance over TCP/IP.
	Mail Exchanger (MX) records are developed to allow non-IP network hosts to have domain addresses.
	Usenet newsgroups proliferate and are reorganized into broad subject clusters according to discussion topics.
	Bay Area Regional Research Network (BARRNet) is established using high-speed links and becomes operational one year later.
1987	Number of Internet hosts surpasses 10,000.
	NSF signs a cooperative agreement with Merit Network, Inc., to manage the NSFNET backbone. IBM and MCI are involved through an agreement with Merit. Later, Merit, IBM, and MCI found Advanced Network Services (ANS), a commercial Internet provider.
	UUNET is founded to provide commercial UUCP and Usenet access.
	CSNET merges into BITNET to form the Corporation for Research and Education Networking (CREN).
	Thousandth RFC: "Request for Comments Reference Guide."
1988	"Worm" burrows through the Internet (November 1), affecting about 6,000 of the 60,000 hosts on the Net and raising consciousness about security problems.
	DARPA forms Computer Emergency Response Team (CERT) in response to the needs exhibited during the "worm" incident.
	DoD sees TCP/IP as an interim protocol and chooses to adopt Open Systems Interface (OSI). U.S. Government OSI Profile (GOSIP) defines the set of protocols to be supported by government-purchased products.
	Los Nettos network created with no federal funding; all support comes from regional network's members in the Los Angeles area.
	NSFNET backbone is upgraded to T1 (1.544 megabits per second).
	California Education and Research Federation network (CERFnet) is founded.
	First Canadian regionals join NSFNET; connected countries now include Canada, Denmark, Finland, France, Iceland, Norway, and Sweden.
1989	Number of Internet hosts surpasses 100,000.
	European service providers form Réseaux IP Européens (RIPE) to ensure the administrative and technical coordination needed for the operation of the pan-European IP Network.
	First relays between a commercial e-mail carrier and the Internet are MCI Mail, through the Corporation for the National Research Initiative (CNRI), and Compuserve, through Ohio State University.
	Growing numbers of hosts and increased complexity of Internet management prompt the creation of a new structure for governance. The Internet Engineering Task Force (IETF) and Internet Research Task Force (IRTF) come into existence under the IAB.
	Australian Academic Research Network (AARNET) is set up.
	Clifford Stoll writes *Cuckoo's Egg,* the real-life tale of a German cracker group that infiltrated numerous computer facilities in the United States.
	Australia, Germany, Israel, Italy, Japan, Mexico, Netherlands, New Zealand, Puerto Rico, and the United Kingdom connect to NSFNET.
1990	ARPANET ceases to exist.
	Electronic Frontier Foundation (EFF) is founded by Mitch Kapor.

Year	Milestone
	Archie, a navigational tool for locating software available on Internet host computers, is developed at McGill University and made available to network users.
	International Standards Organization Development Environment (ISODE) software is developed to provide the DoD with a way to migrate from TCP/IP to OSI. ISODE software allows OSI applications to operate over TCP/IP.
	CA*net formed by ten regional networks as the national Canadian backbone, with direct connection to NSFNET.
	Argentina, Austria, Belgium, Brazil, Chile, Greece, India, Ireland, South Korea, Spain, and Switzerland connect to NSFNET.
1991	NSF lifts restrictions against commercial use of the Internet.
	Commercial Internet eXchange (CIX) Association, Inc., is formed by General Atomics (CERFnet), Performance Systems International, Inc. (PSInet), and UUNET Technologies, Inc. (AlterNet).
	Wide area information servers (WAIS), a method of searching various types of information stored on different computer platforms using natural language queries, is released into the public domain by Thinking Machines Corporation of Cambridge, Massachusetts.
	Gopher, a software designed to organize and help locate computer information files, is developed and released at the University of Minnesota.
	US High Performance Computing Act establishes the National Research and Education Network (NREN).
	NSFNET backbone is upgraded to T3 (44.736 megabits per second).
	NSFNET traffic passes 1 trillion bytes per month and 10 billion packets per month.
	Croatia, Czech Republic, Hong Kong, Hungary, Poland, Portugal, Singapore, South Africa, Taiwan, and Tunisia connect to NSFNET.
1992	Number of Internet hosts surpasses 1 million.
	The Internet Society (ISOC) is chartered for the purpose of promoting global information exchange through technology. ISOC members appoint a council that has responsibility for technical management and direction of the Internet.
	The World Wide Web (WWW) is developed Centre Européen de Recherches Nucléaires (CERN), the European particle physics laboratory in Switzerland. WWW provides access to information files on the Internet through hypertext links and supports graphics, sound, and video as well as text.
	The first MBONE (Multicasting Backbone) audio multicast (March) and video multicast (November) take place.
	IAB reconstituted as the Internet Architecture Board and becomes part of ISOC.
	The World Bank comes on-line.
	Cameroon, Cyprus, Ecuador, Estonia, Kuwait, Latvia, Luxembourg, Malaysia, Slovakia, Slovenia, Thailand, and Venezuela connect to NSFNET.
1993	Number of Internet hosts surpasses 2 million.
	NSF funds a new organization, the InterNIC, which provides specific Internet services: directory and database services (through AT&T), registration services (through Network Solutions, Inc.), and information services (through General Atomics/CERFnet).
	The White House comes on-line.
	Internet Talk Radio is created by Carl Malamud to demonstrate the Internet's broadcast capabilities.
	The United Nations comes on-line.

Year	Milestone
	Congress passes the National Communications Competition and Information Infrastructure Act (NII) in November to "promote a national communications infrastructure" and to "encourage deployment of advanced communications services through competition."
	Mosaic software for browsing the World Wide Web is developed at the National Center for Supercomputing at the University of Illinois. Mosaic takes the Internet by storm, causing a 341,634 percent growth service traffic on the Web in a year. (Gopher's service traffic growth rate for the year is 997 percent.
	Bulgaria, Costa Rica, Egypt, Fiji, Ghana, Guam, Indonesia, Kazakhstan, Kenya, Liechtenstein, Peru, Romania, the Russian Federation, Turkey, Ukraine, the United Arab Emirates, and the Virgin Islands connect to NSFNET.
1994	Number of Internet hosts surpasses 3.8 million.
	The Internet celebrates its twenty-fifth anniversary.
	Communities in the United States begin to be wired directly to the Internet.
	U.S. Senate and House provide information servers.
	Shopping malls arrive on the Internet.
	First cyberstation, RT-FM, broadcasts from Interop in Las Vegas.
	The National Institute for Standards and Technology (NIST) suggests that GOSIP incorporate TCP/IP and drop the "OSI-only" requirement.
	Arizona law firm Canter & Siegel "spams" the Internet by sending thousands of e-mail messages advertising green-card lottery services; Net citizens flame back.
	NSFNET traffic exceeds 10 trillion bytes per month.
	Worms of a new kind—software tools that search Web sites for topics and terms of interest in response to search commands—find their way around the Net. These WWW Worms (W4) are joined by Spiders, Wanderers, Crawlers, and Snakes as the amount of information on the Web expands daily.
	WWW edges out Telnet to become the second most popular service on the Net (behind ftp-data), based on percentage of packets and bytes traffic distribution on NSFNET
	Japan's prime minister comes on-line.
	Britain's Treasury comes on-line.
	New Zealand's prime minister comes on-line.
	First Virtual, the first cyberbank, opens for business.
	The European Research and Education Network Association (TERENA) is formed by the merger of RARE (Réseaux Associés pour la Recherche Européene) and EARN, with representatives from 38 countries as well as from CERN and ECMWF (an international treaty organization).
	Algeria, Armenia, Bermuda, Burkina Faso, China, Colombia, French Polynesia, Jamaica, Lebanon, Lithuania, Macau, Morocco, New Caledonia, Nicaragua, Niger, Panama, Philippines, Senegal, Sri Lanka, Swaziland, Uruguay, and Uzbekistan connect to NSFNET.
1995	Number of Internet hosts surpasses 5 million.
	NSFNET backbone begins to be replaced by a system of interconnected commercial network providers, and U.S. Net subsidies for research and education, funded by the National Science Foundation, are scheduled to end.

Selected Sources

"ARPANET, the Defense Data Network, and Internet." *Encyclopedia of Communications.* Vol. 1, edited by Fritz Froehlich and Allen Kent. New York: Marcel Dekker, 1991.

Cerf, Vinton, as told to Bernard Aboba. "How the Internet Came to Be." In Bernard Aboba, *The Online User's Encyclopedia.* Reading, Mass.: Addison-Wesley, 1993.

Hardy, Henry. "The History of the Net." Master's thesis, School of Communications, Grand Valley State University, Allendale, Michigan, 1993. ftp://umcc.umich.edu/pub/users/seraphim/doc/nethist#.txt

Hauben, Ronda, and Michael Hauben. "The Netizens and the Wonderful World of the Net." http://www.columbia.edu/ ~ hauben/ project_book.html

Kulikowski, Stan, II. "A Timeline of Network History." stankuli@ uwf.bitnet

Quarterman, John. *The Matrix: Computer Networks and Conferencing Systems Worldwide.* Bedford, Mass.: Digital Press, 1990.

APPENDIX B

INTERNET VITAL STATISTICS_____

The size of the Internet and its rate of growth are topics of attention and debate among network analysts. The following charts present some of the most important measures of the recent development of the Internet and highlight the impact of the introduction of the World Wide Web.

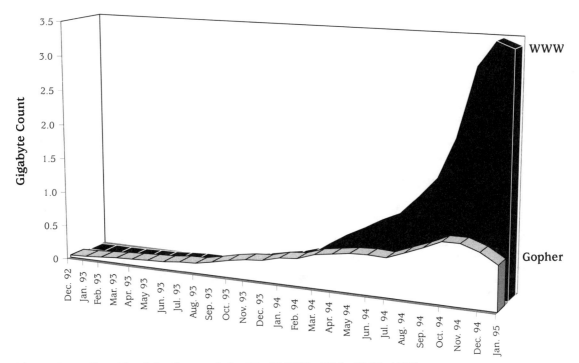

Figure B-a   Growth of Gopher and the World Wide Web (1992–1995)
Source: http://www.cc. gatech.edu/gvu/stats/NSF/merit.html

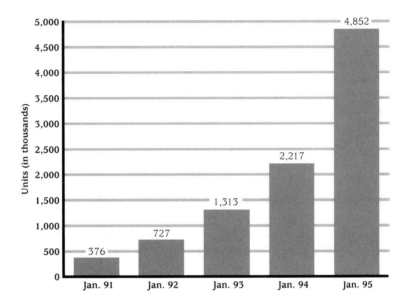

Figure B-b   Growth of Host Computers (1991–1995)

Source: ftp://nic.merit.edu/nsfnet/statistics/history.hosts

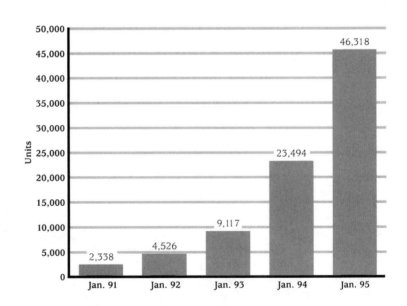

Figure B-c   Growth of Registered Networks (1991–1995)

Source: ftp://nic.merit.edu/nsfnet/statistics/history. netcount

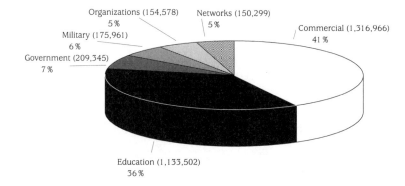

Organizations (154,578)
5%

Networks (150,299)
5%

Military (175,961)
6%

Commercial (1,316,966)
41%

Government (209,345)
7%

Education (1,133,502)
36%

*Figure B-d   Division of
U.S. Domains by Category
(as of January 1995)*
Source: ftp://nic.merit.edu/nsfnet/
statistics/history.hosts

APPENDIX C

A MANAGER'S GUIDE TO INTERNET TERMS_____

This glossary defines the terms most commonly used in discussing the development and implementation of Internet applications. It is based on training material developed by Bolt Beranek and Newman Internet Training Services, Cambridge, Massachusetts.

ACCEPTABLE USE POLICY **(AUP)** A description of specific behavior allowed on a portion of the Internet. Many Internet providers have policies stipulating the way in which the network may be used, but enforcement of such policies varies with the network.

ADVANCED RESEARCH PROJECTS AGENCY NETWORK **(ARPANET)** A pioneering long-haul network established in the early 1970s with funding by ARPA (now DARPA). The ARPANET consisted of individual packet-switching computers interconnected by leased lines. It served as the basis for early networking research, as well as a central backbone, during the development of the Internet. It ceased to exist in 1990.

AMERICAN NATIONAL STANDARDS INSTITUTE **(ANSI)** A private, nonprofit membership organization that coordinates the U.S. voluntary consensus standards system and approves American national standards.

ANONYMOUS **FTP** A protocol that allows users to retrieve documents, files, programs, and other archived data from anywhere in the Internet.

ARCHIE A system for locating, gathering, and indexing information available on the Internet, most frequently used to locate specific software in the extensive files of anonymous FTP archives on the Internet.

ARPANET *See* Advanced Research Projects Agency Network.

AUTHENTICATION The verification of the identity of a person or process; also a component of Internet security software.

BANDWIDTH Technically, the difference, in Hertz (Hz), between the highest and lowest frequencies of a transmission channel. Typically, bandwidth refers to the amount of data that can be sent through a given communications circuit or network cable.

BITNET Because It's Time NETwork, a store-and-forward network established to link academic institutions in 1980, before Internet connectivity was widely available.

CERT *See* Computer Emergency Response Team.

CIX *See* Commercial Internet Exchange.

CLIENT-SERVER SOFTWARE Software designed to facilitate the exchange of information between two connected computers. The "client" runs the user interface, and the "server" stores data and responds to queries. Gopher and World Wide

Web are examples of client-server software that run on the Internet.

Comité Consultatif International de Télégraphique et Téléphonique (CCITT) An agency of the International Telecommunications Union of the United Nations that recommends specifications of networking protocols and related standards.

Commercial Internet Exchange (CIX) The first association of commercial Internet access providers.

Computer Emergency Response Team (CERT) A quasi-governmental body formed by DARPA in November 1988 in response to a widespread security breach on the Internet, CERT works with the Internet community to identify and respond to network security problems, to raise the community's awareness of Internet security issues, and to improve the security of existing systems. CERT provides services such as 24-hour technical assistance for responding to computer security incidents and product vulnerability assistance, and produces technical documents and tutorials.

cracker A person who attempts to access computer systems without authorization and with the intent to cause damage or copy files without permission.

cyberspace A term coined by William Gibson in his fantasy novel *Neuromancer,* published in 1984, to describe the new universe of computers and networked communication. The term is now popularly used to refer to the totality of networks and electronic data.

Data Encryption Key (DEK) A device used for the encryption of message text and for the computation of message integrity checks (e.g., signatures).

Data Encryption Standard (DES) A widely used, standard encryption scheme for encoding messages and data on the Internet.

Dedicated Line A telephone line that is dedicated to communications between computers; also called a lease line.

dialup A temporary, as opposed to dedicated, connection between two computers established over a standard phone line.

Domain Name System (DNS) A general-purpose distributed, replicated, data query service used principally for looking up Internet host addresses that are based on host names rather than on numbers. Host names now used on the Internet are the basis of e-mail and Web addresses. Some important domains are: .com (commercial), .edu (educational), .net (network operations), .gov (U.S. government), and .mil (U.S. military). Countries also have domain names; For example, .us (United States), .uk (United Kingdom), jp (Japan).

European Academic and Research Network (EARN) A European network modeled on BIT-NET with links to many European universities.

electronic mail (e-mail) Software that allows the exchange of messages between individuals, or groups of individuals, on a corporate network or a wide area network like the Internet.

e-mail address The domain-based address or UUCP address used to send electronic mail to a specified destination, either a list or a computer. An example of an e-mail address is "cronin@bcvms.bc.edu."

encryption The encoding of data traveling across the Internet in order to prevent that data from being read by anyone other than the intended recipient.

FAQs *See* Frequently Asked Questions.

File Transfer Protocol (FTP) A protocol that allows a user on one host to access and transfer files to and from another host over a network. FTP is usually also the name of the program the user invokes to execute the protocol.

finger A program that displays information about a particular user, or all users, logged on the local system or on a remote system. A finger can be used to locate Internet users, but it is often disabled by network administrators for security reasons.

Flame To send a strongly worded or inflammatory statement in an electronic-mail message. Unpopular or controversial postings to discussion groups are frequently "flamed."

For Your Information (FYI)   A series of informative papers that convey general information about topics related to TCP/IP or the Internet. FYI is a subseries of Requests for Comment (RFCs), but FYI does not define technical standards or describe protocols.

FreeNet   A community-based Internet access program that usually provides e-mail, information services, interactive communications, and conferencing to local residents. FreeNets are funded by individuals and operated by volunteers. They are part of the National Public Telecomputing Network (NPTN), an organization based in Cleveland, Ohio, that is devoted to making computer telecommunication and networking services as freely available as are public libraries.

Frequently Asked Questions (FAQs)   Lists of questions, and answers to the questions, that are made available to new participants in Internet discussion groups and new users of software tools, to avoid having users repeatedly ask the same questions of such groups.

Gopher   A distributed information service that makes available hierarchical collections of information across the Internet. Gopher uses a simple protocol that allows a single Gopher client to access information from any accessible Gopher server, providing the user with a single "Gopher space" of information.

hacker   A person with expert understanding of the internal workings of computers and computer networks. Distinct from *cracker,* which implies malicious intent.

home page   A graphical multimedia document in page format, which serves as the introductory message on a World Wide Web server. It is similar to a main menu through which related menus and files can be accessed.

host   A computer that allows users to com-

municate with other computers directly connected to a network.

HTML   *See* Hyper/Text Markup Language.

hypermedia   A combination of hypertext and multimedia in a document.

hypertext   A document containing links to other documents; selecting a link automatically displays the connected document.

hyper/text markup language (HTML)   The programming language in which World Wide Web documents are written.

internet   In general, a collection of networks connected to each other using TCP/IP technology. The Internet is the largest internet in the world.

Internet Society (ISOC)   A nonprofit, professional membership organization that (1) facilitates and supports the technical evolution of the Internet; (2) educates the scientific and academic communities, industry, and the public about the technology, uses, and applications of the Internet; and (3) promotes the development of new applications for the system. The development of Internet technical standards takes place under the auspices of the Internet Society, with substantial support from the Corporation for National Research Initiatives under a cooperative agreement with the U.S. government.

InterNIC   A federally funded project to coordinate the services offered by providers of registration, information, and database services to the Internet community.

IRC   A worldwide "party line" protocol that allows Internet users to "converse" with one another in real time. The Internet Relay Chat consists of a network of servers, each of which accepts connections per user from a client program.

LAN   *See* local area network.

Listserv   An automated mailing list distribution system originally designed for the BITNET/EARN network.

LOCAL AREA NETWORK **(LAN)** A connection among computers in a specified local group.

MAIL REFLECTOR A software program that distributes files or information in response to requests sent via e-mail, typically used to implement a discussion group.

MIME *See* Multipurpose Internet Mail Extensions.

MOSAIC World Wide Web client software that provides multimedia searches through files on WWW servers.

MUD *See* Multi-User Domain and Multi-User Dungeon.

MULTIPURPOSE INTERNET MAIL EXTENSIONS **(MIME)** An Internet standard for attaching a variety of file types to a standard e-mail message.

MULTI-USER DOMAIN **(MUD)** An Internet site where users can interact simultaneously.

MULTI-USER DUNGEON **(MUD)** A set of role playing games, modeled on the original Dungeons and Dragons game. These games can involve action, adventure, or magic and are usually based on the Telnet Protocol.

NATIONAL SCIENCE FOUNDATION NETWORK **(NSFNET)** A network established by the National Science Foundation to link U.S. supercomputer sites, facilitating research and education.

NETIQUETTE A pun on the word *etiquette,* referring to proper behavior on a network.

NETWORK INFORMATION CENTER **(NIC)** A source of information, assistance, and services for network users. An example of a NIC is the InterNIC.

NETWORK NEWS TRANSFER PROTOCOL **(NNTP)** A protocol for the distribution, inquiry, retrieval, and posting of news articles.

NETWORK OPERATIONS CENTER **(NOC)** A location from which the operation of a network or an internet is monitored. Additionally, a NOC usually serves as a clearinghouse for connectivity problems and efforts to resolve those problems.

NSFNET *See* National Science Foundation Network.

PACKET A unit of data sent across a network. Also a generic term used to describe a unit of data at all levels of the protocol stack but most correctly used to describe a unit of application data.

POINT OF PRESENCE **(POP)** A site where there exists a collection of telecommunications equipment, usually digital leased lines and multiprotocol routers.

PROTOCOL A formal description of data formats and the rules that two computers must follow to exchange the data.

REQUEST FOR COMMENTS **(RFC)** Begun in 1969, a document series that describes the Internet suite of protocols and related experiments. Not all (in fact, very few) RFCs describe Internet standards, but all Internet standards are written up as RFCs. RFCs are unusual in that the proposed protocols are put forward by members of the Internet research and development community, acting on their own behalf, unlike the formally reviewed and standardized protocols that are promoted by organizations such as CCITT (Comité Consultatif International de Télégraphique et Téléphonique) and ANSI (American National Standards Institute).

ROUTER A device that forwards data between networks using the same protocols. The forwarding decision is based on network layer information and routing tables, which are often constructed by routing protocols.

SERIAL LINE INTERNET PROTOCOL **(SLIP)** A protocol used to run IP over serial lines, such as telephone circuits or RS-232 cables, interconnecting two systems.

SERVER A computer configured to provide information and resources (e.g., file servers over a network, Gopher servers, and Web servers).

SERVICE PROVIDER An organization or a company that provides connections to a part of the Internet.

SIMPLE MAIL TRANSFER PROTOCOL **(SMTP)** A protocol used to transfer electronic mail between computers. This is a server-to-server protocol, so other protocols are used to access the messages.

SIMPLE NETWORK MANAGEMENT PROTOCOL (SNMP) The Internet standard protocol developed to manage nodes on an IP network. This protocol currently manages nodes such as wiring hubs, video toasters, CD-ROM jukeboxes, and so forth.

T1 An AT&T term for a digital carrier facility used to transmit a DS-1 formatted digital signal at 1.544 megabits per second.

T3 A term for a digital carrier facility used to transmit a DS-3 formatted digital signal at 44.746 megabits per second.

TCP/IP *See* Transmission Control Protocol/Internet Protocol.

TELNET The Internet standard protocol for remote terminal-connection service.

TRANSMISSION CONTROL PROTOCOL/INTERNET PROTOCOL (TCP/IP) The suite of transport and application protocols that provide a common way of communicating and sharing data across the Internet.

UNIX-TO-UNIX COPY (UUCP) A facility for copying files between UNIX systems; provided the basis for Usenet.

USENET A collection of thousands of topically named newsgroups, the computers that run the protocols, and the people who read the news and submit news items to the newsgroups. Not all Internet hosts subscribe to Usenet, and not all Usenet hosts are on the Internet. Also called

Network News, Usenet is similar to bulletin boards on other networks.

UUCP *See* UNIX-to-UNIX CoPy.

VERONICA A service similar to Archie that is built into Gopher and will allow searches of all Gopher sites for menu items (e.g., files, directories, and other resources).

WAIS *See* wide area information servers.

WHOIS An Internet program which allows users to query a database at the InterNIC contaIng information about people and other Internet entities (e.g., domains, networks, and hosts). The information for people includes the name of a person's company and the person's address, telephone number, and e-mail address.

WIDE AREA INFORMATION SERVERS (WAIS) A distributed information service for looking up information in databases across the Internet. The service offers simple natural-language input, indexed searching for fast retrieval, and a "relevance feedback" mechanism that ranks search results by relevance to the search request.

WORLD WIDE WEB (WWW) A hypertext-based, distributed information system created by researchers at Centre Européen de Recherches Nucléaires (CERN) in Switzerland. The Web allows users to create, edit, and browse hypertext documents.

WWW *See* World Wide Web.

APPENDIX D

SELECTED BUSINESS RESOURCES ON THE WORLD WIDE WEB

The growth of business information on the Internet has kept pace with the surge of commercial interest in the World Wide Web. The following Web sites are representative of the diversity of business resources available. Each site is represented by a uniform resource locater (URL), the standard addressing scheme for the Web.

Accounting and Taxes

Accounting Net	http://www.scu.edu.au/ANetHomePage.html
Accounting Web	http://www.rutgers.edu/Accounting/raw.html
Internal Revenue Service	http://www.ustreas.gov/treasury/bureaus/irs/irs.html
Taxing Times	http://www.scubed.com/tax/index.html

Banking and Electronic Commerce

Bank America	http://www.bankamerica.com/
CommerceNet	http://www.commerce.net
First Virtual	http://www.fv.com
World Bank	http://www.worldbank.org

Business Schools and Education

Boston College	http://www.bc.edu/bc_org/avp/csom
Business Education Sites on the Internet	http://raider.mgmt.purdue.edu/HTML.bused.html
Dartmouth	http://www.dartmouth.edu/pages/tuck/tuckhome.html
Harvard	http://www.hbs.harvard.edu
MIT	http://www ~ sloan.mit.edu

Stanford	http://gsb ~ www.stanford.edu/home.html
Internet Training Resources:	http://www.brandonu.ca/ ~ ennsnr/Resources/ Welcome.html

Demographics

Demographic Summaries 1994	http://www.upclose.com/upclose/demomenu/demomenu.htm
Internet User Surveys	http://tig.com/IBC/index.html
Nielsen Media Research	http://www.nielsenmedia.com/demo.htm
U.S. Census Data	http://www.census.gov

Financial Information Services

American Stock Exchange	http://www.amex.com
Chicago Mercantile Exchange	http://www.interaccess.com:80/cme/
Dow Jones Industrial Average	http://www.secapl.com/secapl/quoteserver/djia.html
Financial Services Technology Consortium	http://www.llnl.gov/fstc
Mutual Fund Information	http://networth.galt.com
NASDAQ Financial Executive Journal	http://www.law.cornell.edu/nasdaq/nasdtoc.html
New York Stock Exchange	http://www.cob.ohio-state.edu/dept/fin/nyse.htm
SEC Corporate Reports	http://town.hal.org/edgar/edgar.html
Stock Market Quotes	http://www.ai.mit.edu/stocks/graphs.html

Human Resources and Employment

Career Mosaic	http://www.service.com:80/cm/
Networks for Recruiters	http://nero.aa.msen.com/occ06.html
OnLine Job Services	http://rescomp.stanford.edu/jobs.html

Internet Directories

Clearinghouse for Subject-Oriented Internet Resources	gopher://gopher.una.hh.lib.umich.edu/11/inetdirs
Desktop Internet Reference	http://www.clark.net/pub/iistserv/dir1.html
Finding People on the Internet	http://alpha.acast.nova.edu/netservices.html
Institute of Management and Administration	http://ioma.com/ioma/

InterNIC Directory of
  Directories   http://ds.internic.net/ds/dsdirofdirs.html

Yahoo Business Resources   http://www.yahoo.com

Yanoff's Special Internet
  Connections   http://www.uwm.edu/Mirror/inet.services.html

U.S. Government

Department of Commerce   http://www.doc.loc.gov

FedWorld   http://www.fedworld.gov

House of Representatives
  and Senate   http://thomas.loc.gov

White House   http://www.whitehouse.gov

Appendix E

HOME PAGES OF CONTRIBUTORS AND THEIR ORGANIZATIONS

BBN PLANET CORPORATION

URL: http://www.bbnplanet.com

BBN Planet Corporation (formerly BBN Internet Services Corp.) is a subsidiary of Bolt Beranek and Newman Inc., a diversified high-technology company founded in 1948. The BBN Planet home page provides a company overview, product announcements, information about training programs, and other value-added services.

Welcome to BBN Planet's On-line Information Service.

BBN Planet, formerly BBN Internet Services Corporation, offers comprehensive Internet service packages to business and organizations worldwide.

 Hot News: Find out what s new at BBN Planet.

 Service Offerings: Internet access and value-added services.

 Customer Profiles: Find out how our customers are using the Internet.

 Contact us for more information on any of our services.

 Learn about Job Opportunities at BBN Planet and apply right now.

Bolt Beranek & Newman, Inc. Corporate Home Page

MARY J. CRONIN

URL: http://fenris.novalink.com:80/cronin/index.html

Cronin's home page provides excerpts from books and articles she has written about electronic commerce and commercial applications on the Internet.

Doing Business on the Internet
by Mary J. Cronin

Table of Contents

Exceprts
> Chapter 2: A Manager s Guide
> Chapter 4: Intermarketing
> Chapter 8: Putting the Network to Work

Previews: Forthcoming books
> *Doing More business on the Internet*
>> -expanded and updated with World Wide Web cases
> *Global Advantage: Competing in a Networked World*
>> -Internet applications and strategies around the world
> *Internet Strategy Handbook*
>> -detailed Internet studies from Fortune 500 companies

DIGITAL EQUIPMENT CORPORATION

URL: http://www.digital.com

Digital opened the first commercial home page on the Web in October 1993. Its current version features product information, a message from Digital's CEO, electronic versions of customer publications, product information, and support services. Users can also "test drive" software running on Digital's Alpha systems via the Web server.

digital

Click on an area of interest

Greeting
A word from Bob Palmer
Chairman of the Board, President and CEO

Company Financials & Contacts

Careers

WHAT'S NEW FROM DIGITAL

QuickIndex

Flash!

Digital outlines bold new Corporate Strategy

Customer Periodicals

InfoCenters

Service, Training and Support

 Directory
Information Links by Subject

Products & Services

Reading Rooms

New Technology and Research

OTHER WEB SERVERS

About   Browse   Search   Feedback   Help

DOW JONES

URL: http://bis.dowjones.com

The Dow Jones home page contains information, products, and services from Dow Jones's Business Information Services Group (BIS) and Business Information Services International (BISI). It also provides product and pricing information on Dow Jones News/Retrieval, DowVision, private investor services, reference services, and Personal Journal. Commercial versions of software for some of the products and services are available for downloading.

Where the Web gets down to business.

[What's New | About Business Information Services | Other Dow Jones Sites]

[Customized News Services | Research Services | Electronic Publications]

GENENTECH, INC.

URL: http://www.gene.com

The Genentech external web server is currently under development. At the present time, it includes information about a program to support high school biology teachers called "Access Excellence." Plans for expansion include a corporate overview, press releases, and employment opportunities.

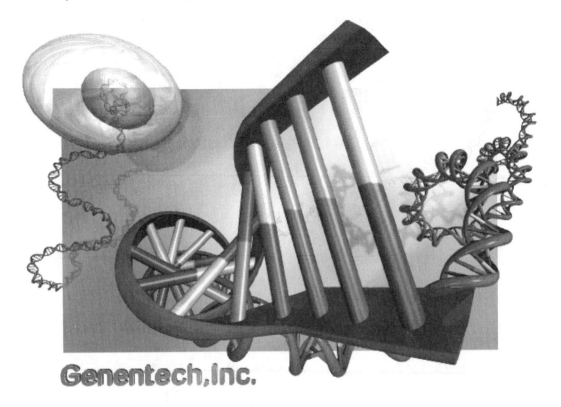

Genentech, Inc. is a pioneer biotechnology company that discovers, develops, manufactures and markets human pharmaceuticals for significant unmet medical needs. The company has headquarters in South San Francisco, California and is traded on the New York and Pacific Stock Exchanges under the symbol GNE.

"Genentech Space is currently under construction. Please check back here for more information on Genentech's people, products and programs as we continue development of this area.

Please check out Access Excellence, our national educational program, that puts high school biology teachers in touch with their colleagues, scientists and critical sources of new scientific information through an online network.

Genentech supports investigators in academic institutions throughout the world by supplying key reagents for their research with the Collaborative Research Materials Program.

LOCKHEED MARTIN

URL: http://www.lmsc.lockheed.com/

The home page for Lockheed Missiles and Space (LMSC), a part of the newly merged Lockheed Martin Corporation, contains facts about the company, copies of official press releases, some technical highlights of the company, and a link to the Lockheed Martin corporate home page.

Lockheed Martin Missiles & Space

Lockheed Martin Missiles & Space, headquartered in Sunnyvale, CA, is a major aerospace and defense company specializing in the development of space systems, missiles, and other high technology products.

Missiles & Space is a proud part of Lockheed Martin Corporation.
'Letting The Future In'

The following information is available from our World-Wide Web pages.

 ## About Missiles & Space

The Company Fact Sheet and contacts for the Public Information Office.
On-line transcriptions of Press Releases. Here's our latest:
- Space Shuttle to Deliver Lockheed Martin Solar Panels to Russian Space Station

Please visit our photo gallery.

The Star, Missiles & Space's company newspaper.

Interested in working at Missiles & Space? See our job opportunities.

 ## Some Technical Highlights

TRACE -- Transition Region and Coronal Explorer: investigating the relations between magnetic fields and plasma structures on the sun. A project of the Stanford-Lockheed Institute for Astrophysical and Space Research, for NASA.

Lockheed ATM Project -- Lockheed Martin Missiles & Space and Asynchronous Transfer Mode (ATM) networking for the California Research and Education Network

BADGER -- The Bay Area Digital GeoResource: a model for public/private shared access to earth science data over the internet

THAAD -- Theater High Altitude Area Defense

 ## On-line services

Lockheed organizations offering services over the Internet.

THE MALOFF COMPANY

URL: http://www.branch.com:80/maloff/

The Maloff Company home page provides an overview of capabilities and services, summary reports of company surveys and research papers, and access to Joel Maloff's speaking calendar.

The Maloff Company, Internet Consultants

- Statement of Capabilities
- The Maloff Company Services
- Web Outsourcing Survey
- The Maloff Company Speaking Calendar
- The Value of Internetworking and the Internet
  An article written by the Maloff Company
- 1993-1994 Internet Service Provider Marketplace Analysis
  The executive summary of the survey done by the Maloff Company

Joel H. Maloff, Internet Consultant
The Maloff Company
10371 N. Territorial Rd.
Dexter, MI
48130 U.S.A.
Telephone (313) 426-1331
Internet: joel@maloff.com

WWW Space Provided by Branch Internet Services Inc.

MILLIPORE CORPORATION

URL: http://www.millipore.com

In addition to a fully searchable product catalog, the Millipore home page offers technical support query forms, corporate financial information, research reports, and new product announcements. Special "hyperfilters" for pharmaceutical and microelectronic customers provide comprehensive pointers to relevant resources elsewhere on the Internet.

Thanks for stopping at Millipore. We're a company that focuses on applying "purification technology" to critical research and manufacturing problems. There are over 3,500 of us worldwide. 10,000 products and systems, and 40 years of expertise in applications ranging from bacteria testing of water, to sterilization of biopharmaceutical proteins, to eliminating contamination from gases used in manufacturing the latest and hottest semiconductor device.

What's New | Products and Services | Applications | Investors | Technical Support | Employment Opportunities

Subscribe to a MilliGram!

We encourage comments about this server!

Copyright 1994 Millipore Corporation 80 Ashby Road, Bedford, MA 01730-9125 USA. All right reserved.

OPEN MARKET, INC.

URL: http://www.openmarket.com

Open Market, Inc. was founded in 1994 to enable merchants of any size or type to quickly and easily create a storefront on the Internet. Among the other features of the Open Market Home Page are an extensive, searchable directory of other commercial sites on the Internet, in-depth product descriptions, on-line demonstrations, and job opportunities at Open Market.

SCHLUMBERGER

URL: http://www.slb.com

The Schlumberger home page offers information about the company and its divisions around the world, shareholder news, overviews of products and services, and an employee directory. Additional features are an extensive collection of petroleum-related resources and the career opportunities section.

What's New at Schlumberger

NEW Schlumberger Plc Business Review 1994 An annual review of SLB's presence in the U.K. (August 3, 1995)

NEW SLB Second Quarter Earnings and Dividend (July 20, 1995)

NEW **Schlumberger introduces PLATFORM EXPRESS** A revolution in wireline logging (July 21, 1995)

- About Schlumberger
- Shareholder News
- Publications & Presentations
- Services & Products
  - Electricity Management NEW
- Career Opportunities
- Petroleum Related Resources
- Employee & Site Location Directory
- Search this server

If you have any questions or comments, please send a message to our WWW administrator Jim Protos. If your Web browser does not support forms, send e-mail to protos@slb.com

INDEX

ABOUT THE CONTRIBUTORS

Tom Anderson is the director of corporate communications at Millipore. He supports the company's marketing and communications efforts with investors, employees, and customers. At Millipore, he has sponsored and developed multimedia, print, software, public relations, database, and advertising programs. Anderson has been a champion of Millipore's Internet implementation efforts since early 1994, using various internal and external resources to create a strong Web site for customers worldwide. He has a master's degree in English literature from Boston College and a degree in chemistry from Holy Cross College.

Marian Bremer is a senior information specialist at BBN Systems and Technologies, a division of Bolt Beranek and Newman, Inc. She also manages BBN's Corporate Information Center in Cambridge, Massachusetts. Prior to joining BBN in 1984, Bremer worked in academic, public, and corporate libraries in Switzerland, Italy, and the United States. Bremer has organized many successful programs to introduce librarians to Internet resources. She is currently the president of the Boston Chapter of the Special Libraries Association and has worked on the SLA's Networking Committee at the national level.

Mary J. Cronin is a professor of management in the Department of Operations and Strategic Management at the Carroll School of Management, Boston College. She is the author of *Doing Business on the Internet: How the Electronic Highway Is Transforming American Business* (Van Nostrand

Reinhold, 1994) and *Global Advantage on the Internet* (Van Nostrand Reinhold, 1996), as well as numerous articles on Internet strategies for business. Dr. Cronin has more than 20 years of experience in information management, networking, and technology. She received her Ph.D. from Brown University and her master of library science degree from Simmons College.

Gregory P. Gerdy is the director of Enterprise Products at Dow Jones Business Information Services, where he oversees product management and marketing of all enterprisewide information products for DowVision and Dow Jones News/Retrieval. Gerdy was responsible for the business planning and development of DowVision and was instrumental in the development of Internet services for Dow Jones. Prior to joining Dow Jones in 1983, Gerdy was a database editor for The New York Times Information Service. He has spoken about on-line and Internet services at conferences sponsored by Online/CD-ROM, Seybold, Internet World, Networks Expo, and the Public Relations Society of America. A former volunteer with the United States Peace Corps in Manila, Gerdy has a B.A. in political science from Davidson College, and a master's degree in international affairs from Ohio University.

Gail Grant is the vice president for business development at Open Market, Inc., responsible for evaluation of the firm's potential technology partners and long-term product requirements. She is also the chairman of CommerceNet's Network Services Working Group, which is working to facilitate the development, standardization, and deployment of protocols, applications, and technologies that provide authentication, privacy/encryption, and certification services over the Internet in a secure and interoperable manner. Prior to joining OMI in 1994, Grant was manager of the Internet Alpha Program at Digital Equipment Corporation. She has previously held development and development management positions at Bolt Beranek and Newman in Cambridge, Massachusetts, and in Cardiac Research at Massachusetts General Hospital.

Scott Guthery, a scientific advisor in Schlumberger's Austin Research Center, is currently coordinating the company's Technology Watch effort and building a content-driven alert and document-distribution system called The Refinery. Previously at Schlumberger he served as chief software architect for the company's well logging system and initiated the development of the Schlumberger Data Model for oilfield information. Prior to joining Schlumberger, he worked at Yourdon, Mathematica, and Bell Laboratories. Guthery holds a Ph.D. in probability and statistics from Michigan State University.

Russ Jones is director of the Program Office for Digital Equipment Corporation's Internet Business Group. In addition to developing Digital's cross-functional Internet communications strategy, Jones designed and implemented Digital's World Wide Web server. Jones is a frequent speaker at international conferences on the uses and implications of the Internet and the World Wide Web. He is the co-author of *Managing Internet Information Services* (O'Reilly & Associates, 1995).

Joel H. Maloff is founder and president of The Maloff Company. Involved in telecommunications since 1974, he has been a key participant in the Internet since 1987. He was executive director of CICNET (the Big Ten universities' research network throughout the midwestern United States) and, more recently, vice president of client services (sales and marketing) for Advanced Network & Services. Maloff writes and speaks frequently about business use of the Internet.

John "Scooter" Morris is manager of the Technology Development group in the Scientific Computing Department of Genentech, Inc., where he focuses on software architectures to support the scientific computing environment for Genentech's large scientific community. Morris served as co-chair of the 1992 Conference on Human Factors in Computing Systems (CHI '92) and continues to be active in the ACM SIGCHI community as the information director. Morris received his doctorate in medical information science from the University of California at San Francisco and has a B.A. in physics, a B.S. in biology, and a B.S. in information and computer science from the University of California at Irvine. His interests are in software architecture and user interfaces appropriate in the scientific environment.

Steve L. Swenson is the chief software engineer for simulation-based design for the Research & Development Division of Lockheed Missiles and Space Company, a Lockheed Martin Company. With degrees in engineering from the University of California at Los Angeles and the University of Santa Clara, Swenson has more than 20 years experience in software development and the application of computers to solve business problems. In the last ten years, teams he has led have developed and delivered computer systems supporting re-engineered division and company business processes. His goal is continuing innovation utilizing the best of current and nascent technologies.